The Frozen Peas
Cookbook

Recipe notes
- Eggs are always medium (UK)/large (Aus/US).
- Butter is always unsalted.
- Herbs are always fresh, unless specified otherwise.
- Both metric and imperial measures are used in this book. Follow one set of measurements throughout, not a mixture, as they are not interchangeable.
- All spoon measurements are level, unless specified otherwise.
- Tablespoon measures: We have used 15ml (3 teaspoon) tablespoon measures.

Published in 2025 by Murdoch Books,
an imprint of Allen & Unwin

Murdoch Books UK
Ormond House
26–27 Boswell Street
London WC1N 3JZ
Phone: +44 (0) 20 8785 5995
murdochbooks.co.uk
info@murdochbooks.co.uk

Murdoch Books Australia
Cammeraygal Country
83 Alexander Street
Crows Nest NSW 2065
Phone: +61 (0)2 8425 0100
murdochbooks.com.au
info@murdochbooks.com.au

For corporate orders and custom publishing, contact our business development team at salesenquiries@murdochbooks.com.au

Publisher: Céline Hughes
Project Editor: Lisa Pendreigh
Cover and Series Designer: Clare Skeats
Page Layout: Megan Ellis
Photographer: Mowie Kay
Food Stylist: Troy Willis
Prop Stylist: Max Robinson
Senior Production Controller, UK: Jess Brisley
Production Manager, Australia: Natalie Crouch

Text, design and photography
© Murdoch Books 2025

The moral right of the author has been asserted.

Murdoch Books Australia acknowledges the Traditional Owners of the Country on which we live and work. We pay our respects to all Aboriginal and Torres Strait Islander Elders, past and present.

All rights reserved. No part of this publication may be reproduced, stored in a retrieval system or transmitted in any form or by any means, electronic, mechanical, photocopying, recording or otherwise, without the prior written permission of the publisher.

ISBN 978 1 761500657

A catalogue record for this book is available from the British Library

A catalogue record for this book is available from the National Library of Australia

Colour reproduction by Born Group, London, UK

Printed by 1010 Printing International Limited, China

10 9 8 7 6 5 4 3 2 1

SAMUEL GOLDSMITH

The Frozen Peas Cookbook

100 everyday recipes for the most versatile ingredient in your freezer

murdoch books
London | Sydney

Contents

Introduction
6

Storecupboard Saviours
10

Pasta and Rice
30

One-Pot Wonders
56

Family Feasts
80

Midweek Meals
102

Sides, Sauces and Snacks
130

Sweet Peas
158

Index
167

Cook's Index
172

Acknowledgements
175

Introduction

Peas, glorious peas. The emeralds of the vegetable world are easily the most useful frozen vegetable. What's more, because they're frozen so quickly after picking, they retain their flavour, texture, colour and nutritional value. In my humble opinion, frozen is best. Unless, of course, you're able to pick them straight from the garden immediately before cooking while they're still tender and sweet. The fresh peas that grace the supermarket shelves are usually too old to compare favourably to their frozen counterpart.

The science of freezing has been developed over hundreds of years. I'm not joking when I say that it was championed by Clarence Birdseye (though I cannot find any evidence that he was ever a captain). He was not the first to observe that freezing can keep food edible for an extended period, but he certainly helped the frozen food industry become what it is today. It is, of course, important to note that much of the inspiration came from those communities that had been freezing food (or using ice to store food) for hundreds, if not thousands, of years.

Although we recognise the benefits of frozen foods and are comfortable using them in our cooking, it took a long time for it to catch on – we are talking decades – partly because the technology took a while to develop before it produced the quality we enjoy today. It also took trial and error of different types of vegetable to see which work. Peas are one of the best examples of a vegetable that remains close in taste, texture and appearance to its fresh counterpart. This is thanks to how quickly they're frozen (usually within two and a half hours of picking).

Key to the success of freezing now is that food is frozen quickly to ensure that quality is retained. The technology has become much more advanced and peas are graded, like a student waiting to be picked for a school sports team, before they're selected for their destination. Those graded highly will be used as straight up frozen peas while those deemed to be of lesser quality will be used in things like ready meals.

Once selected, those being frozen will first be washed and then either immersed in hot water or sprayed with hot water or steam to blanch them quickly so that the peas keep their glorious bright green colour and retain their flavour. Immersing the peas in the hot water also kills off any bacteria that can both cause the peas to spoil and be passed on to the consumer. (For the same reason, some manufacturers state within the packet instructions that you should cook their frozen peas for at least 2 minutes to eliminate any risk of harmful bacteria.) The peas are then cooled, much like if you were blanching at home, so that they stop cooking and the colour remains.

The blanched peas are then taken through to the flow freezer (via a conveyor belt). The freezing is done by passing the peas through -38°C (-36°F) air until they reach -18°C (-0°F), which takes around 8 minutes. This can also involve a rotating drum to ensure speed and consistency. Optical sorting of the frozen peas then takes place as they're passed through an infrared scanner to ensure there are no foreign bodies, such as insects or growing debris, followed by a metal detector. They're then stored until they need to be packed and sold. Each batch will also be sampled to ensure the quality is kept to a high standard.

That entire process – from the picking to the packing – all happens in 150 minutes combined. I find that hard to believe, but it's true, which is why the frozen pea manages to retain so much of its 'just-picked' flavour.

INTRODUCTION

There are generally two types of frozen pea that you'll find in the shops:

Garden peas The classic choice which are picked at their peak to give a delightfully sweet, green, tender sphere. They're podded and graded, with the best ones being selected for freezing. They then travel through a tunnel and are cryogenically frozen using liquid nitrogen to freeze them individually and quickly.

Petits pois These can be a separate cultivar or they can be the same variety of pea as those sold as garden peas but, as the name suggests to those who have studied a little French, they are smaller. This is because they're picked earlier, before full maturity, which gives a sweeter flavour and a more tender skin. They're frozen in the same way as garden peas.

It's easy to relegate peas to simply a veg spooned on the side of a main meal but they really are incredibly versatile. They also don't have to be merely stirred through as an afterthought. Easy to blitz into a smooth purée, they can make a simple sauce more animated or blitz them briefly to finely chop them when incorporating into cakes and other bakes. Mashing also works nicely (you can crush them with your fingers, which I find super satisfying) as an alternative to finely chopping or to break them down a little – this isn't always necessary but I find that they sometimes combine better with other ingredients when they've been broken down a little. That said, when in their full spherical form, there's something satisfying about biting through them; the texture and the flavour really is that of one of the best vegetables out there.

While peas aren't always the lead ingredient in a recipe, much like Judi Dench in *Shakespeare in Love*, Emily Blunt in *Devil Wears Prada* and Octavia Spencer in *The Help*, they do have the ability to steal the show even though they're supporting a bigger star. It's why I love them; you know that they'll always bring something to the party.

Aside from the recipes you'll find in each chapter, peas are also a saving grace when you need a simple side and have run out of time – I've often used them when I have a meat and a carb but I have forgotten about the side dish. (Obviously, now you've got this book on your shelf, that'll never happen to you...) If you're not in love with frozen peas already, I hope this book will prove to you just how versatile they are. And if they already feature heavily in your culinary line-up, then I hope this book will give you some new favourites to add to your repertoire.

Key to recipe symbols

% suitable for batch cooking

❄ suitable for freezing

V vegetarian

VG vegan

GF gluten free

DF dairy free

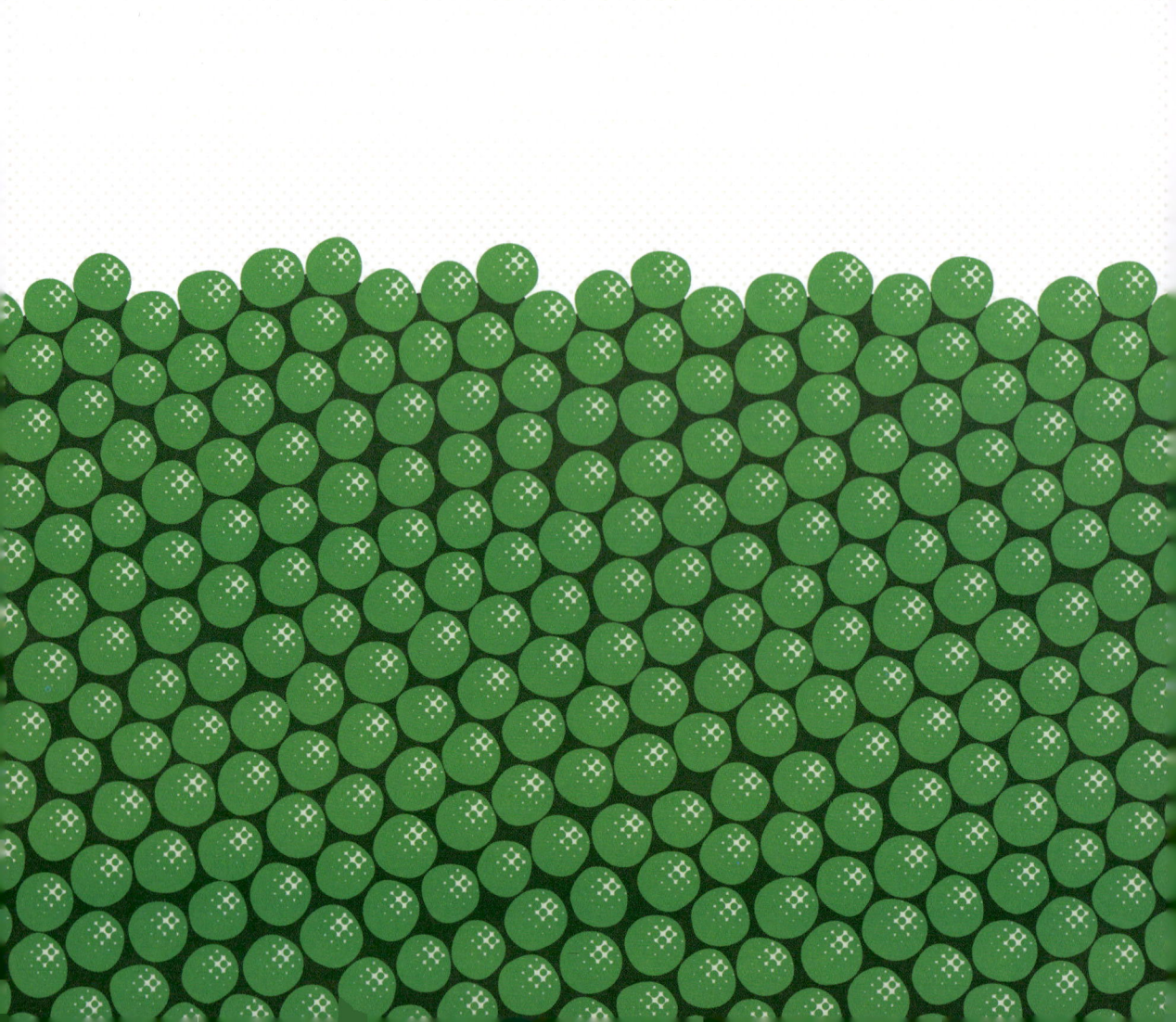

Storecupboard Saviours

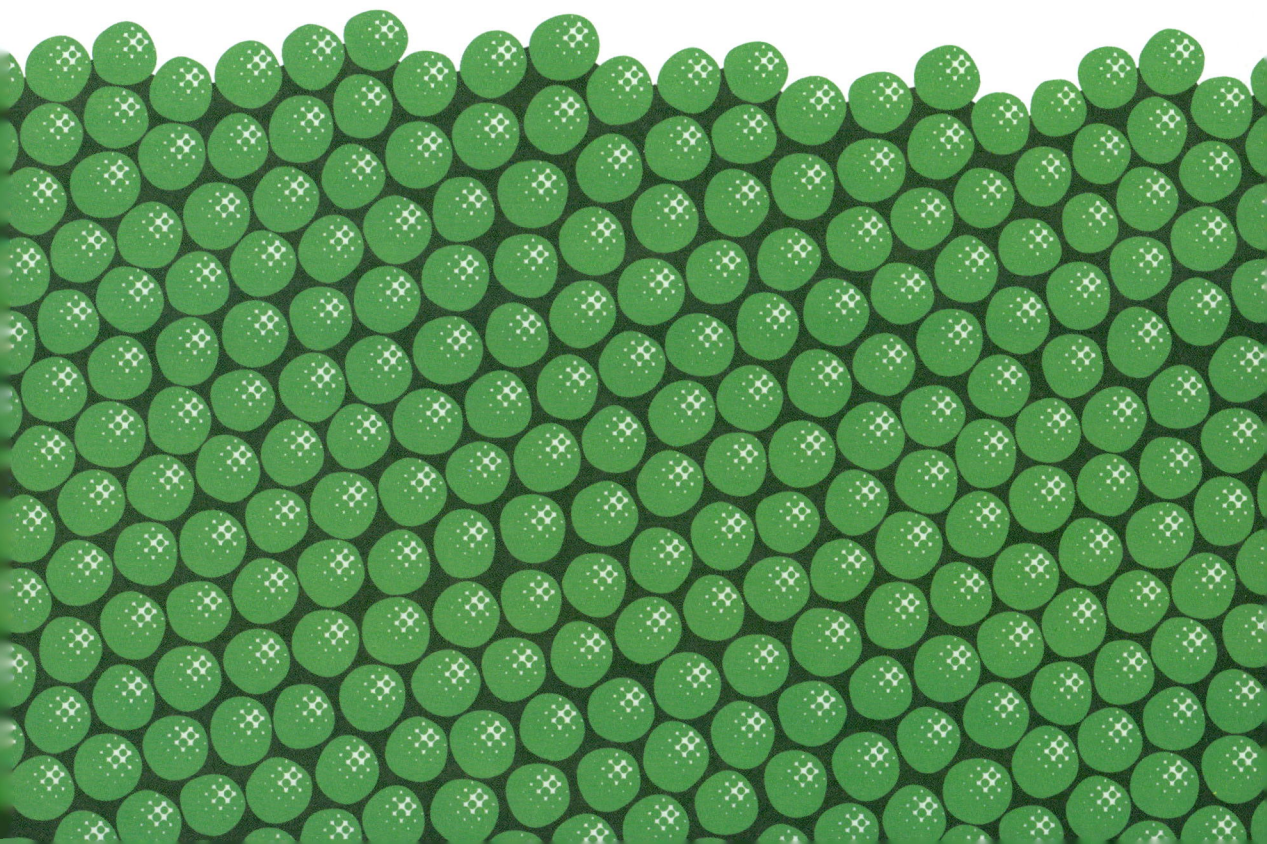

Spring Pea Soup

Cold soups are perfect for when the weather heats up – they're refreshing and cooling. Frozen peas help cool down the dish quicker and their sweetness is great in the sun. This one uses ingredients often found lying around in the kitchen, so you can make it last minute if you've got friends round or just fancy a little something in the sunshine.

SERVES 8

- 1 teaspoon sunflower or vegetable oil
- 1 bunch (around 8) spring onions (scallions), sliced
- 1 garlic clove, crushed or finely grated (shredded)
- 750ml (25fl oz) vegetable stock (gluten-free, if necessary)
- 500g (1lb 2oz) frozen peas, plus an extra handful of peas to garnish, defrosted according to the packet instructions
- 150ml (5fl oz) natural yogurt or plant-based alternative yogurt
- A few sprigs of fresh herbs, such as parsley and mint, to garnish (optional)
- Freshly ground black pepper

Heat the oil in a large frying pan (skillet) or saucepan over a medium heat. Add the spring onions and fry for a few minutes or until softened and beginning to brown. Stir in the garlic and cook for 1 minute.

Pour in the stock and bring to a simmer. Turn off the heat.

Tip the peas into the hot stock, stir to mix everything together and then bring the stock back to a simmer.

Blend the soup until smooth. (I use a food processor for this, rather than a handheld stick (immersion) blender, because it results in a smoother soup.)

Check the temperature of the soup. If it's cold enough, it can be served straight away. If it's not cold enough, chill the soup in the fridge for 1 hour or so. (You can prepare this soup the day before and store in the fridge until ready to serve.)

Serve the soup in bowls, cups or glasses with a spoonful of yogurt stirred through each portion. Scatter a handful of extra peas over the top of the soup along with a handful of fresh herbs to garnish, if you like. Season with plenty of freshly ground black pepper.

Herb it up If you want to give the soup a little herby kick, try adding a couple of tablespoons of soft herbs like parsley, mint or tarragon when blending the soup.

Quick Rustic Chicken and Bean Stew

The words quick and stew don't usually go together. However, by using ready cooked meat as well as tinned tomatoes and frozen peas, you can get a comforting dish on the table in a fraction of the time it takes to cook a 'proper' stew.

SERVES 4

1 tablespoon sunflower, vegetable or olive oil
1 red onion, roughly chopped
2 carrots, roughly chopped
2 celery sticks, roughly chopped
2 large potatoes, chopped into small chunks
1 tablespoon Italian seasoning, mixed dried herbs or a few sprigs of rosemary or thyme
1 × 400-g (14-oz) tin chopped tomatoes
1 × 400-g (14-oz) tin beans (cannellini/white kidney beans, red kidney beans or borlotti/cranberry beans all work well) or lentils
750ml (25fl oz) vegetable or chicken stock (gluten-free, if necessary)
250g (9oz) cooked chicken, shredded into bite-sized pieces
200g (7oz) frozen peas
Salt and freshly ground black pepper
Crusty bread, sliced and buttered, to serve (optional)

Heat the oil in a large, heavy-based saucepan with a lid over a medium-low heat. Add the onion, carrots and celery and cook with the lid on, stirring occasionally, for 8–10 minutes or until soft but not golden.

Tumble in the potatoes and stir through the seasoning or herbs, then cook for a further 2 minutes.

Tip in the tomatoes and beans, then pour over the stock. Pop on the lid and gently simmer for 10 minutes, then remove the lid and cook for a further 5 minutes or until the carrots are tender.

Stir through the chicken and frozen peas and cook for 3 minutes, or until the peas are warmed through and tender. Season well with salt and freshly ground black pepper.

Serve the stew in bowls with buttered slices of crusty bread, if you like.

Frozen Veg and Pea Broth

Though this is a book dedicated to the wonder that is the frozen pea, there are many other excellent frozen vegetables. Here, I use a bag of mixed frozen veg that includes peas; if you've only got the peas, you can just use more or add a little extra frozen spinach. This is purposefully simple for those days when you're running on empty in the fridge and freezer department, but feel free to use this recipe as a base to play with. Just remember the frozen veg doesn't take long to cook.

SERVES 4

2 teaspoons sunflower or vegetable oil
1 onion, finely chopped
2 teaspoons dried mixed herbs or a few rosemary or thyme sprigs
2 tablespoons tomato paste (concentrated purée) or harissa paste
750ml (25fl oz) vegetable or chicken stock
300g (10½oz) frozen mixed vegetables (which includes peas)
4 blocks frozen spinach (or up the mixed veg by an extra handful or two)
200g (7oz) thick-cut ham or cooked chicken, shredded or chopped
Salt and freshly ground black pepper

Heat the oil in a large saucepan over a medium heat. Add the onion and fry for 4–5 minutes or until soft and beginning to turn golden.

Sprinkle the mixed herbs into the onions and cook for 1 minute. Stir in the tomato paste and pour in the stock, then bring to a simmer.

Tip in the mixed frozen vegetables, spinach and ham or chicken. Season well with salt and pepper, then bring to a simmer and cook for 2 minutes or until the veg has warmed through and is tender.

Ladle the broth into individual bowls to serve.

Cook's tip If you want to add some carbs, try stirring in 50–75g (1¾–2½oz) rice, orzo or other small pasta shapes (or even some broken up spaghetti) and cooking for 8–10 minutes in the stock before adding in the frozen veg. Because the rice or pasta will absorb some of the liquid, you may need to add a little extra water or stock if the broth is a bit thick or there's not enough to serve four.

Ramen Noodles with Pea and Miso Broth

I usually have all of these ingredients in my kitchen at any one time. It's also an easy recipe to tweak – swap the ramen noodles for ready-made gyoza (or use both) and stir in a bit of leftover cooked chicken. You could also add sliced chillies or boiled eggs (halved) to garnish, if you like.

SERVES 2

½ tablespoon sunflower or vegetable oil
4 spring onions (scallions), sliced or ½ onion, chopped
500ml (17fl oz) miso or ramen broth (from a packet or made using 1–2 tablespoons miso paste and 500ml (17fl oz) vegetable stock or hot water)
100g (3½oz) kale, shredded (or use 4 blocks frozen spinach)
125–150g (4½–5½oz) ramen noodles
100g (3½oz) frozen peas
1 red chilli, sliced (optional)
Chilli crisp oil, to serve (optional)

Heat the oil in a saucepan over a medium heat. Add the onions and fry for a few minutes or until soft and beginning to turn brown.

Pour in the broth along with 300ml (10fl oz) water, bring to a simmer, then add the kale and noodles, cover the pan with a lid and cook for 3 minutes. Add the peas, cover again with a lid, bring back to a simmer and cook for 2 minutes – you may need to adjust the timings depending on the variety of noodles you buy, so check the packet instructions.

Ladle the noodles and broth into individual bowls. Top each bowl with chilli slices and serve with chilli crisp oil, if you like.

Cook's tip If you've made your own miso broth using miso paste, you'll probably want to season it a little – start with ½ teaspoon of soy sauce and a pinch of sugar, then add a little more to taste and stop when you're happy.

Sausage, Courgette, Pea and Harissa Pasta

When I get home from work, I often find that I don't quite have everything needed to make a certain dish. That's when I go on a bit of a fridge raid in the hope I won't have to go back out to the shops. This recipe came out of one of those moments. It's pretty flexible, so if you don't have the exact ingredients, you can make swaps – bell peppers are great in place of the courgette (zucchini), for example, or leave it out and add spinach along with the peas.

SERVES 2

200g (7oz) dried pasta (fusilli or penne both work well)
1 tablespoon oil
4 sausages (vegetarian or vegan, if preferred), each cut into 4
1 onion, chopped
1 courgette (zucchini), grated (shredded)
1 large garlic clove, crushed or finely chopped
2 roasted red bell peppers from a jar (or about 8 if they're piquante peppers), chopped
2 tablespoons harissa paste
1 tablespoon tomato paste (concentrated purée)
150g (5½oz) frozen peas
Salt and freshly ground black pepper

Bring a large pan of salted water to the boil. Add the pasta to the pan and cook according to the packet instructions; this should take around 8–10 minutes. Drain the pasta, reserving a cup of the pasta cooking water, and set aside.

Heat the oil in the same pan over a medium heat. Add the sausage pieces and onion and fry for around 5 minutes or until the sausage has browned and the onion has softened.

Tip in the courgette and cook for 6–8 minutes. You want any liquid to be released and the courgette to soften and reduce a little, but try not to cook off all the liquid as it's useful for the sauce.

Add the garlic and roasted bell peppers to the pan and cook for 1 minute, then stir in the harissa paste and tomato paste and a splash of the reserved pasta water. Cook for a few minutes over a medium-low heat – the sausages should be cooked through by this point. Scatter in the frozen peas.

Return the cooked pasta to the pan along with a few tablespoons of the reserved pasta water. Stir everything together, turn up the heat to medium and cook for a couple of minutes so the pasta is nicely coated and the peas are warmed through. If needed, pour in a little more of the pasta water; the pasta should have a nice gloss to it. Season well with salt and freshly ground black pepper before serving.

Macaroni Cheese

A comfort food classic, macaroni cheese can usually be whacked together solely with items from the back of your fridge and cupboards. Frozen peas are a simple way not only to add some veg but also to break through the beige. In this recipe, I blend the peas with the sauce thanks to a suggestion from my German friend Anja, who says she thinks she learnt it from a Jamie Oliver recipe for cabbage in a white sauce. Sometimes I also stir in a little spreadable cheese to give it an extra-cheesy pop. Because who doesn't love cheesy pop.

SERVES 4–6

400g (14oz) dried macaroni pasta
500ml (17fl oz) whole (full-fat) milk
50g (1¾oz) butter
50g (1¾oz) plain (all-purpose) flour
2 tablespoons spreadable cheese or 2 cheese triangles (optional)
175g (6oz) mature Cheddar cheese, grated (shredded)
300g (10½oz) frozen peas, defrosted according to the packet instructions

Bring a large pan of salted water to the boil. Add the pasta to the pan and cook for 2 minutes less than given in the packet instructions. Once cooked, drain well and set aside.

Pour the milk into a heatproof jug (pitcher) and heat in the microwave in 30 second blasts until steaming, making sure it doesn't boil over. (This step is optional, however I find it speeds up the sauce-making process.)

Melt the butter in a pan over a low heat. When the butter begins to sizzle, stir in the flour to make a smooth paste. Once all the flour is combined, cook the paste for 1–2 minutes. Gradually add the milk, a ladleful at a time, stirring continuously until all the milk is fully incorporated. Once all the milk has been added, you will have a glossy, thick sauce. If there are any lumps, use a whisk. (Although if you're using a non-stick pan, do not use a metal whisk.)

Remove the pan from the heat and stir the spreadable cheese, if using, and all but around 50g (1¾oz) of the Cheddar into the sauce until melted. Stir in the defrosted peas and then blend with a handheld stick (immersion) blender until you have a light green sauce. (You can blend as little or as much as you like, really, keeping the peas chunky or until very smooth, or you don't have to blend them at all.)

Preheat the oven to 200°C/180°C fan/390°F/gas 6.

To assemble the bake, combine the cooked pasta with the cheese sauce – you can do this either in the pan used to cook the pasta or in a large bowl. Tip the cheesy pasta mixture into a large ovenproof dish and scatter over the remaining cheese.

Bake in the hot oven for 30–40 minutes or until the top is golden and the sauce is bubbling.

Variation: Macaroni cheese with bacon breadcrumbs Macaroni cheese is excellent with bacon folded through and bacon breadcrumbs on top. Fry 200g (7oz) bacon lardons for 5–6 minutes or until golden. Set aside three-quarters of the lardons. Cook the remaining lardons until deep golden brown, then leave to cool. Once cool, chop finely into 'bacon dust'. Fold the reserved lardons into the sauce with the pasta, then pile everything in a baking dish. Combine the bacon dust with 75g (2½oz) panko breadcrumbs and a handful of grated (shredded) mature Cheddar. Scatter this on top of the macaroni cheese before baking.

Tuna Cheesy Pasta Bake

Before I met my partner, Gareth, I always made tuna pasta bake this way. He thought it was sacrilegious because he preferred the tomato-based version (which I included in my first book, *The Tinned Tomatoes Cookbook*). However, I've since won him round and we both love both versions, so we flick between the two. This one still holds a special place in my heart though.

SERVES 4–6

400g (14oz) dried pasta (I use penne or conchiglie)
500ml (17fl oz) whole (full-fat) milk
50g (1¾oz) butter
50g (1¾oz) plain (all-purpose) flour
1 teaspoon Dijon or English mustard
200g (7oz) mature Cheddar cheese, grated (shredded)
2 × 145-g (5½-oz) tins tuna in spring water, drained
250g (9oz) frozen peas (frozen sweetcorn kernels also work well)
Handful of parsley, finely chopped (optional)
75g (2½oz) panko breadcrumbs (optional)

Bring a large saucepan of salted water to the boil. Add the pasta to the pan and cook for 6–8 minutes (or 2 minutes less than given in the packet instructions) or until almost tender. Once cooked, drain well and set aside. (I tend to use the same pan to make everything and also to bake the pasta bake in, so I move onto step two after I've cooked the pasta, but you can follow step two while the pasta is cooking.)

Pour the milk into a heatproof jug (pitcher) and heat in the microwave in 30 second blasts until steaming, making sure it doesn't boil over. (This step is optional, however I find it speeds up the sauce-making process.)

Melt the butter in a pan over a low heat. Once melted, stir in the flour and cook for 1–2 minutes or until combined into a smooth paste. Gradually add the milk, a ladleful at a time, stirring well between each addition until completely absorbed. Once all the milk has been added and you have a thick sauce, bring to a simmer for 1 minute to cook out the flour.

Remove the pan from the heat and stir the mustard and two-thirds of the Cheddar into the sauce. Continue to stir until the cheese has melted, then add in the tuna, frozen peas and half the chopped parsley, if using. Season well with salt and freshly ground black pepper.

Preheat the oven to 200°C/180°C fan/390°F/gas 6.

To assemble the bake, either tip the pasta into the pan with sauce and mix everything together or put the pasta into a large ovenproof dish, pour over the sauce and carefully mix to combine. You can also mix everything together in a bowl and tip into a large ovenproof dish.

If using the breadcrumbs, combine them with the remaining Cheddar and parsley, then scatter the mixture over the top (or just scatter over the remaining cheese and parsley).

Bake in the hot oven for 30–40 minutes or until the top is golden and the sauce is bubbling.

Cheese and Pea Omelette

While it may seem like a simple suggestion and an obvious recipe, I often find that it's these kinds of dishes that inspire me the most when I'm struggling to decide what to cook. Usually because I've already got everything in the kitchen. I like an omelette but I often find I'm wanting it to taste a bit fresher, and the peas are a great way to achieve that.

MAKES 1

40g (1½oz) frozen peas
3 eggs
1 tablespoon butter
40g (1½oz) mature Cheddar cheese, finely grated (shredded)
Chives or parsley, chopped, to serve (optional)
Freshly ground black pepper

Place the peas in a heatproof bowl and cover them in freshly boiled water to defrost. Leave for 2 minutes, then drain. Leave for a few minutes to dry off a little.

Crack the eggs into a bowl or jug (pitcher), add a big pinch of black pepper, then beat everything together. Set aside.

Heat the butter in a small to medium frying pan (skillet) over a medium heat. Once sizzling, pour in the beaten eggs. Let the eggs cook until the base of the omelette has started to set.

Using a fish slice, move part of the edge of the omelette and allow any runny egg on top to move into its space. Work like this until no more runny egg will move off. Cook until the top of the omelette is set.

Turn down the heat, add the cheese and peas to one half of the omelette. Flip the other half over the top and leave to cook for a few minutes or until the cheese has melted and the peas have warmed through.

Transfer the omelette to a plate and scatter over some chopped herbs, if you like.

Cook's tip There are lots of options for omelettes. Where I add the cheese and peas above, you could add cooked bacon, fried mushrooms or swap the Cheddar for Gruyère. The key thing is that whatever ingredient you add is already cooked or only needs warming through because it doesn't have long to cook.

STORECUPBOARD SAVIOURS

Ricotta, Pea and Pesto Tart

One of the recipes from my first book, *The Tinned Tomatoes Cookbook*, that drew people in was the Tomato, Cheddar and Pesto Tart – it's incredibly simple to make and such a crowd pleaser. This is a similar dish, though a completely different flavour and a much fresher vibe thanks to the peas and lemon.

SERVES 4–6

1 × 320-g (11-oz) packet ready-rolled puff pastry
150–200g (5½–7oz) frozen peas
250g (9oz) ricotta
1 egg
Zest and juice of ½ lemon
4 tablespoons Genovese basil pesto
Salt and freshly ground black pepper

Preheat the oven to 200°C/180°C fan/390°F/gas 6.

Unroll the puff pastry sheet and lay it on a non-stick baking tray. Score along each side of the pastry, around 3cm (1 inch) in from the edges, to create a border – take care not to cut all the way through the pastry. Prick inside the border all over with a fork. Bake in the hot oven for 10–15 minutes or until light golden brown and puffed up.

While the pastry cooks, tip the peas into a heatproof bowl – if you'd like to scatter some whole peas over the top for decoration, use 200g (7oz). Pour freshly boiled water over the peas and leave for 2 minutes to defrost, then drain.

Put 150g (5½oz) of the peas, 175g (6oz) of the ricotta, the egg, lemon zest and juice into a blender with a good pinch of salt and freshly ground black pepper. Pulse until combined and the peas have broken down a little – you can go as chunky as you like here.

Remove the pastry from the oven and, using a spoon or fork, push down the puffed pastry inside the border to create a pastry case. Spread the pea and ricotta mixture over the centre of the pastry case – it's easier to start from the outside and work your way in. Return the tart to the hot oven for 8 minutes.

Remove the tart from the oven, then dot over the remaining ricotta, scatter over the 50g (1¾oz) of whole peas, if using, and spoon dollops of the pesto on top.

Bake in the hot oven for 10–15 minutes or until the ricotta is a little golden and the pastry is golden and cooked through.

Cook's tip For a cheesier tart, grate (shred) a little Cheddar, Parmesan or vegetarian or vegan Italian hard cheese over the top of the filling in the final 10 minutes.

Beef and Frozen Veg Pasties

The pasty – a classic British dish. This is not a traditional recipe because it's lacking in swede and potato, but it's unapologetically simple to make and most of the ingredients you'll already have in the freezer or can grab from a local store. If you can't find stir-fry beef, then you can slice a steak into strips. It's also possible to use puff pastry, however, I find that shortcrust is easier to roll again, if you need to. If you've got any leftover filling, freeze it for a later date or fold it through some cooked rice for a speedy lunch.

MAKES 4

1 tablespoon sunflower or vegetable oil
1 × 300-g (10½-oz) pack stir-fry beef strips or 300g (10½oz) skirt steak, sliced
150g (5½oz) frozen soffritto mix
25g (¾oz) butter
150g (5½oz) frozen peas or frozen veg mix
2 × 320-g (11-oz) packets ready-rolled shortcrust pastry
Flour, for rolling out
1 egg, beaten, to glaze
Salt and freshly ground black pepper

Heat half the oil in a frying pan (skillet) over a medium heat. Add the beef and fry until browned all over, then tip into a bowl with the juices from the pan.

Add the remaining oil to the pan, then fry the soffritto mix until warmed through and any water has evaporated. Next, add the butter and, once melted, tip the soffritto mix into the bowl with the beef.

Stir the frozen peas or frozen veg mix into the beef, then season really well with salt and freshly ground black pepper. Set aside.

Preheat the oven to 220°C/200°C fan/430°F/gas 7.

On a lightly floured surface, unroll the pastry. Cut out circles around 20cm (8 inches) in diameter. (The easiest way to do this is to trace around a side plate or base of a cake tin.)

Spoon 2–3 heaped tablespoon of the beef mixture into the centre of each pastry circle. Brush either a little water or egg around the mixture, then fold one side of the pastry circle over the other to cover the filling. Using your fingers, press down on the edges of the pastry circle to seal. (I find that nothing works better than your own fingers, especially with shop-bought pastry, as it doesn't always seem to stick well. You can also use a fork or edge of a knife to press down and create a pattern as well as sealing tighter.)

At this point, you can freeze the uncooked pasties for up to 3 months.

Arrange the pasties on a baking tray, then brush them all over with the beaten egg. Make two small slits in the top of each pasty to let any steam escape. Bake in the hot oven for 20–30 minutes or until the pastry is cooked and golden. If cooking the pasties from frozen, bake them for slightly longer – around 45 minutes.

Variation: Chicken tikka masala pasties Try mixing up the filling for these pasties. Replace the beef by frying 200g (7oz) chicken breast strips with 1 tablespoon of tikka masala curry paste, then mix in 2 tablespoons of water. Cook until the water has evaporated a little and the chicken is coated in a tikka masala sauce. Stir this through the cooked soffritto mix and frozen peas, then continue as directed above.

Egg Fried Rice

Were it not for roast potatoes and Marmite on toast, I would firmly come out in favour of rice being the best carb. Rice pudding is one of my favourite puddings and a simple fried rice is one of my go-to quick meals. I've given rough quantities here for the rice because the amount doesn't need to be exact – and you can add more or less of the veg, too. You can have this dish as part of a wider meal, but I tend to enjoy it on its own as a simple supper when I've got little time and even less in the fridge.

SERVES 3–4

2–3 tablespoons sunflower or vegetable oil
100g (3½oz) bacon lardons (optional)
1 onion, finely sliced
400–500g (14–17½oz) cooked long-grain rice
200g (7oz) frozen peas
3 eggs, beaten
4 spring onions (scallions), finely sliced, to serve (optional)
Soy sauce or chilli crisp oil, to serve (optional)

Heat 2 tablespoons of the oil in a frying pan (skillet) over a medium heat. Add the lardons, if using, and fry for a couple of minutes until the fat is beginning to release a little.

Stir in the onions and fry until beginning to turn golden and the lardons are becoming crispy, around 4 minutes.

If you haven't used the lardons, add another 1 tablespoon of oil. Stir in the rice and fry for 2 minutes to coat the rice in the oil.

Tip in the frozen peas and fry for a few minutes until they are warmed through and tender.

Pour in the egg, leave for 2 minutes and then stir everything together. Continue to cook until all the egg is set.

Divide the rice between bowls and scatter over the spring onions (scallions), if using. Serve with a drizzle of soy sauce or chilli crisp oil, if you like.

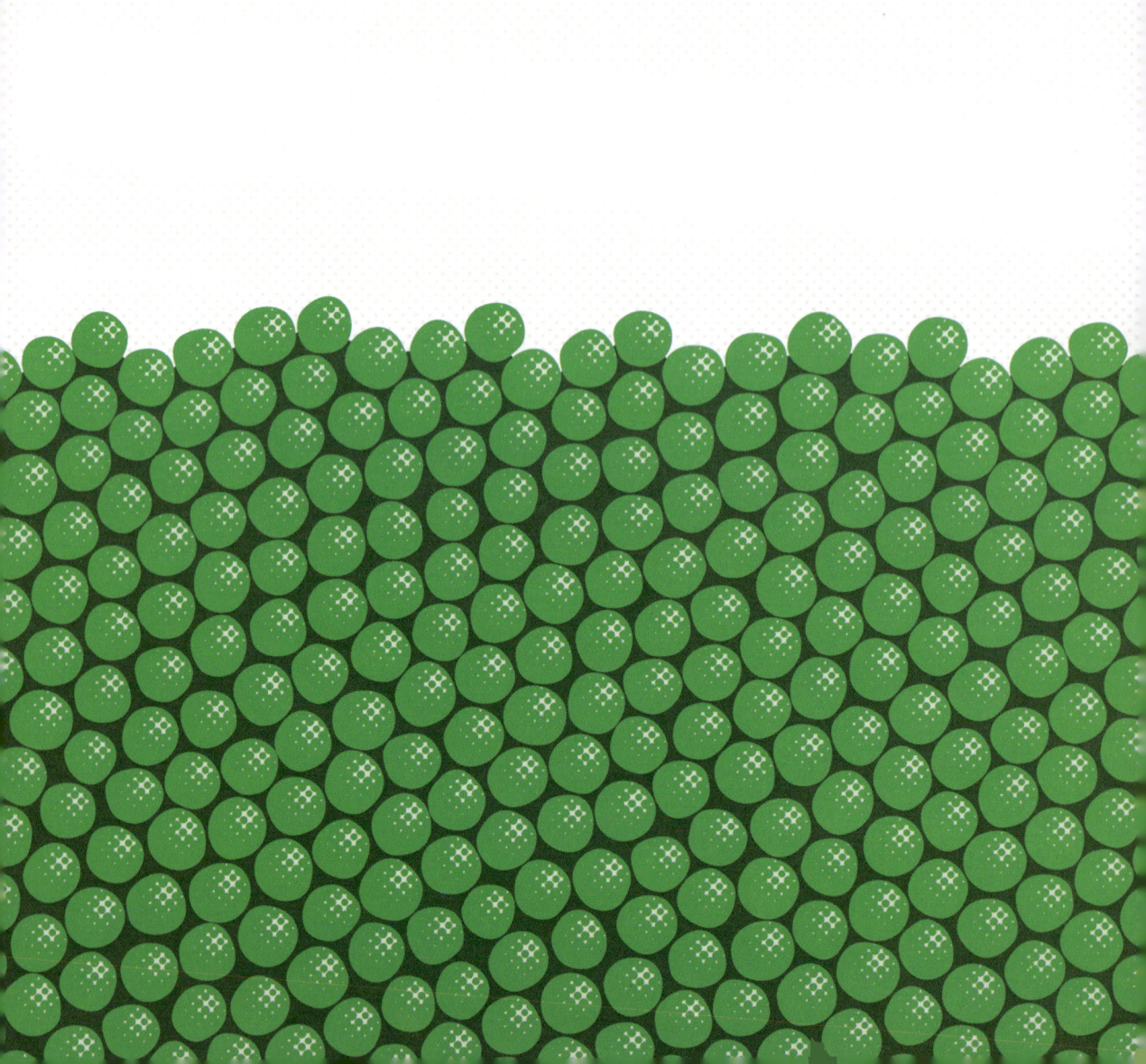

Pasta and Rice

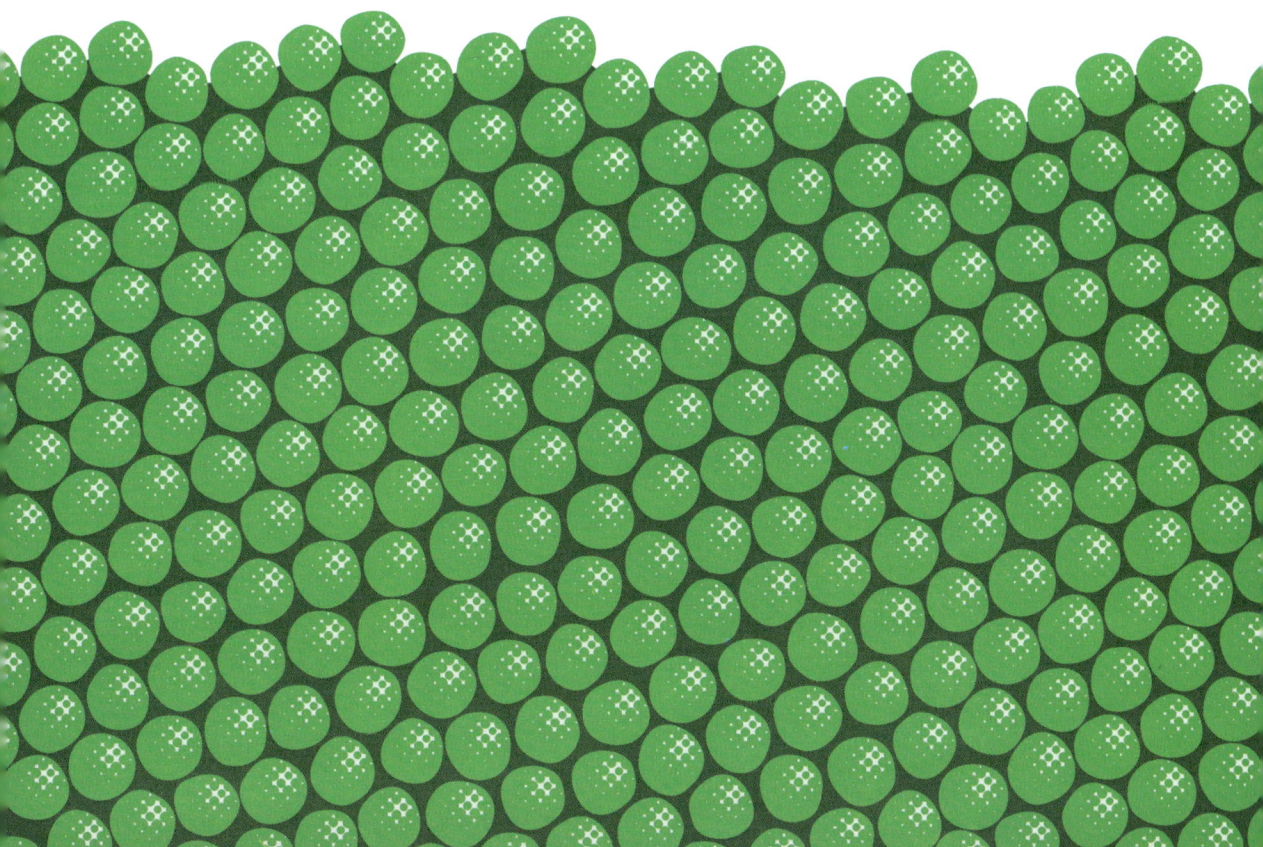

Asparagus and Pea Linguine

This is a super simple pasta dish, which makes an elegant and quick midweek meal. If asparagus is out of season, add in a few blocks of frozen spinach instead. This isn't a blow-your-socks-off-with-flavour kind of dish; it's light and delicate and I'm here for it. I love zesty dishes so I will often use a whole lemon, but I've included half here because you can always add more!

SERVES 2

200g (7oz) dried linguine
1 tablespoon olive oil
½ red onion or 1 shallot, sliced
1 garlic clove, crushed or finely sliced (optional)
200g (7oz) asparagus, trimmed and cut into bite-sized pieces
160g (5½oz) frozen peas
Zest and juice of ½ lemon
2 heaped tablespoons cream cheese or double (heavy) cream
Salt and freshly ground black pepper

Bring a large pan of salted water to the boil and cook the linguine according to the packet instructions. Reserve a cup of the pasta cooking water before draining.

While the pasta is cooking, heat the oil in a pan over a medium heat and fry the red onion or shallot for 4–5 minutes until softened and lightly golden.

Stir through the garlic and cook for 1 minute. Add in the asparagus with 1 tablespoon of the pasta water and cook for 2 minutes. Stir in the frozen peas, lemon zest and season with salt and freshly ground black pepper. Splash in a little of the pasta water (about 3 tablespoons should be enough). Cook until the asparagus and peas are warmed through and tender, about 2–3 minutes.

Mix through the cream cheese or cream and the lemon juice, to taste.

Tip in the cooked pasta and mix everything together, then cook for 30 seconds or so to allow the pasta and sauce to mingle. If you like a slightly thinner sauce, add a little more of the pasta water.

As the dish cools, the cream cheese will 'dry' a little. I like this texture, but if you prefer it glossy then definitely add a good extra splash of pasta water.

Cook's tip To trim your asparagus, simply bend the spear gently and it will naturally snap where the woody bit ends. You can use the trimmed ends in soups or stocks, or have a nibble.

Cheesy Peas Pasta (AKA Ham and Cheese Pasta)

When my friend Julie had a deli in Tufnell Park, this was her most popular dish. Julie is an amazing cook – and friend – so much so that she was one of the original MasterChef winners, so I couldn't turn this recipe down! Essentially a ham and pea pasta, her cheesy peas pasta is comforting and very popular with kids. If you're serving to children, you can leave out the wine, but it does burn off so there shouldn't be any alcohol in the finished dish.

SERVES 2

150g (5½oz) dried pasta (short pasta is ideal, such as penne and fusilli)
80g (3oz) frozen peas
2 tablespoons olive oil
80g (3oz) ham, pancetta or streaky bacon, cut into small pieces
1 shallot or 2 spring onions (scallions), finely chopped
75ml (2½fl oz) white wine
½ vegetable stock cube or 1 teaspoon vegetable stock powder
100ml (3½fl oz) double (heavy) cream
2 tablespoons grated (shredded) Parmesan
Freshly ground black pepper

Bring a large saucepan of salted water to the boil. Cook the pasta according to the packet instructions, around 10–12 minutes. With 2 minutes of the cooking time left, add in the frozen peas. Bring back to the boil and cook for 2 minutes. Once cooked, drain, reserving a cup of the pasta cooking water. Set aside.

While the pasta is cooking, heat the olive oil in a frying pan (skillet) over a medium heat. Add the pancetta pieces and fry until they start to turn golden.

Add the chopped shallot or spring onions to the frying pan and cook gently until it starts to turn golden brown. Pour in the wine and turn the heat up a little. Crumble in the stock cube and simmer.

Tip the pasta, peas and 2 tablespoons of the reserved pasta water into the frying pan. Stir in the cream and simmer for a couple of minutes until it thickens.

Season with a little freshly ground black pepper and stir in the Parmesan. Serve immediately.

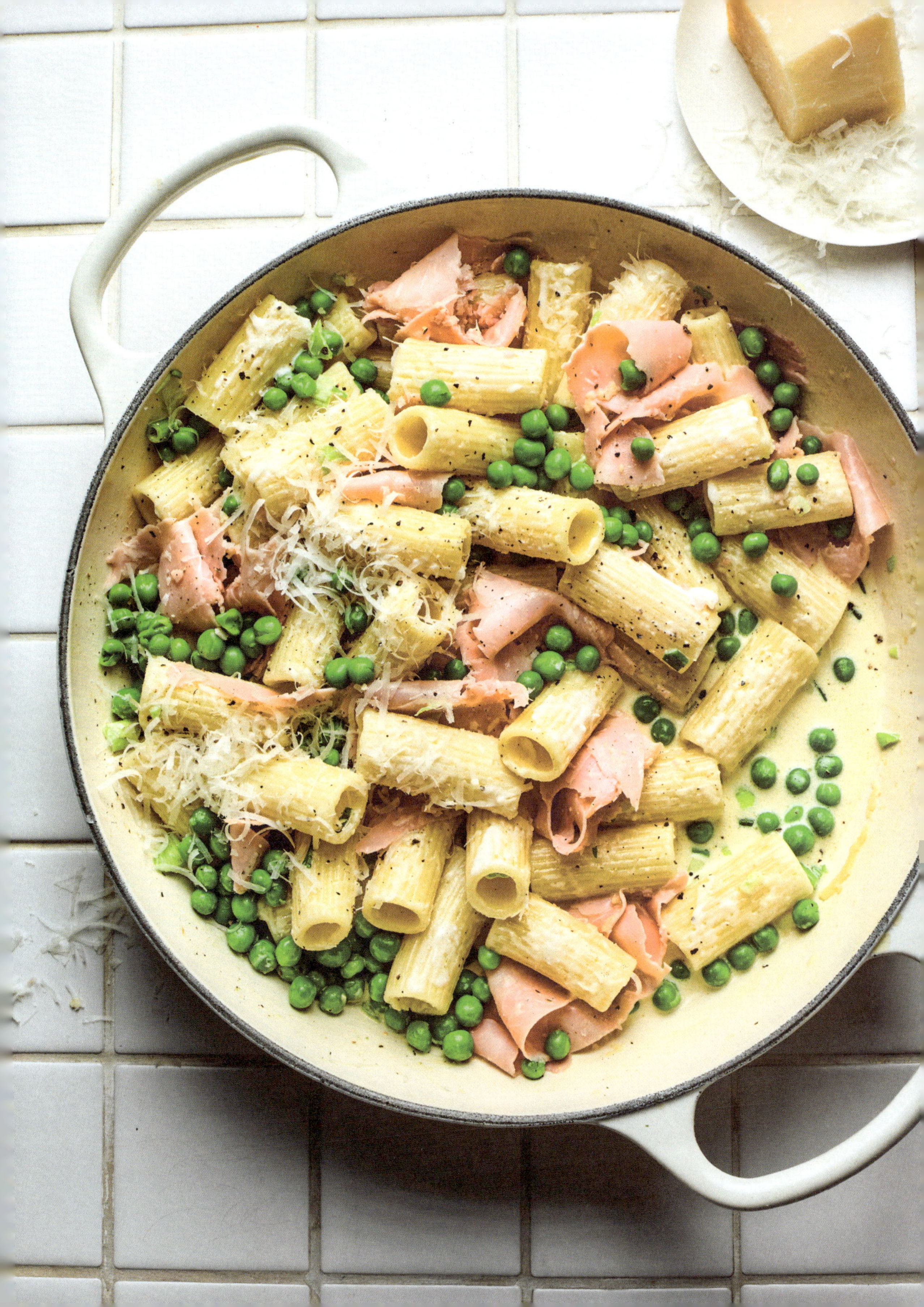

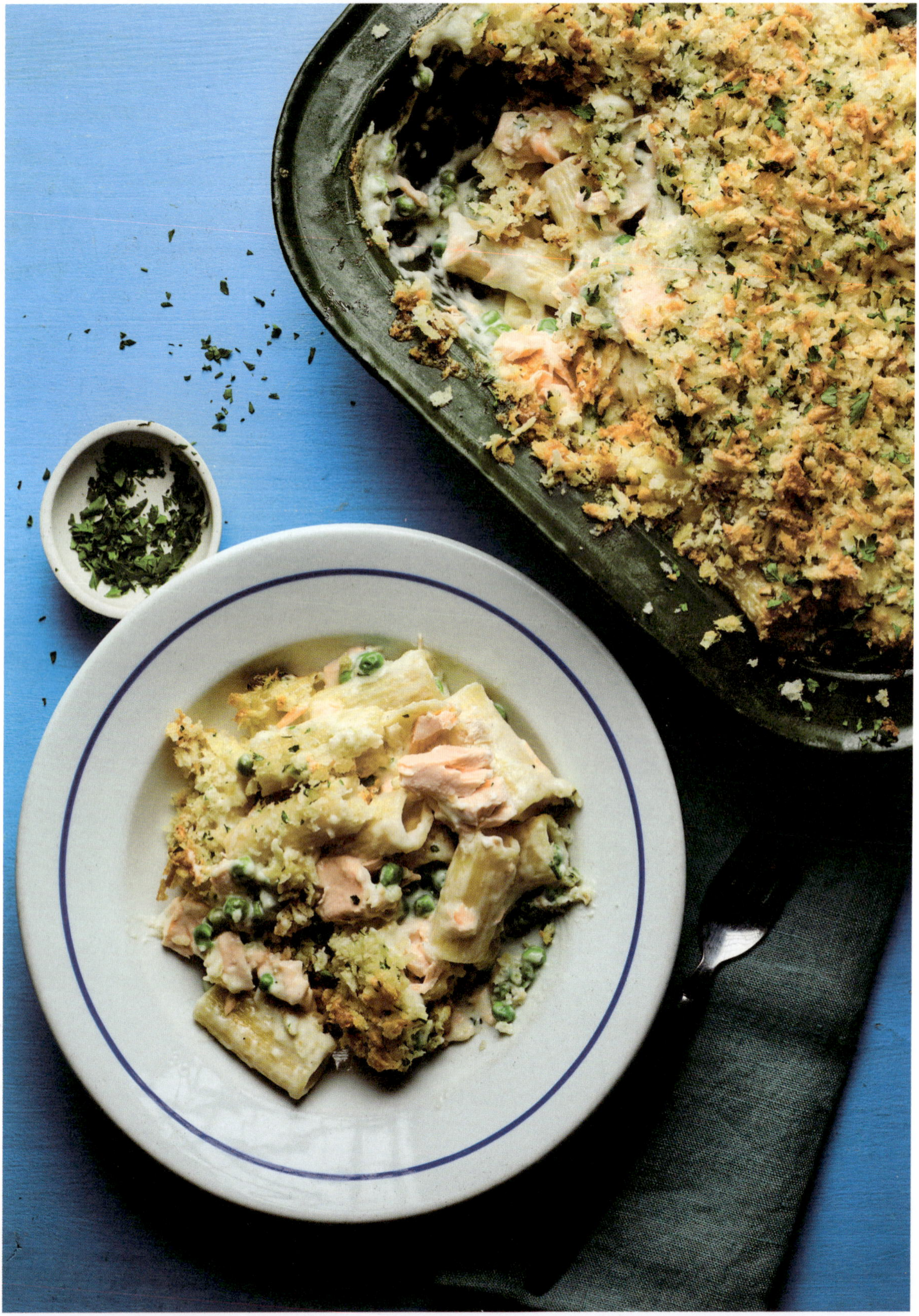

Salmon and Pea Pasta Bake

When I was young, my dad and step mum made a similar dish for a simple supper. The sauce is quite thick, but you can add an extra 100ml (3½fl oz) milk if you prefer it looser. This pasta bake can be prepared ahead of time – just pop it in the fridge and cook it for 10–15 minutes longer than given in the recipe below. Other veg like sweetcorn, broccoli and chopped green beans also work well here, as do some chopped sun-dried tomatoes.

SERVES 4

- 400g (14oz) dried pasta (penne or rigatoni works well)
- 4 skinless salmon fillets
- 500ml (17fl oz) whole (full-fat) milk
- 50g (1¾oz) butter
- 50g (1¾oz) plain (all-purpose) flour
- 150g (5½oz) mascarpone
- 250g (9oz) frozen peas
- 75g (2½oz) mature Cheddar cheese, grated (shredded)
- 75g (2½oz) panko breadcrumbs
- Handful of parsley, finely chopped

Bring a large saucepan of salted water to the boil and cook the pasta according to the packet instructions. With 4 minutes of the cooking time left, add the salmon fillets to the pan, laying them on top of the pasta. After the 4 minutes, carefully remove the salmon fillets and set them on a plate. Drain the pasta and set aside. (You can pop the pasta back in the pan, if you like – this is a good place to mix everything for the pasta bake. And if it's an ovenproof pan, you can even use it to cook the pasta bake in.)

Preheat the oven to 200°C/180°C fan/390°F/gas 6.

Pour the milk into a heatproof jug (pitcher) and heat in the microwave in 30 second blasts until steaming, making sure it doesn't boil over. (This step is optional, however, I find it speeds up the sauce-making process.)

Melt the butter in a small pan over a low heat. When the butter begins to sizzle, stir in the flour to make a paste. Once the flour is all combined, cook the paste for 1–2 minutes. Gradually pour in the milk a ladleful at a time, stirring continuously until all the milk is fully incorporated. Bring to a simmer and cook for 1 minute.

Remove the pan from the heat and stir in the mascarpone with a good pinch of salt and freshly ground black pepper and mix until combined.

Pour the sauce over the pasta, then flake in the salmon (don't worry if it's not fully cooked through) and stir in the frozen peas. Transfer everything to an ovenproof dish or ovenproof pan, then level the top of the pasta.

Combine the Cheddar cheese, breadcrumbs and parsley, then scatter over the top of the pasta.

Bake in the hot oven for 20–30 minutes or until bubbling and the crumb topping is golden.

PASTA AND RICE

Orecchiette with Peas and Pancetta

I don't know what it is about orecchiette, but I get posh vibes from it. It feels like the fancier cousin of penne and fusilli. Maybe it's just because I didn't see it around when I was younger or maybe it's because it tends to be sold in the higher-end supermarkets. That said, you can still pick up a pack pretty cheaply. I've combined it with the classic partnership of peas and pancetta.

SERVES 4

400g (14oz) dried orecchiette
1 tablespoon olive oil
1 onion, finely chopped
300g (10½oz) pancetta, chopped or bacon lardons
2 garlic cloves, crushed or finely grated (shredded)
1 teaspoon smoked paprika
1 × 400-g (14-oz) tin chopped tomatoes or cherry tomatoes
1 tablespoon tomato paste (concentrated purée)
300g (10½oz) frozen peas
Parmesan or mature Cheddar cheese, grated (shredded), to serve (optional)
Salt and freshly ground black pepper

Bring a large saucepan of salted water to the boil. Cook the orecchiette according to the packet instructions. Drain, reserving a cup of the pasta cooking water, and set aside.

Meanwhile, heat the oil in a pan or large frying pan (skillet) over a medium-low heat. Add the onion and fry for 8–10 minutes or until soft but not golden.

Tip in the pancetta and cook for a few minutes so the pancetta releases its fat, then turn up the heat to medium and fry for a few minutes until the pancetta is golden around the edges.

Stir in the garlic, cook for 1 minute, then add the paprika and cook for a further 1 minute.

Pour in the chopped tomatoes and squeeze in the tomato paste. Season with salt and freshly ground black pepper and cook for 5 minutes over a low heat.

Tip in the cooked pasta and frozen peas along with a splash or two of the reserved pasta water, if you need to thin the sauce. Stir and cook for 2 minutes until the peas are warmed through and tender.

Serve with a scattering of Parmesan or Cheddar, if you like.

Cook's tip Although I recommend orecchiette here, you can use any shape of dried pasta really – I've made this with penne, fusilli and conchiglie and all work well. You can also add in other veg like bell peppers, spinach and courgettes (zucchini).

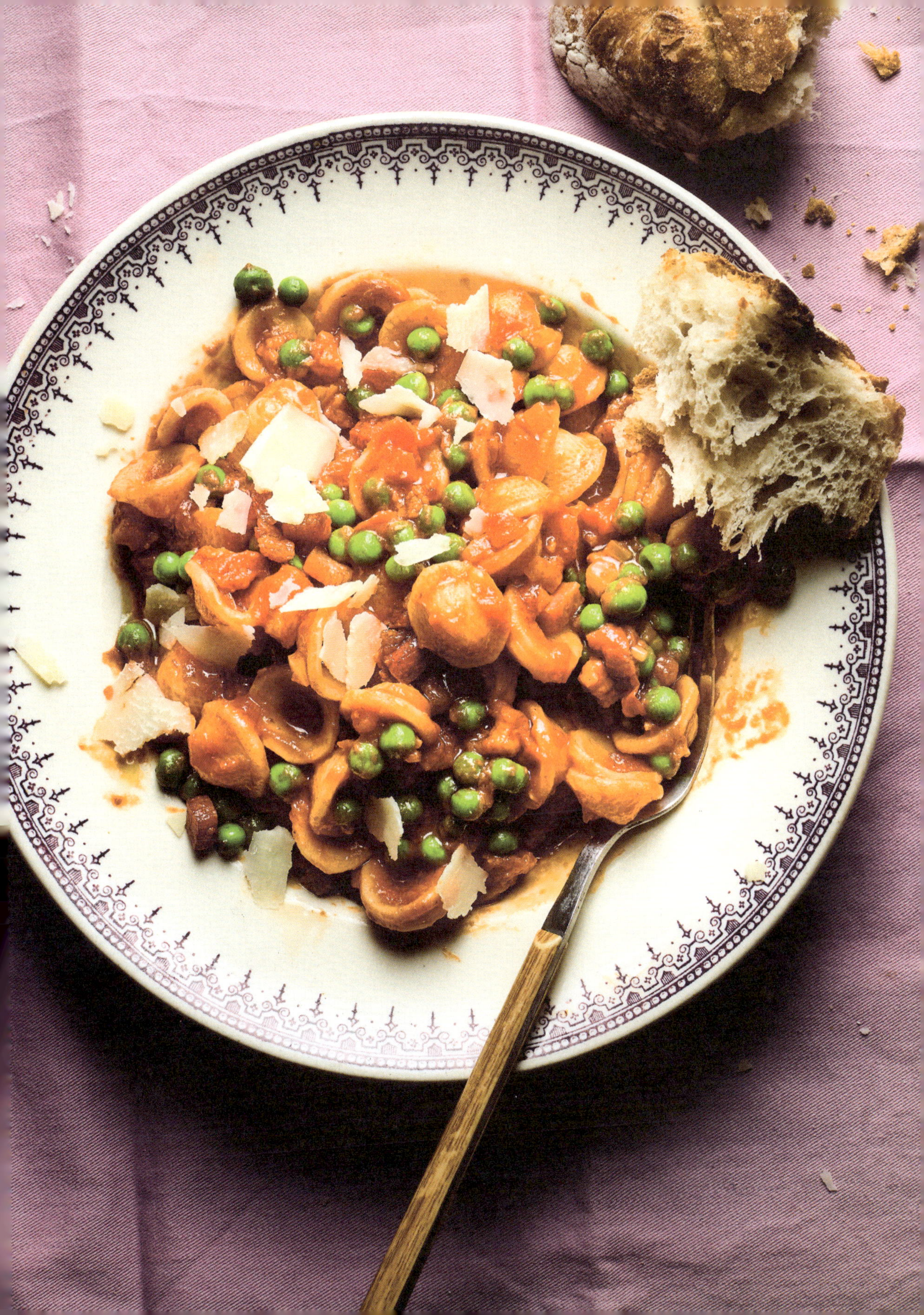

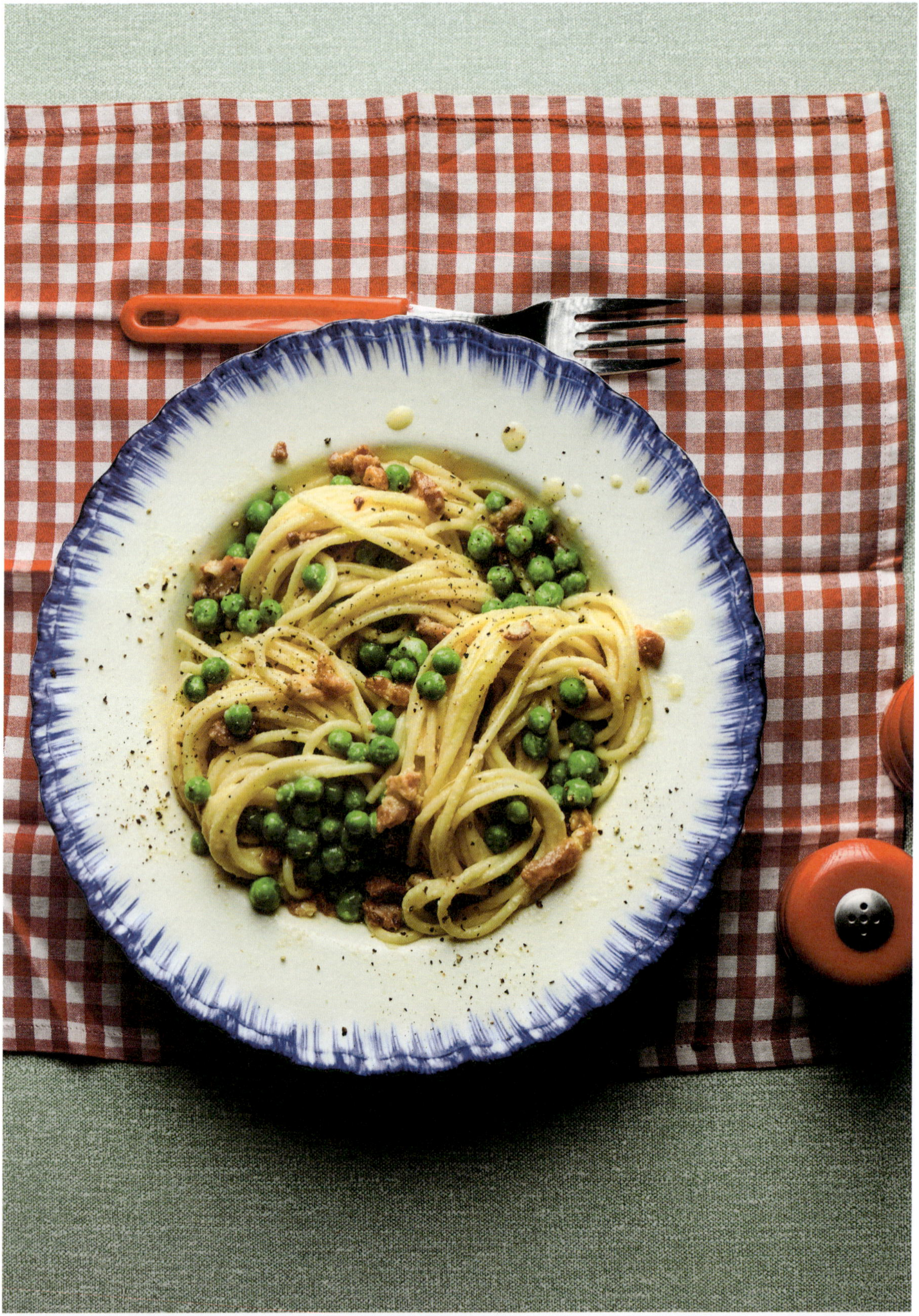

Rosie's Carbonara

My friend Rosie makes the best carbonara, and this is how she does it. Second only to a McDonald's breakfast, carbonara is the perfect hangover cure and it's simple enough to make when you're suffering from one. Rosie's version doesn't usually have peas in, but she's given me permission to slip some in. The peas add a great pop of colour and I like the addition of the texture, too. Plus, sometimes you need one of your five-a-day.

SERVES 2

200g (7oz) dried spaghetti
150g (5½oz) frozen peas
125g (4½oz) smoked pancetta lardons or chopped smoked streaky bacon
2 egg yolks
50g (1¾oz) Parmesan, finely grated (shredded)

Bring a large saucepan of salted water to the boil. Cook the spaghetti according to the packet instructions. With 2 minutes of the cooking time left, add in the frozen peas. Bring back to the boil and cook for 2 minutes. Once cooked, drain, reserving a cup of the pasta cooking water. Set aside.

While the pasta is cooking, fry the pancetta or chopped bacon in a frying pan (skillet) until crisp and the oil has been released. Set aside.

In a large bowl, mix the egg yolks and Parmesan together with enough of the reserved pasta water to make a thin, paste-like texture – you should only need about 75ml (2½fl oz). If the pasta hasn't finished cooking yet, scoop a little out of the pan.

Once cooked, tip the pancetta or bacon, pasta and peas into the bowl with the egg mixture and toss everything together – the egg will set in the residual heat of the pasta. Season well with lots of freshly ground black pepper, then serve immediately.

One-Pot Orzo with Peas, Mushrooms and Bacon

Although this is a one-pan dish, I do like to fry off my mushrooms first before mixing them back in because I prefer a properly browned mushroom. If you're not fussy then you can fry them with the onions. Peas, here, are a great way to add some more veg. They also mix well with all the other flavours.

SERVES 4

400–500g (14–17½oz) mushrooms, depending on the pack size, sliced
1 tablespoon olive oil
1 red onion, finely chopped
200g (7oz) bacon lardons
1 tablespoon tomato paste (concentrated purée)
1 teaspoon dried mixed herbs
200g (7oz) dried orzo
750ml (25fl oz) vegetable or chicken stock
200g (7oz) frozen peas
Handful of parsley, finely chopped, to serve (optional)
Parmesan, grated (shredded), to serve (optional)
Freshly ground black pepper

Heat a large frying pan (skillet) or saucepan with a lid over a medium heat. Add the mushrooms and dry fry until they've released their moisture and it starts to evaporate. Drizzle in half of the oil and fry the mushrooms for a few minutes until beginning to brown. Remove from the pan and set aside.

Drizzle in the remaining oil and tip in the onions. Turn down the heat to medium-low and fry the onion for 8–10 minutes or until softened but not golden.

Mix in the bacon and turn up the heat to medium. Fry for a few minutes until golden and starting to crisp.

Stir in the mushrooms and any juices along with the tomato paste and mixed herbs, then mix in the orzo and fry for a minute before adding the stock and a good seasoning of freshly ground black pepper.

Put the lid on the pan and bring to the boil, turn down the heat and simmer for 8 minutes. Remove the lid to check how much liquid is left; if it's still quite soupy then keep the lid off and simmer for 2–4 minutes until the orzo is almost tender and the stock has been absorbed.

If the dish starts to become too dry, add a little more water or stock – you want a small amount of liquid, but it shouldn't be swimming. Stir in the frozen peas and mix everything together. Cook for 2 minutes until the peas are warmed through and tender, plus everything else is hot. Again, add a little extra water or stock if you need to.

Serve with a scattering of parsley and freshly grated (shredded) Parmesan, if you like.

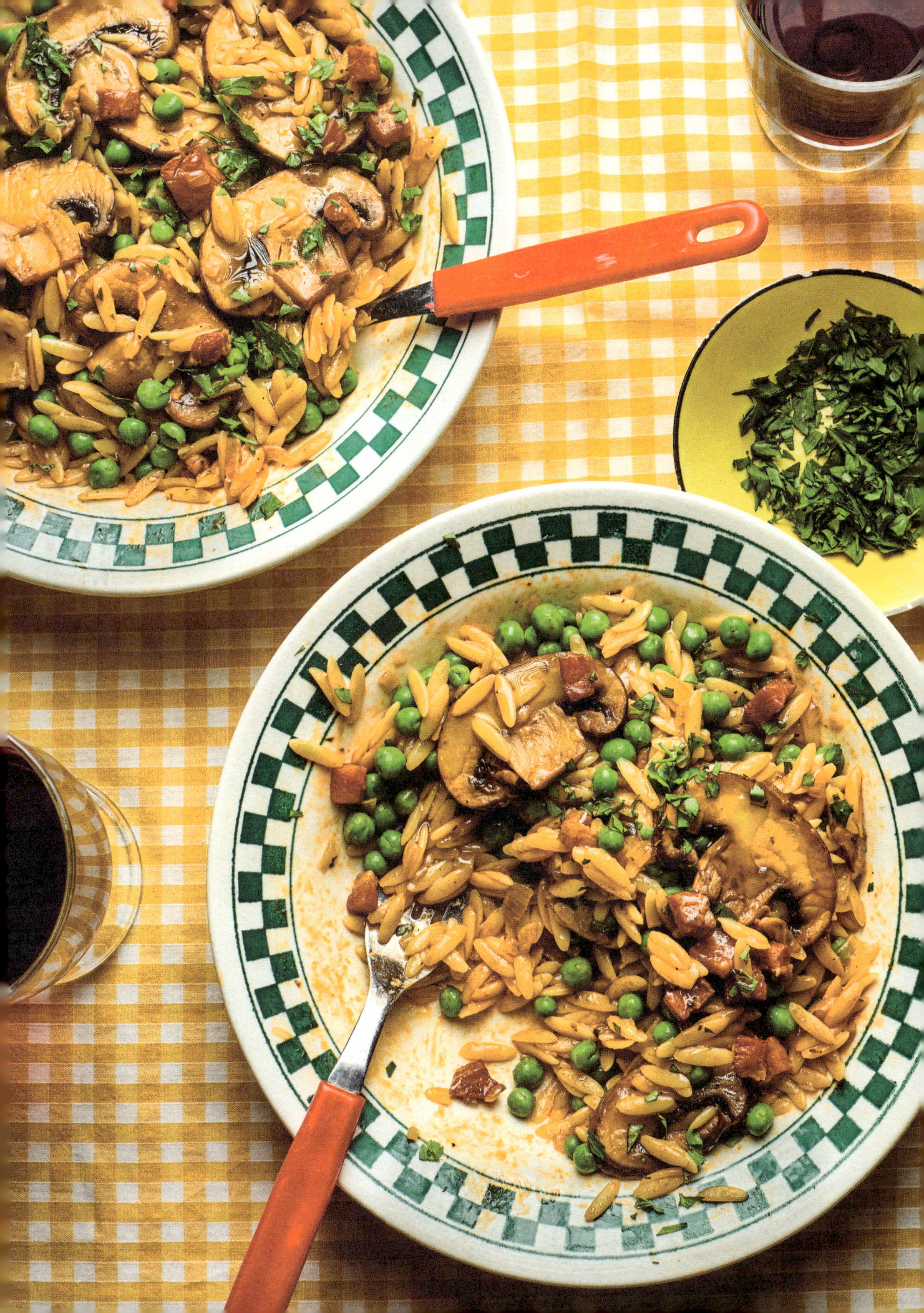

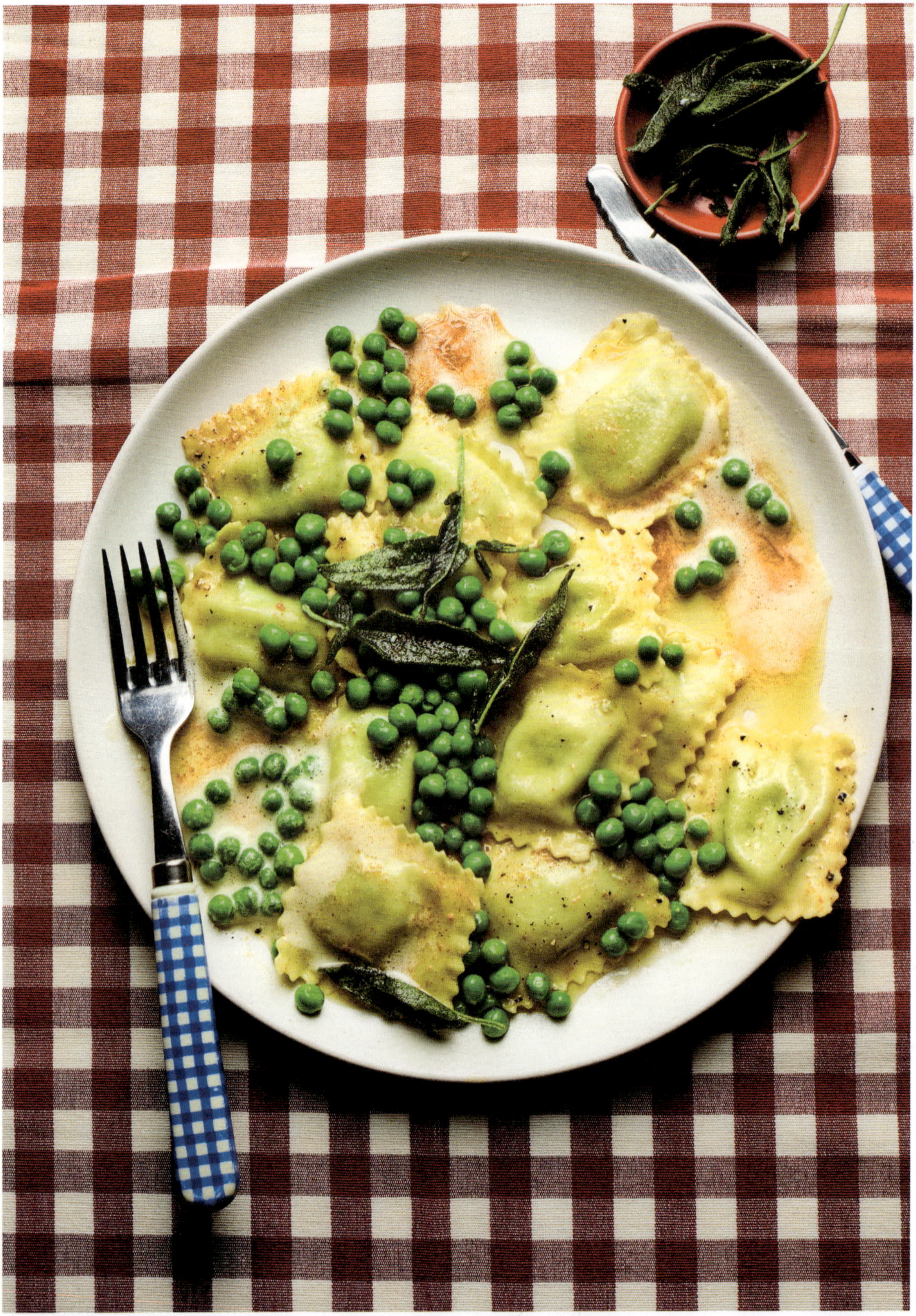

Ravioli with Sage Brown Butter

Supermarket ravioli is great for a speedy dinner. They're often on the shelves alongside a ready-made sauce, but I much prefer to make one at home and this is a super-quick option. Plus brown butter sounds fancy, so you'll feel like an Italian nonna in no time (although they would definitely make the ravioli themselves). This is where frozen peas really come into their own.

SERVES 2

75g (2½oz) butter
Handful of sage leaves (around 10 leaves), sliced or 1–2 tablespoons of picked thyme leaves
1 × 300-g (10½-oz) pack prepared ravioli (vegetarian if necessary, I tend to use spinach and ricotta)
175g (6oz) frozen peas (frozen spinach also works well)
Parmesan or vegetarian or vegan Italian hard cheese, finely grated (shredded), to serve
Freshly ground black pepper

Melt the butter in a frying pan (skillet) over a low heat and then cook for 6–8 minutes or until the butter starts to show brown specks (this is the milk solids in the butter toasting).

Carefully stir in the sage or thyme leaves (they will sizzle), cook for 30 seconds longer and then leave to stand with the heat off.

Bring a large saucepan of salted water to the boil and then tip in the ravioli and frozen peas and cook for 2–3 minutes (or however long the packet says to cook the pasta).

Drain the pasta and stir it into the sage brown butter in the frying pan. Alternatively, pop the ravioli back in the saucepan and stir the sage brown butter into the pasta.

Serve the ravioli in bowls with a scattering of freshly grated (shredded) Parmesan and a good grind of black pepper.

PASTA AND RICE

Tuna and Pea Pasta

This is a 'holiday' pasta dish – a recipe for which you don't need to buy all the usual storecupboard staples (oil, tomato paste, etc) that quickly crank up the shopping spend. It's tasy as it is, but you can add your favourite seasonal veg.

SERVES 2

1 × 145-g (5½-oz) tin tuna in oil
1 shallot or ½ small red onion, finely chopped or sliced
Zest and juice of ½ lemon
200g (7oz) dried spaghetti or penne
450ml (15fl oz) vegetable or chicken stock
100g (3½oz) frozen peas
Parmesan, to serve (optional)
Salt and freshly ground black pepper

Drain the tuna and reserve the oil. Put 2 tablespoons of oil into a frying pan (skillet) with a lid, heat over a low heat, add the shallot or onion and fry for 6–8 minutes or until soft.

Stir in the lemon zest and juice, then scatter in the pasta. Pour in the stock, season with salt and freshly ground black pepper and bring to a simmer. Put the lid on the pan and simmer for 8–10 minutes or until the pasta is almost cooked.

Scatter in the frozen peas and stir in the tuna, pop the lid back on the pan and cook for 2 minutes or until the peas have warmed through and the pasta is fully cooked.

Divide the pasta between two individual bowls and grate over some Parmesan, if you like.

Chorizo and Pea Pasta

If you own my first book, *The Tinned Tomatoes Cookbook*, you'll know chorizo, tomato and pasta make a winning dinner. Peas add a vibrancy to the dish.

SERVES 4

½ tablespoon olive oil
1 red onion, finely sliced
150g (5½oz) chorizo, chopped
2 garlic cloves, crushed or finely grated (shredded)
½ tablespoon smoked paprika
½ tablespoon dried mixed herbs
1 × 400-g (14-oz) tin chopped tomatoes
400g (14oz) dried pasta (penne works well)
200g (7oz) frozen peas
Salt and freshly ground black pepper

Heat the oil in a saucepan over a medium-low heat. Add the onion and fry for 10–12 minutes or until soft but not golden.

Tip in the chorizo, turn up the heat to medium and fry for 5 minutes or until turning golden. Stir in the garlic and cook for 1–2 minutes, then stir in the paprika and dried herbs.

Pour in the tomatoes, then add a couple of tablespoons of water to the tin, swill it around before pouring into the pan. Season well, stir and leave to simmer while you cook the pasta.

Bring a saucepan of salted water to the boil. Cook the pasta according to the packet instructions. A few minutes before the end, tip in the frozen peas, bring back to the boil and cook for 2 minutes. Drain, reserving a little pasta cooking water.

Tip the drained pasta and peas into the pan with the sauce. Stir everything together well, adding a little of the pasta water, if necessary. Serve immediately.

Pea Risotto

Although cooking a risotto can sometimes seem a bit daunting, it's actually a pretty simple dish to make. As with any traditional Italian dish, it's important to point out that this varies from the classic version in that I use courgette (zucchini) in the soffritto. You don't have to; I just find that the flavour complements the peas well without clashing with the bright green colour. If I'm adding a cooked veg to a risotto, I usually blitz or mash most of it before stirring it in – for example, with roasted squash or beetroot.

SERVES 4

250g (9oz) frozen peas
2 tablespoons olive oil
1 onion, finely chopped
1 courgette (zucchini), finely chopped
1 teaspoon dried mixed herbs or 1 tablespoon picked thyme leaves
200g (7oz) risotto rice (arborio or carnaroli both work well)
175ml (6fl oz) white wine
750ml (25fl oz) hot vegetable or chicken stock
40g (1½oz) butter
40g (1½oz) Parmesan or vegetarian hard cheese, finely grated (shredded)
Salt and freshly ground black pepper

Place the frozen peas in a heatproof bowl and cover in freshly boiled water to defrost. Leave to sit for 2 minutes, then drain. Blitz two-thirds of the peas in a food processor or using a handheld stick (immersion) blender. Set aside both the blitzed peas and whole peas.

Heat the oil in a large frying pan (skillet) or saucepan with a lid over a medium-low heat. Add the onion and courgette and fry, with the lid on, for 10–12 minutes or until soft. Keep an eye on the mixture to ensure it doesn't start to brown, giving it a stir every couple of minutes. Mix in the herbs and cook for a further 1 minute.

Remove the lid from the pan, tip in the risotto rice and cook for a couple of minutes or until the rice starts to turn translucent around the edges. Turn up the heat to medium, pour in the wine and cook until it's been absorbed. Season well with salt and freshly ground black pepper.

Add the hot stock, one ladleful at a time, stirring a little and simmering until absorbed. Keep going until the rice is al dente (cooked but with a slight bite) – you might not need to use all the stock and the risotto shouldn't be soupy, rather it should be quite creamy in texture.

Remove the pan from the heat, then stir in the blitzed peas, butter and most of the cheese. Stir until the butter and cheese has melted. Fold through the whole peas.

Spoon the risotto into bowls and serve with a scattering of Parmesan and a few cracks of freshly ground black pepper.

PASTA AND RICE

Risi e Bisi

In the traditional version of this Venetian classic, fresh peas are used. If you grow your own, or live next to someone kind enough to share theirs, they are preferable. However, with frozen peas being preserved so quickly, you get a much better flavour than if you use fresh peas that have been hanging around for ages. Risi e bisi means rice and peas in the Venetian dialect and the dish was often used to herald the start of spring when served at the feast of Saint Marco on 25th April. The great thing about frozen peas is that you don't have to wait for the start of spring; you can enjoy this dish all year round.

% GF

SERVES 4

2 tablespoons olive oil
1 onion, finely chopped
125g (4½oz) pancetta, chopped
250g (9oz) vialone nano risotto rice (see tip below)
125ml (4½fl oz) white wine or vermouth (optional)
600–800ml (20–27fl oz) hot vegetable or chicken stock (gluten-free, if necessary)
500g (1lb 2oz) frozen peas
50g (1¾oz) butter
60g (2oz) Parmesan, finely grated (shredded), plus extra to serve
Salt and freshly ground black pepper

Heat the oil in a large saucepan or deep frying pan (skillet) over a gentle heat. Add the onion and fry for 8–10 minutes or until soft but not golden.

Stir in the pancetta and turn up the heat a little to medium-low. Fry the pancetta until it has started to release its fat and become a little golden round the edges.

Tip in the rice and stir to coat the grains in the oil. Turn up the heat to medium, then fry for a minute or so until the rice starts to go a little translucent round the edges.

Pour in the wine, if using, and simmer for a few minutes until almost all absorbed. Follow with a ladleful of the stock and simmer, stirring continuously, until absorbed. Continue using up the stock until you have a thick but soupy consistency and the rice is almost tender. (You may not need to use all the stock, but if you haven't added the wine you may need to use a little more.) Season with salt and freshly ground black pepper.

Tip in the frozen peas, stir to mix them with the rice and cook for 2–3 minutes or until warmed through. Remove the pan from the heat and stir in the butter and Parmesan until melted. Serve with a little more grated (shredded) Parmesan and freshly ground black pepper on top.

Cook's tip Vialone nano is the risotto rice traditionally used for this dish and most other soupy risotto dishes. If you can't find it, swap it out for carnaroli risotto rice.

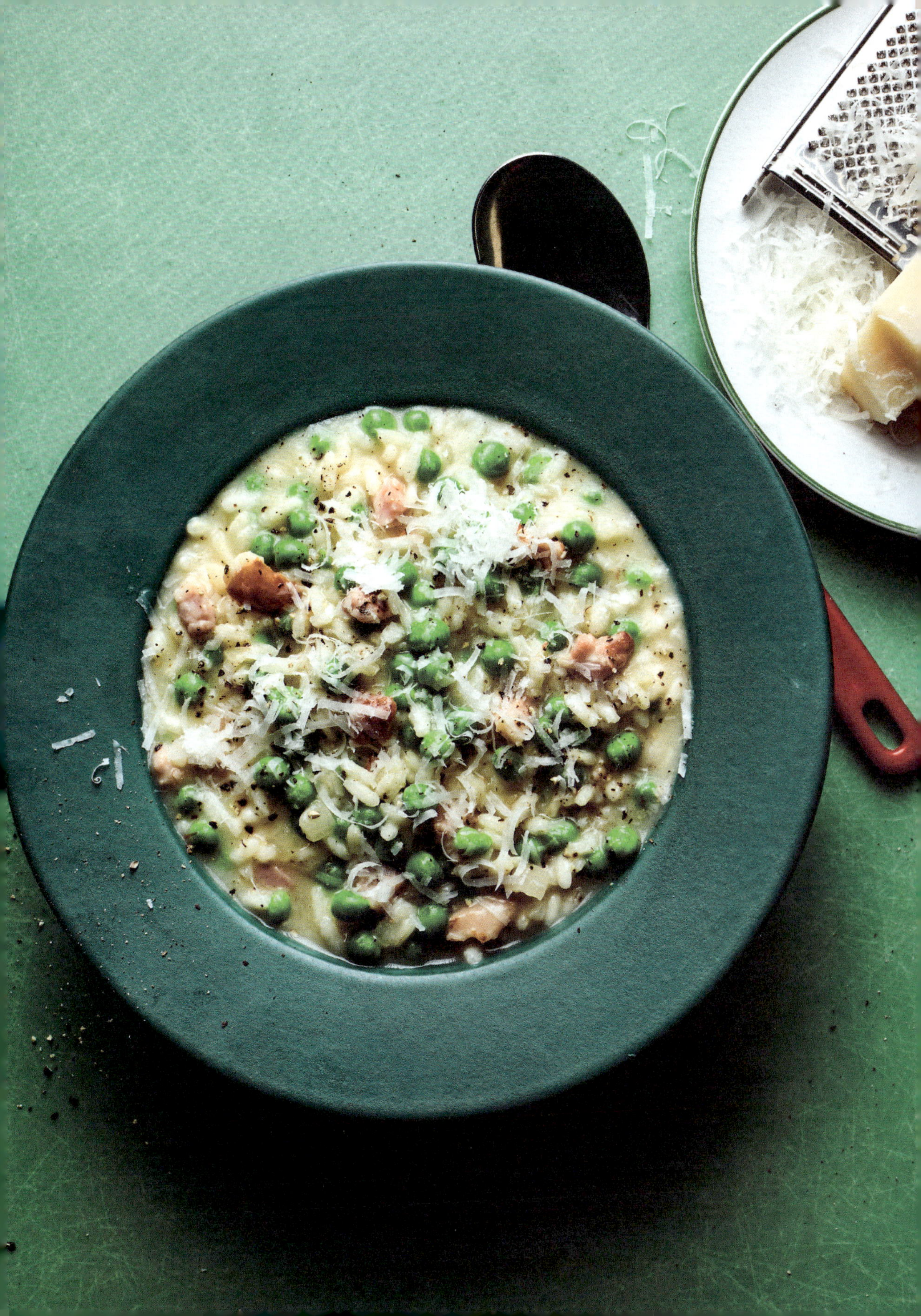

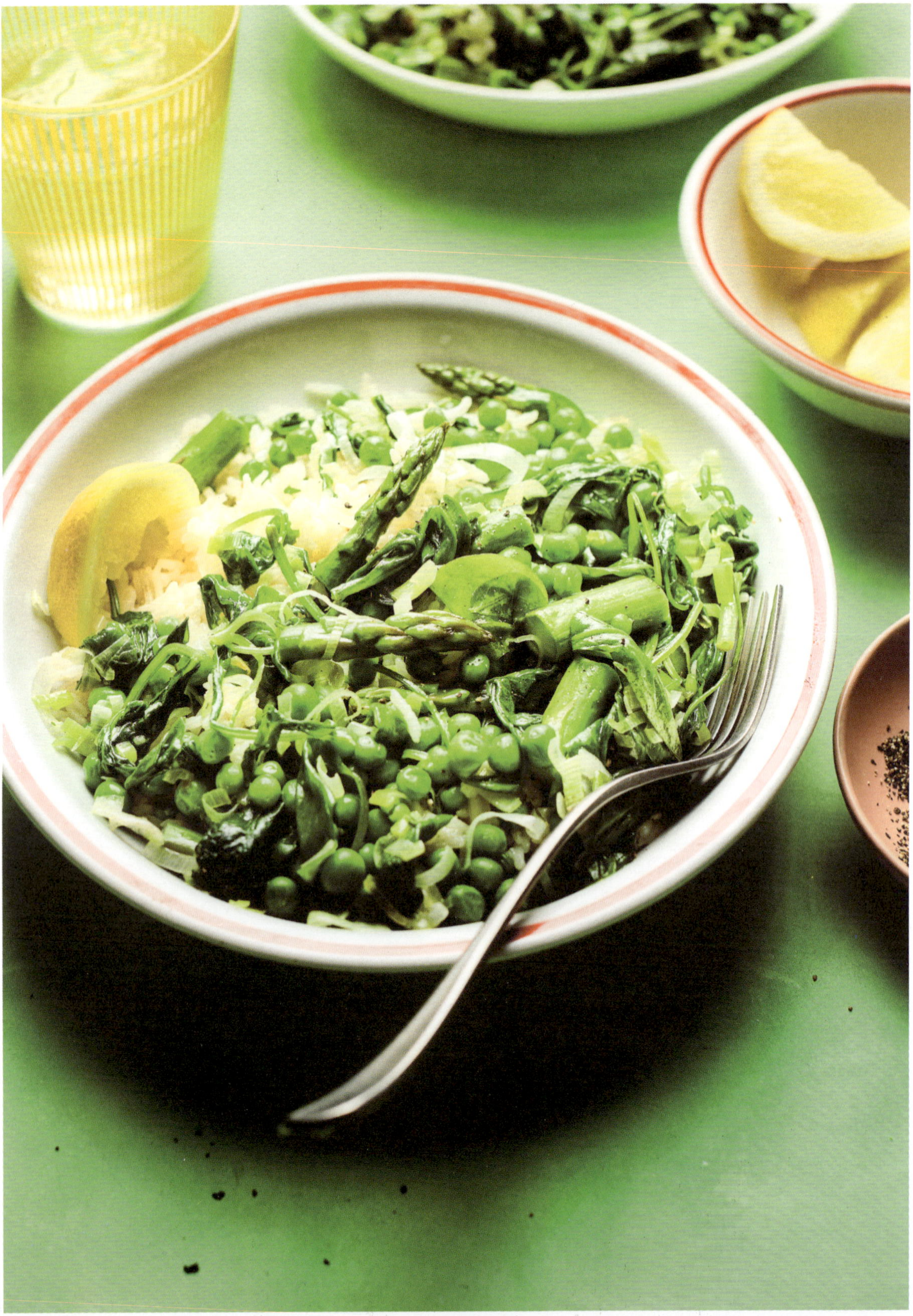

Arroz de Primavera

Translated as 'spring rice', this dish uses seasonal ingredients alongside rice to create a bright dish that's great as a side or veggie midweek meal. As we know, spring ingredients aren't always in season, which is why frozen peas and its frozen siblings are so handy. If it's not spring, feel free to swap some of the fresh ingredients for their frozen counterparts (or something similar).

% ❄ V VG GF DF

SERVES 6–8

300g (10½oz) long-grain white rice
600ml (20fl oz) vegetable stock (gluten-free, if necessary)
4 tablespoons olive oil
1 leek, halved lengthways and finely sliced
200g (7oz) asparagus, trimmed and cut into bite-sized pieces
150g (5½oz) spinach
200g (7oz) frozen peas
Handful of parsley, finely chopped
1 lemon, cut into 4 wedges
Salt and freshly ground black pepper

Rinse the rice a few times to remove as much of the starch as possible. Ideally, you should do this until the water runs clear. (I don't like to waste too much water, however, so I tend to do this a maximum of 3 or 4 times.)

Put the rice into a pan with the stock and simmer until the rice is cooked, around 10–15 minutes. If it gets too dry, top up with a little water. Once cooked, drain and set aside.

Drizzle the oil into a saucepan or large frying pan (skillet) and heat over a medium-low heat. Stir in the leeks and cook for 5–6 minutes until softened, then stir in the asparagus and spinach and cook until the spinach has wilted and most of the liquid has evaporated.

Tip in the frozen peas and season really well with salt and freshly ground black pepper. Mix everything together and cook for 2–3 minutes until the peas are warmed through and tender.

Stir in the rice until well combined.

Serve with a scattering of parsley and lemon wedges for squeezing over.

Flavourings I love the gentle flavour of this dish and so I don't like to drown it in other strong tastes. However, if you'd like to give things a bit more oomph, you could simply add a garlic clove or two. You could also play around with the herbs – try dill, tarragon or chervil – and add the zest of the lemon wedges when you add the asparagus.

Jewelled Couscous

I love a couscous side. It's so quick to cook as you literally just cover the couscous grains in boiling water, so this is really not a tricky dish to make. I like to use a range of colourful ingredients, which glisten like a platter of jewels. You can play around with the ingredients; I basically use salad ingredients and soft herbs with a few nuts and dried fruits, but you could add goats' cheese or feta, harissa or a dressing – it's totally up to you. My only suggestion would be to have a taste each time you add an ingredient and see how you feel.

% ❄ V VG GF DF

SERVES 4–6

250g (9oz) dried couscous
150g (5½oz) frozen peas
Zest and juice of 1 lime
75g (2½oz) sultanas or raisins (a mix of colours is great)
1 red or yellow bell pepper, deseeded and finely chopped
150g (5½oz) cherry tomatoes, quartered (or a handful of sun-dried tomatoes when not in season)
100g (3½oz) pomegranate seeds
Handful of parsley or coriander (cilantro), finely chopped
50g (1¾oz) nuts or seeds (pumpkin seeds/pepitas, sunflower seeds or hazelnuts all work well), chop any large nuts
3 tablespoons extra virgin olive oil
Salt and freshly ground black pepper

Put the couscous, frozen peas, lime zest, a good pinch each of salt and freshly ground black pepper into a heatproof bowl and then pour over 300ml (10fl oz) boiling water and the lime juice. Leave for 5–10 minutes or until the couscous has absorbed the water.

Fold all the remaining ingredients into the couscous and then pile everything onto a platter before serving.

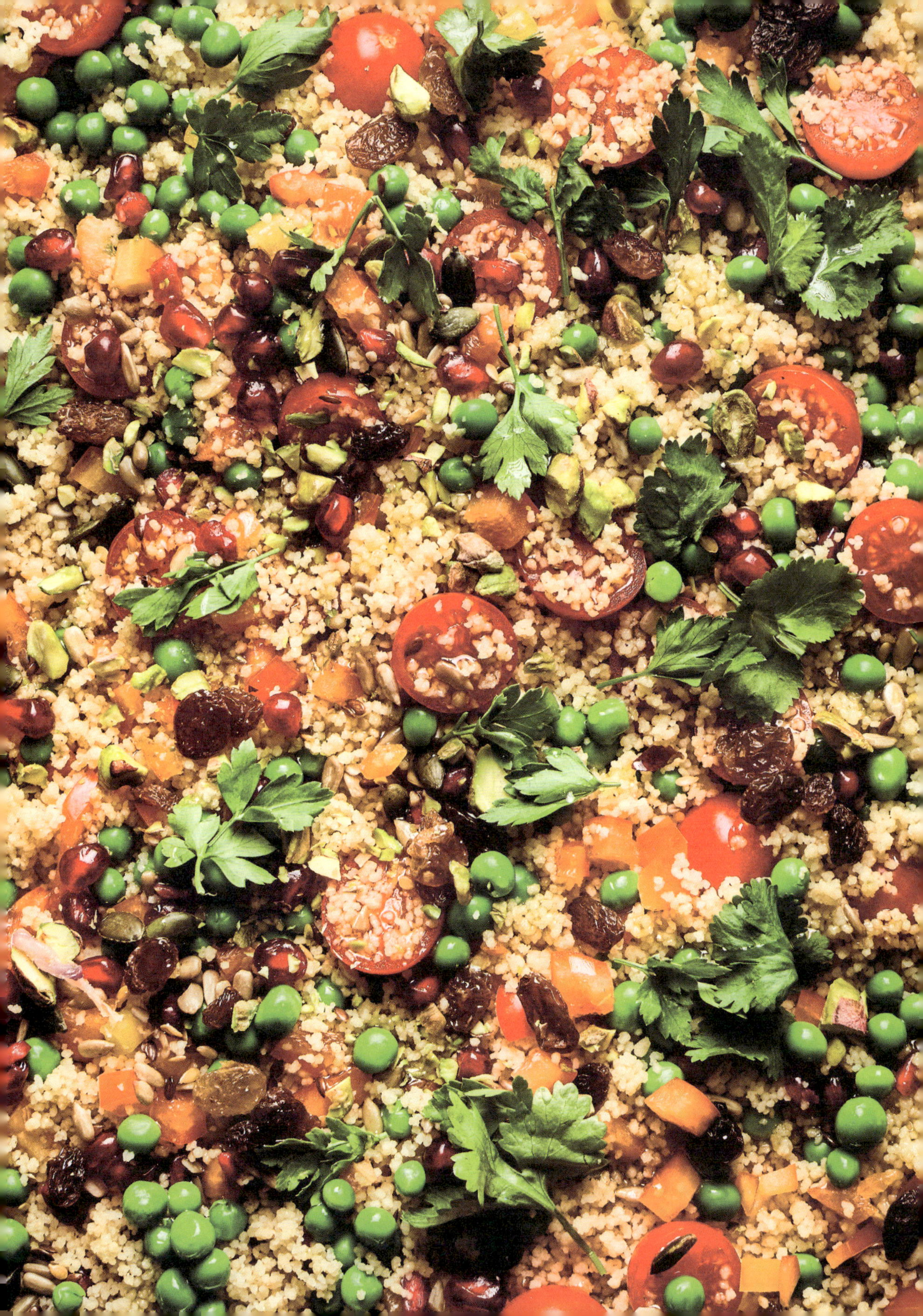

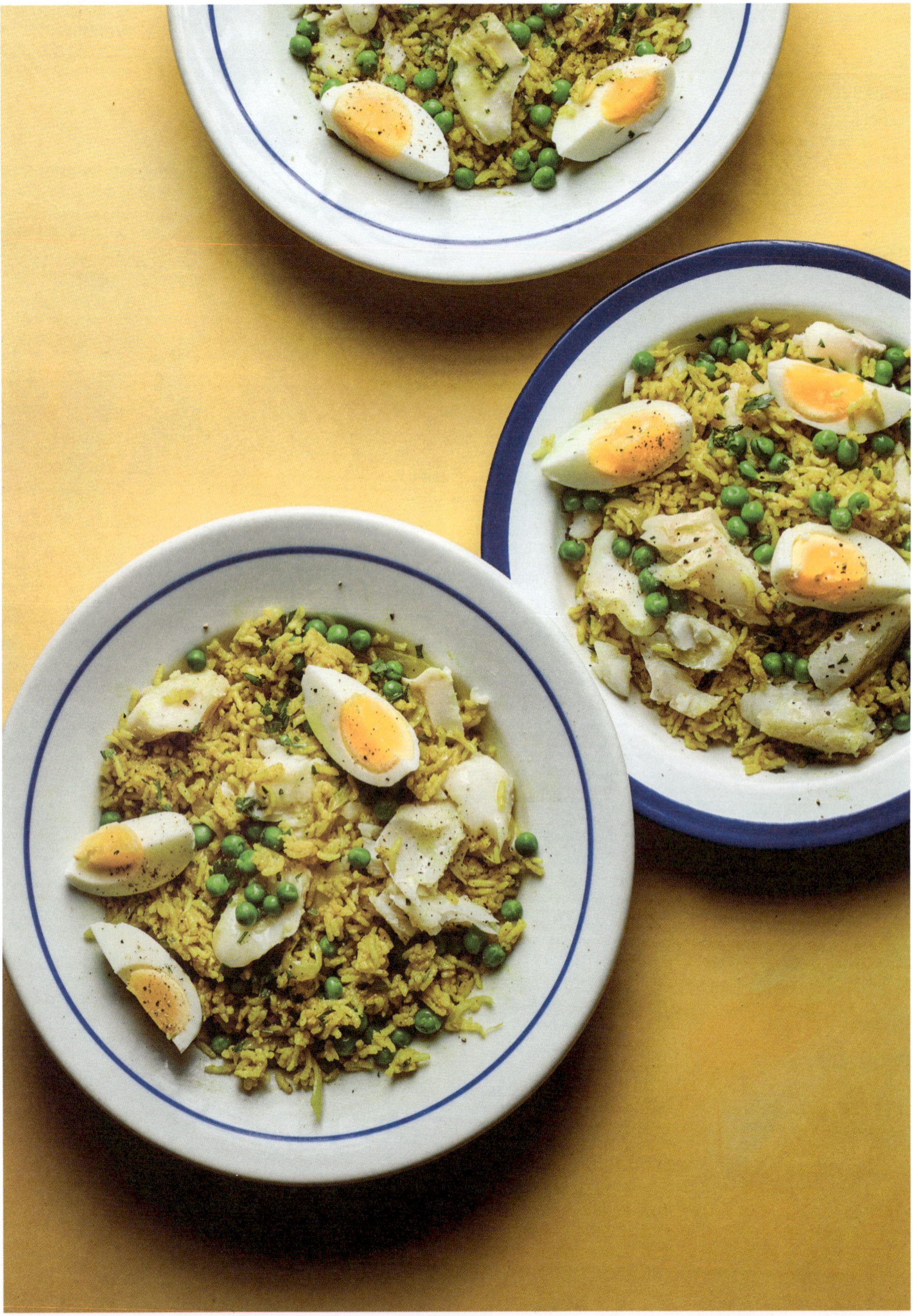

Kedgeree

I was told that kedgeree is one of the four things beginning with K that the Victorians introduced as breakfast, along with Kellogg's, kippers and kidneys. Now, I've no idea if that's true, but it's a fun piece of dinner-party trivia. I prefer kedgeree as a brunch or a more involved dinner and I like to use undyed smoked haddock. Here, the sweetness of the peas really helps to cut through the smokiness of the fish.

SERVES 4-6

- 200ml (7fl oz) whole (full-fat) milk
- 200ml (7fl oz) vegetable stock (gluten-free, if necessary)
- 400g (14oz) smoked fish (haddock, trout or salmon all work well)
- 175g (6oz) frozen peas
- 250g (9oz) basmati rice
- 1 tablespoon oil
- 50g (1¾oz) butter
- 1 onion, sliced
- 1 garlic clove, crushed or finely grated (shredded)
- 1 tablespoon mild curry power
- ½ teaspoon ground turmeric
- 4 eggs
- Handful of parsley, finely chopped
- Salt and freshly ground black pepper

Pour the milk and stock into a saucepan with a lid. Bring to a simmer, then add the fish and cook for 3 minutes. Add the frozen peas and cook for a further 2 minutes or until the fish is cooked through. Drain the fish and peas, reserving the poaching liquid. Pour the liquid into a jug (pitcher) and top up with water so it measures 500ml (17fl oz).

Rinse the rice a few times until the water is running almost clear. Drain and set aside.

Heat the oil in a pan over a medium heat, add half the butter and, once melted, fry the onion for 4–5 minutes or until softened and beginning to brown. Stir in the garlic and fry for 1 minute. Stir in the curry powder and ground turmeric, then cook for 1 minute.

Tip the rice into the pan and stir well so every grain is coated in the spiced oil. Fry the rice for a few minutes until slightly nutty then pour over the reserved poaching liquid. Cover the pan with a lid and bring to a simmer. Turn down the heat until just simmering and cook for 10–15 minutes or until the rice is tender. Remove the pan from the heat and set aside, leaving the rice in the pan.

Meanwhile, cook the eggs to your preference. Bring a pan of water to the boil and cook for 7–10 minutes depending on how soft or hard you want your yolks. Transfer the eggs to a bowl of cold water, then peel once cool enough to handle. (Sometimes this is easier to do under cold running water.) Slice each egg into four.

When ready to serve, assemble the dish by folding the fish, remaining butter and chopped parsley through the rice, then season to taste. Either spoon the kedgeree onto individual plates or onto a serving platter then top with the eggs.

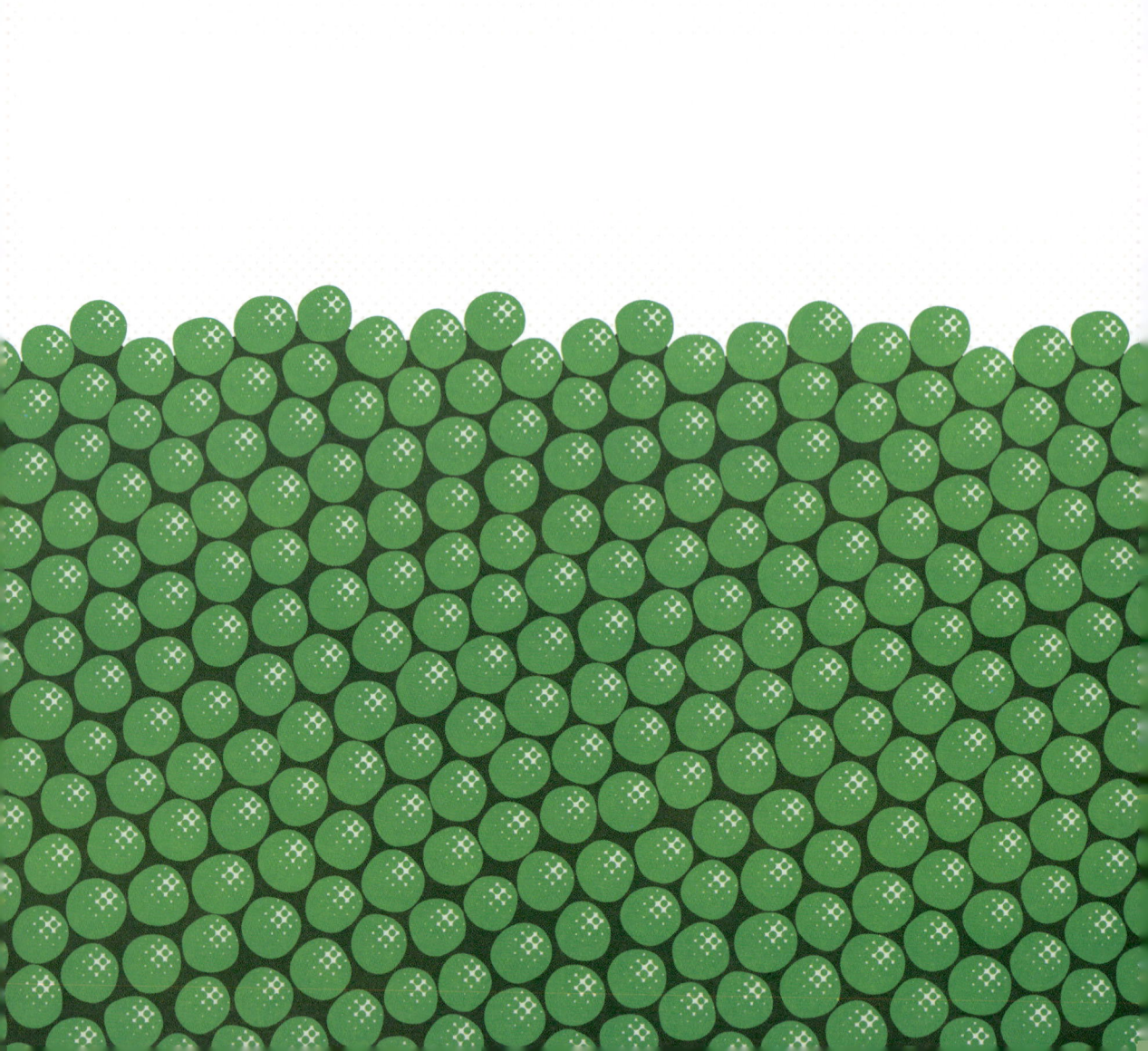

One-Pot Wonders

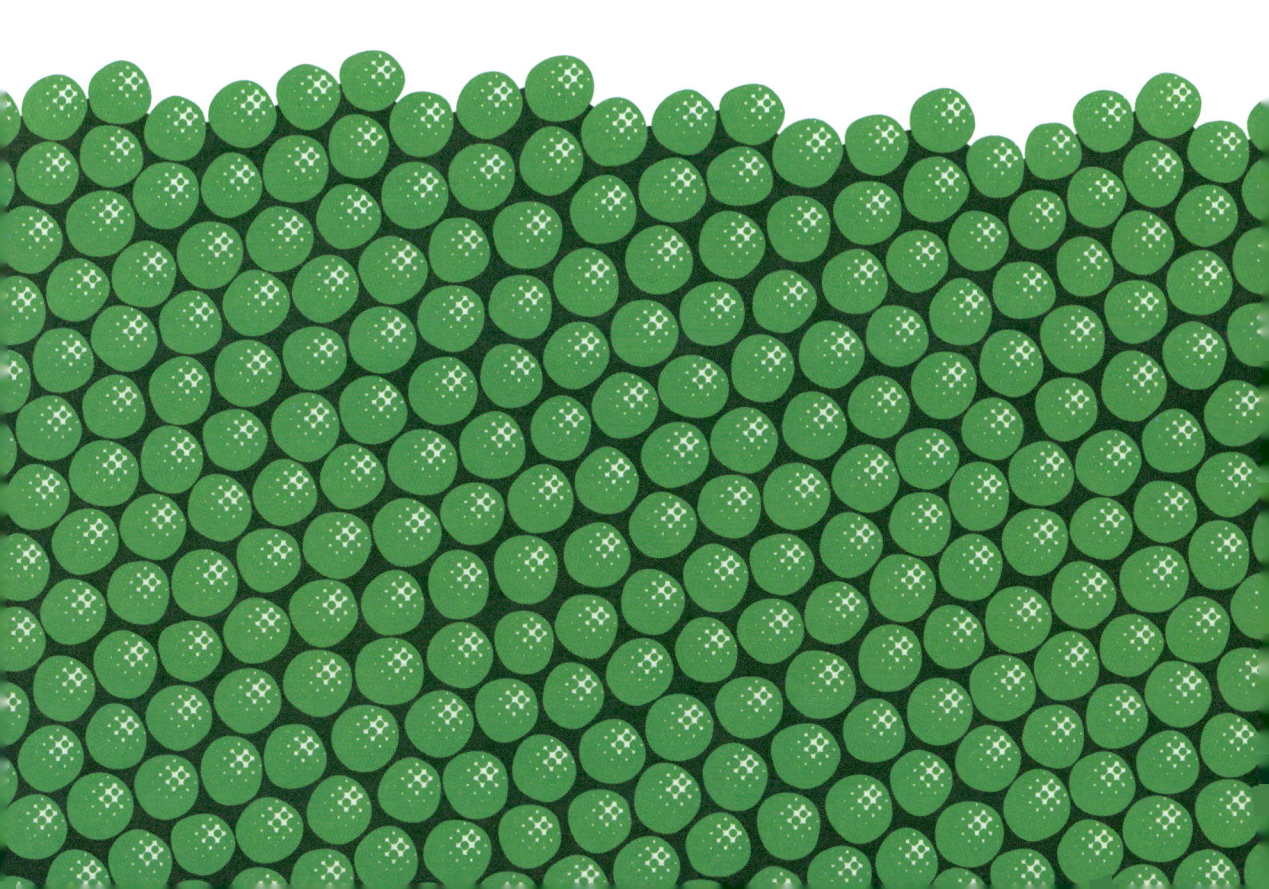

Norwegian-esque Fish Soup

On our first visit to Bergen, having taken the incredibly scenic train route from Oslo, we were told we *had* to try the Bergensk Fiskesuppe. There was a torrential downpour (we soon found out from the locals that this was a common occurrence) so we quickly dived into a kind-of-marquee that was set up outside the fish market. We ordered the soup. It was creamy and delicious, incredibly simple and made using whatever fish they had caught that morning; perfect for a cold, rainy day. This is an homage to that soup.

% **GF**

SERVES 2–4

1 tablespoon sunflower or vegetable oil
1 large leek, halved lengthways and sliced
350g (12½oz) potatoes, roughly chopped
2 carrots (about 250g/9oz), thinly sliced
1 garlic clove, crushed or finely grated (shredded)
750ml (25fl oz) fish stock
500g (1lb 2oz) sustainably caught fish (any white fish, salmon and trout all work well), roughly chopped
250ml (9fl oz) whole (full-fat) milk
200g (7oz) frozen peas
200g (7oz) raw king prawns (jumbo shrimp), frozen is fine (optional)
Handful of parsley or chives, roughly chopped, to serve
1 lemon, cut into wedges, to serve
Crusty bread, to serve (optional)

Heat the oil in a large saucepan over a medium heat. Add the leeks and fry for a few minutes or until fragrant and beginning to soften. Stir in the potato and carrots and fry for a few minutes more, then add the garlic and cook for 1 minute. If you're using parsley to serve, you could also add the stems here.

Pour in the stock and simmer for 15–20 minutes or until the potato and carrots have softened. Season well, then add in the fish and cook for 3–5 minutes or until almost cooked. Pour in the milk and tip in the frozen peas and prawns, if using. Cook for 3–5 minutes or until the prawns have turned pink and all the veg is tender.

Serve with a scattering of chopped herbs, the lemon wedges for squeezing over and crusty bread. I like to serve the lemon wedges alongside the soup as opposed to squeezing the lemon in before serving, as people seem to tolerate it differently.

> **Cook's tip** There's no hard-and-fast rule as to the fish in this dish; use whatever you can find or whatever you have in the fridge or freezer. If you like, you could also add mussels as well as – or instead of – the prawns (shrimp). If possible – and if you can afford it – buy sustainably caught fish. If it carries the MSC logo, you can usually be sure it's sustainably caught.

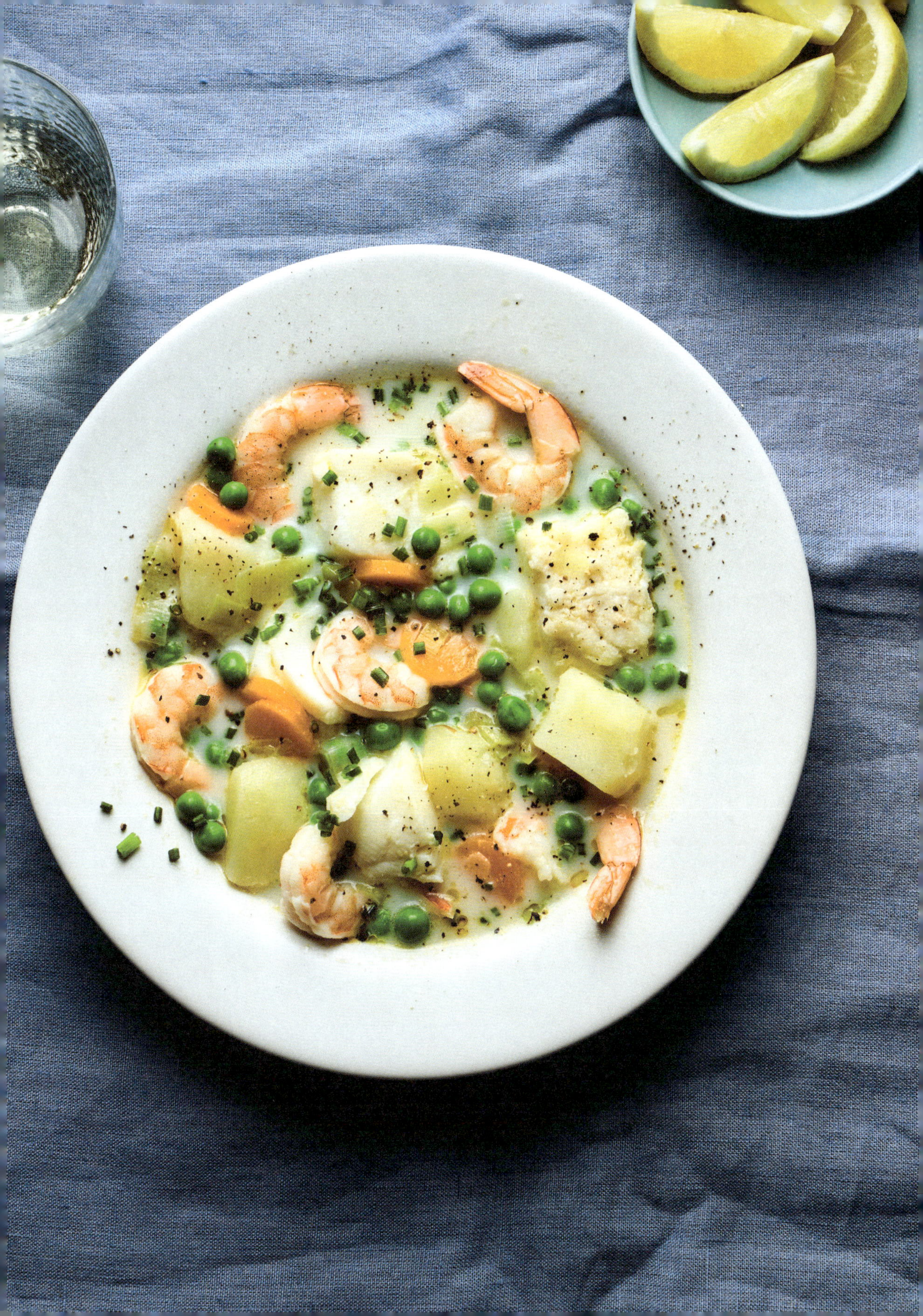

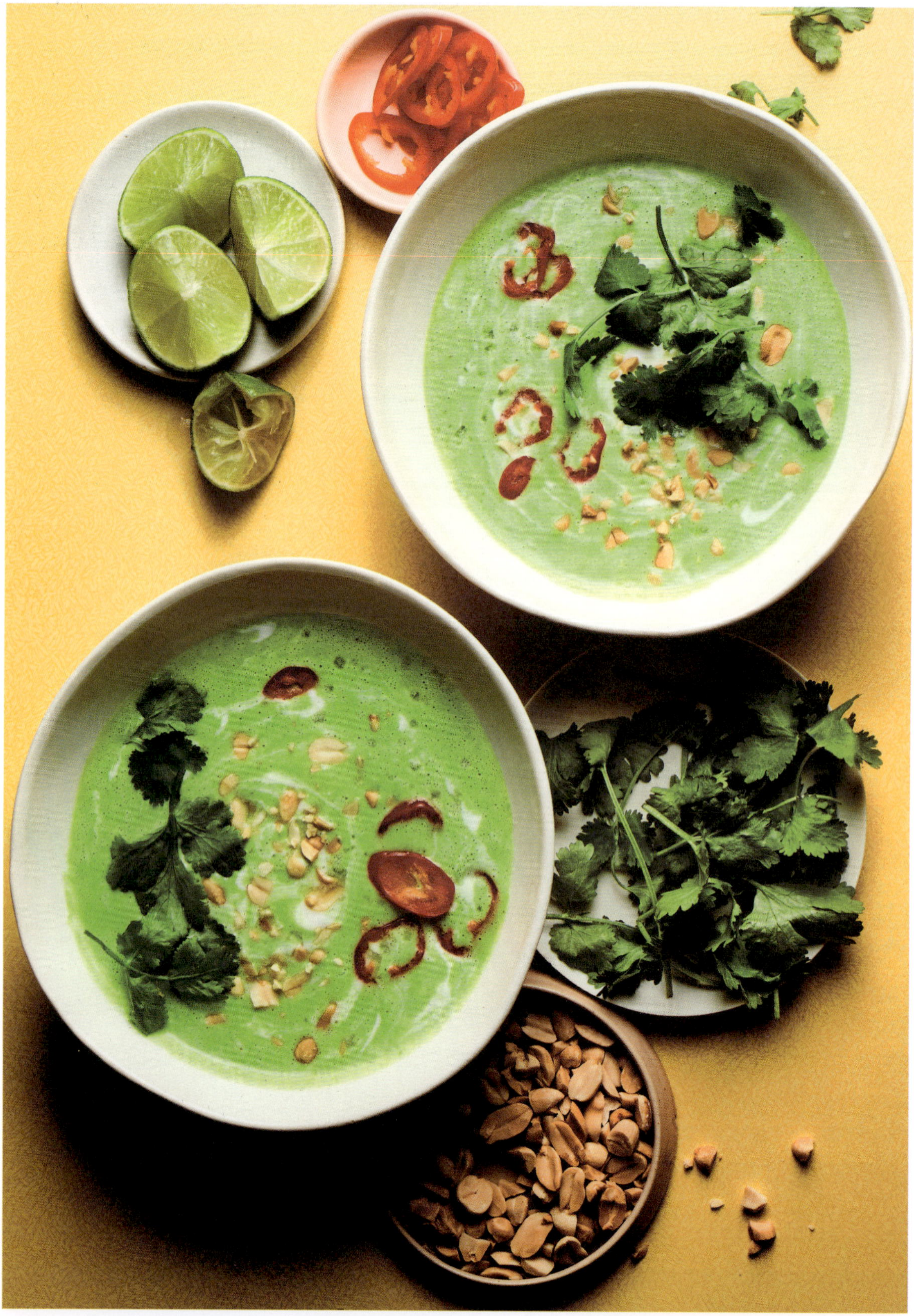

Thai-Spiced Pea and Coconut Soup

When I told my friend Lindsay that I was writing a cookbook based around frozen peas, she insisted that I include this chilled soup. Anyone who knows Lindsay will appreciate that you always follow her direction because she's the Queen of Good Advice, although I have made a few little tweaks to her original recipe. If you're not a chilled soup fan, this is also lovely warm.

% ❄ V VG GF DF

SERVES 4

- 1 tablespoon sunflower or vegetable oil
- 1 onion, finely chopped
- 1 lemongrass stick, tough outer leaves removed, finely sliced
- Large handful of coriander (cilantro), leaves and stalks separated, both chopped
- 1 large garlic clove, crushed or finely grated (shredded)
- 2 tablespoons Thai green curry paste (vegetarian or vegan, if necessary)
- Zest and juice of 1 lime
- 500ml (17fl oz) vegetable or chicken stock (gluten-free, if necessary)
- 1 × 400-ml (14fl-oz) tin full-fat coconut milk, shaken to combine
- 500g (1lb 2oz) frozen peas
- 1 red chilli, sliced (deseeded if you prefer it milder)
- Handful of unsalted peanuts, chopped

Heat the oil in a large pan over a medium heat. Add the onion and lemongrass and fry for 4–5 minutes or until the onion has softened and the lemongrass smells fragrant. Stir in the coriander stalks and garlic, then cook for 1 minute. Add the curry paste and lime zest and cook for a further 1 minute, stirring until everything is coated in the paste.

Pour in the lime juice, stock and all but a couple of tablespoons of the coconut milk, then bring to a simmer. Add the frozen peas, bring everything back to a simmer and cook for 2–3 minutes or until the peas are warmed through and tender.

Blitz the soup either in a blender or using a handheld stick (immersion) blender until smooth. Leave to cool to room temperature or chill in the fridge until cold.

Ladle the soup into bowls, drizzle over a little coconut milk, then scatter over the coriander leaves, red chilli slices and chopped peanuts.

Cook's tip You can also make this meaty by adding some shredded cooked chicken when you add the peas.

Pea and Mint Soup

Pea and mint is such a classic combination, it just works. Fresh mint gives a much nicer, more natural flavour, but if you only have dried mint to hand, go sparingly – perhaps add only half a teaspoon at a time and taste as you go.

% ❄ V VG GF DF

SERVES 4

1 tablespoon sunflower or vegetable oil
1 onion, chopped
1 potato (around 200g/7oz), cut into small cubes
1 garlic clove, chopped
500ml (17fl oz) vegetable stock
400g (14oz) frozen peas
2 mint sprigs, leaves picked and chopped
Juice of ½ lemon
4 tablespoons natural yogurt (optional)
Salt and freshly ground black pepper

Heat the oil in a large saucepan over a gentle heat. Fry the onion for 10–12 minutes or until soft but not golden. Stir in the potato and garlic and fry for 1–2 minutes to soften a little.

Pour in the stock, bring to the boil and then simmer for 10–15 minutes or until the potato has softened. Tip in the frozen peas and mint, season well with salt and freshly ground black pepper. Bring back to a simmer and cook for 3–5 minutes or until the peas have warmed through.

Blitz with a handheld stick (immersion) blender. At this point, thin the soup by adding freshly boiled water, if you like.

Squeeze in the lemon juice to taste, then ladle the soup into bowls and serve with a drizzle of yogurt, if you like, and a crack of black pepper.

The soup can be frozen (without yogurt), for up to 3 months.

Pea and Watercress Soup

The pepperiness of watercress goes really nicely with the sweetness of peas. I've occasionally used rocket (arugula) in the past, which also works well.

% ❄ V VG GF DF

SERVES 4

1 tablespoon sunflower or vegetable oil
8 spring onions (scallions), chopped
1 potato (around 200g/7oz), chopped
2 garlic cloves, finely chopped
500ml (17fl oz) vegetable stock
400g (14oz) frozen peas or petits pois
80g (3oz) watercress
Juice of ½ lemon
A few chives, snipped, to serve (optional)
Salt and freshly ground black pepper

Heat the oil in a large saucepan over a gentle heat. Setting aside a small handful of the green parts, add the spring onions and fry for 6–8 minutes or until soft. Stir in the potato and garlic, then cook for 2 minutes.

Add the stock, bring to a simmer and cook for 10–15 minutes or until the potato has softened. Turn the heat down to a gentle simmer, stir in the frozen peas and watercress, then cook for 2–3 minutes or until the watercress has wilted and peas have warmed through. Season with a little salt and plenty of freshly ground black pepper.

Blitz with a handheld stick (immersion) blender. Squeeze in the lemon juice to taste, then ladle the soup into bowls. Serve with the spring onion greens and a few chives, if you like.

Pea and Ham Soup

Peas and pork go well together in many guises – ham, pancetta, bacon, sausages, the list goes on… In a soup, I love how the pinkness of the ham pops against the vibrant green soup. It's a great dish to serve at a relaxed dinner.

SERVES 4

1 tablespoon sunflower or vegetable oil
1 onion, chopped
1 potato (around 200g/7oz), chopped
2 garlic cloves, finely chopped
400ml (14fl oz) chicken or vegetable stock (gluten-free, if necessary)
200ml (7fl oz) whole (full-fat) milk (or use stock)
300g (10½oz) frozen peas or petits pois
175g (6oz) thick-cut ham, roughly chopped, or shredded ham hock
Salt and freshly ground black pepper

Heat the oil in a large saucepan over a gentle heat. Fry the onion for 10–12 minutes or until soft but not golden. Stir in the potato and garlic and fry for 1–2 minutes to soften a little.

Pour in the stock and milk and bring to the boil over a medium heat. Reduce to a simmer. Tip in the frozen peas, bring back to a simmer and cook for a few minutes or until the peas are warmed through. Season with salt and freshly ground black pepper.

Blitz with a handheld stick (immersion) blender. At this point, thin the soup by adding freshly boiled water, if you like.

Stir all but a handful of the ham into the soup. Place the pan over a gentle heat for 2 minutes to warm the ham.

Ladle the soup into bowls and scatter over a little of the reserved ham. Add a crack of black pepper to each bowl.

The soup can be frozen for up to 3 months.

Chorizo, Pea and Pearl Barley Stew

Having a speedy stew up your sleeve is great for when the weather turns cooler. What I love about this recipe is that the flavours mean that it also suits the warmer weather too – the lemon and peas help here. In fact, it's one of the many benefits of frozen peas – you get to use a spring/summer ingredient all year round.

SERVES 4

- 1 tablespoon sunflower, vegetable or olive oil
- 200g (7oz) cooking chorizo, roughly chopped
- 1 onion, sliced
- 1 leek, sliced
- 2 garlic cloves, crushed or finely grated (shredded)
- 1½ teaspoons smoked paprika
- 1½ teaspoons dried mixed herbs
- Zest and juice of 1 lemon
- 150ml (5fl oz) white wine
- 200g (7oz) pearl barley
- 600ml (20fl oz) vegetable or chicken stock
- 200g (7oz) frozen peas
- Crusty bread, to serve

Heat the oil in a large saucepan with a lid over a medium heat. Add the chorizo and fry for 4–5 minutes until it's started to release its oil and is turning golden. Remove from the pan, leaving the oil behind.

Stir the onion, leek and ½ teaspoon salt into the chorizo. Fry for 6–8 minutes or until beginning to brown. Stir in the garlic, smoked paprika, dried mixed herbs and lemon zest, then season with salt and pepper and cook for 1 minute.

Pour in the white wine, then simmer for 1–2 minutes or until the wine has reduced.

Stir in the pearl barley and mix to combine everything, then cook for 1 minute before pouring in the stock. Pop the lid on then bring to a simmer. Cook for 10 minutes, then mix in the chorizo and cook for a further 10 minutes. Remove the lid, cook for 10 minutes, then stir in the frozen peas, bring back to a simmer and cook for 2–3 minutes or until the peas are warmed through and tender.

Just before serving, stir through the lemon juice to taste, ladle the stew into bowls and serve with crusty bread.

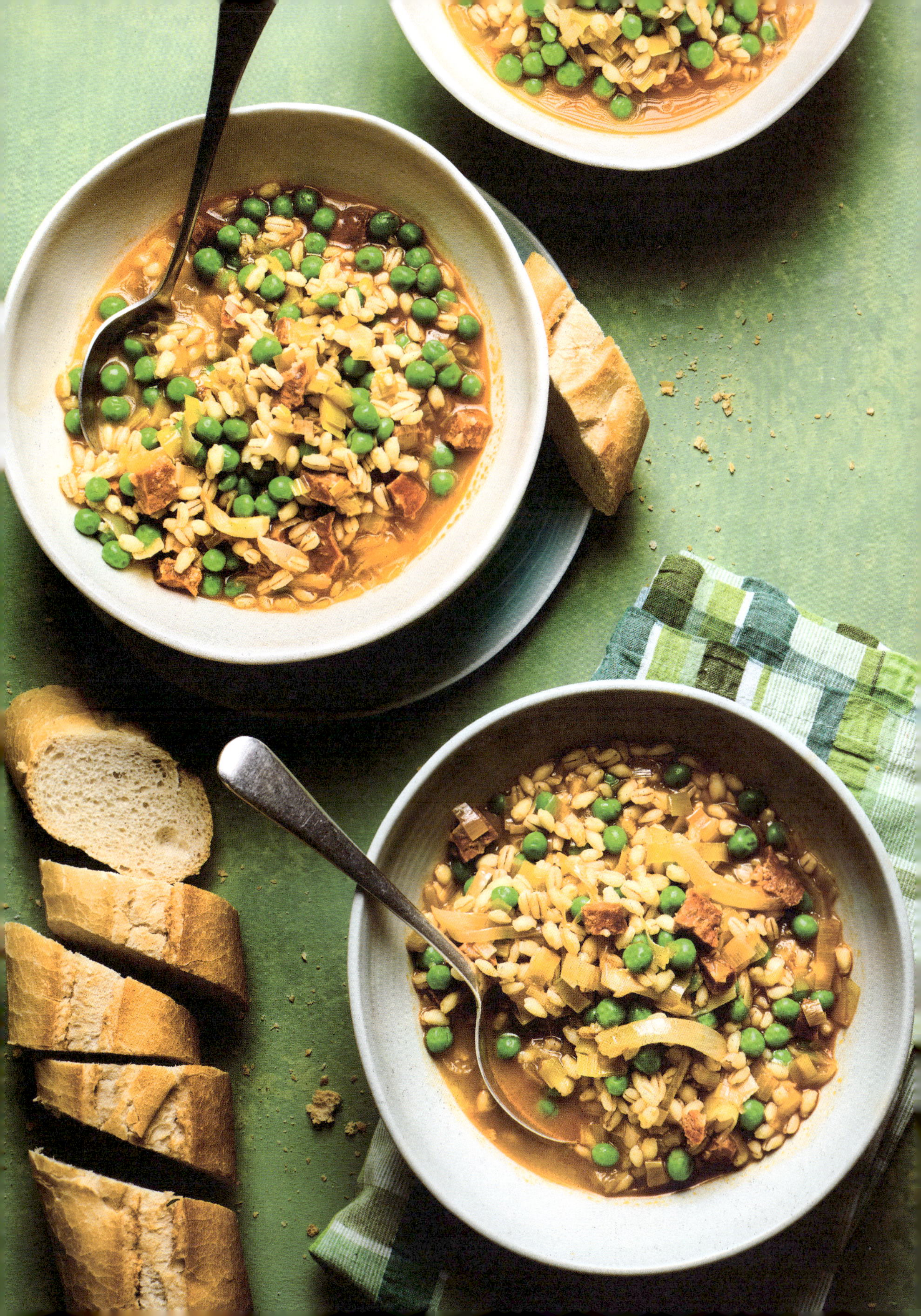

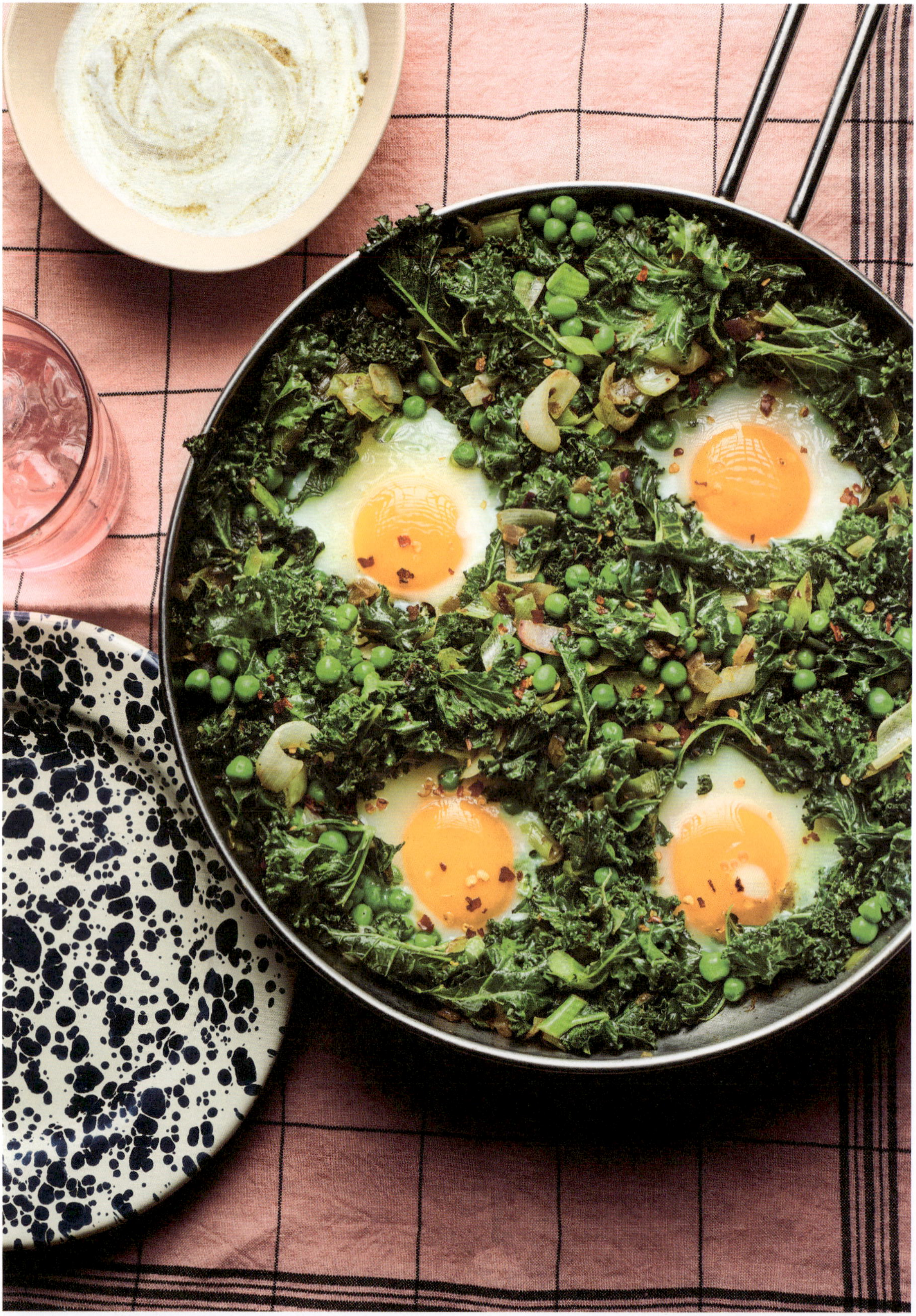

Green Shakshuka

This is very different in flavour to the shakshuka you'll likely be used to, which is made with tomatoes. What I love about this version is that you can switch up the greens depending on what's in season – I always include the frozen peas because they're great all year round.

% V GF DF

SERVES 4

2 tablespoons olive oil
1 leek, halved lengthways and sliced
1 red onion, finely chopped
2 garlic cloves, crushed or finely grated (shredded)
1 teaspoon ground coriander
½ teaspoon ground cumin, plus an extra pinch to serve
½ teaspoon chilli flakes (optional), plus an extra pinch to serve
150g (5½oz) kale, cavolo nero, spring greens or chard, finely sliced
225g (8oz) frozen peas
4 eggs
75g (2½oz) Greek yogurt or plant-based alternative yogurt

Heat the oil in a large frying pan (skillet) with a lid over a medium-low heat. Add the leek and onion and fry, with the lid on but stirring occasionally, for 8–10 minutes or until softened but not golden.

Remove the lid and stir in the garlic, then cook for 1 minute before sprinkling in the ground coriander, cumin and chilli flakes, if using. Cook for 1 minute, making sure that the spices don't burn.

Stir in the kale (or other greens) and frozen peas along with 75ml (2½fl oz) water. Put the lid back on the pan and simmer for 3–4 minutes or until the kale has wilted and peas have warmed through.

Make 4 wells in the greens. Crack an egg into each one. (You can crack the egg into a cup or glass first, if that's easier for you.) Put the lid on the pan and cook for 3–5 minutes or until the egg white is cooked and the yolk is a little runny. (You can cook for longer if you want a completely set egg yolk.)

Dollop over the yogurt and add a pinch each of ground cumin and chilli flakes, if you like.

Mussels in a Creamy White Wine Sauce

I love how versatile mussels are; they're delicious cooked solely in white wine or even just in a little stock, but there's something rather decadent about a creamy sauce. Adding the peas to the sauce at the end makes it feel more substantial. I recently enjoyed the most amazing mussels at a restaurant in the Meat Packing District of Copenhagen; they were from a very local supplier and I can only think that was what made the difference.

SERVES 2

200g (7oz) frozen peas, defrosted according to the packet instructions
150ml (5fl oz) double (heavy) cream
1 tablespoon olive oil
1 small onion, finely chopped
1 garlic clove, crushed
150ml (5fl oz) white wine
1kg (2lb 4oz) live mussels, scrubbed and debearded

TO SERVE
Small handful of parsley, finely chopped
French fries or thick slices of crusty bread (optional)

Put the peas in a colander and rinse with freshly boiled water. Shake the colander, then tip roughly two thirds of the peas into a food processor or blender. Add the cream and season with salt and pepper, then blitz until as smooth as your food processor or blender can manage. Set aside.

In a large saucepan with a lid, heat the oil over a medium-low heat. Add the onion and fry for 8–10 minutes or until softened, then add the garlic and fry for a further 1 minute.

Pour in the white wine and bring to a simmer.

Discard any broken or open mussels (give them a flick first to see if they make any movement; if they do, they're fine.) Add the mussels to the pan with the remaining whole peas, give them a stir, pop on the lid and cook for 2 minutes. Pour in the blended pea and cream mixture and cook for a further 2–3 minutes or until the mussels are cooked. Discard any mussels that have not opened.

Scatter over the chopped parsley and then stir. Serve with French fries or slices of crusty bread, if you prefer.

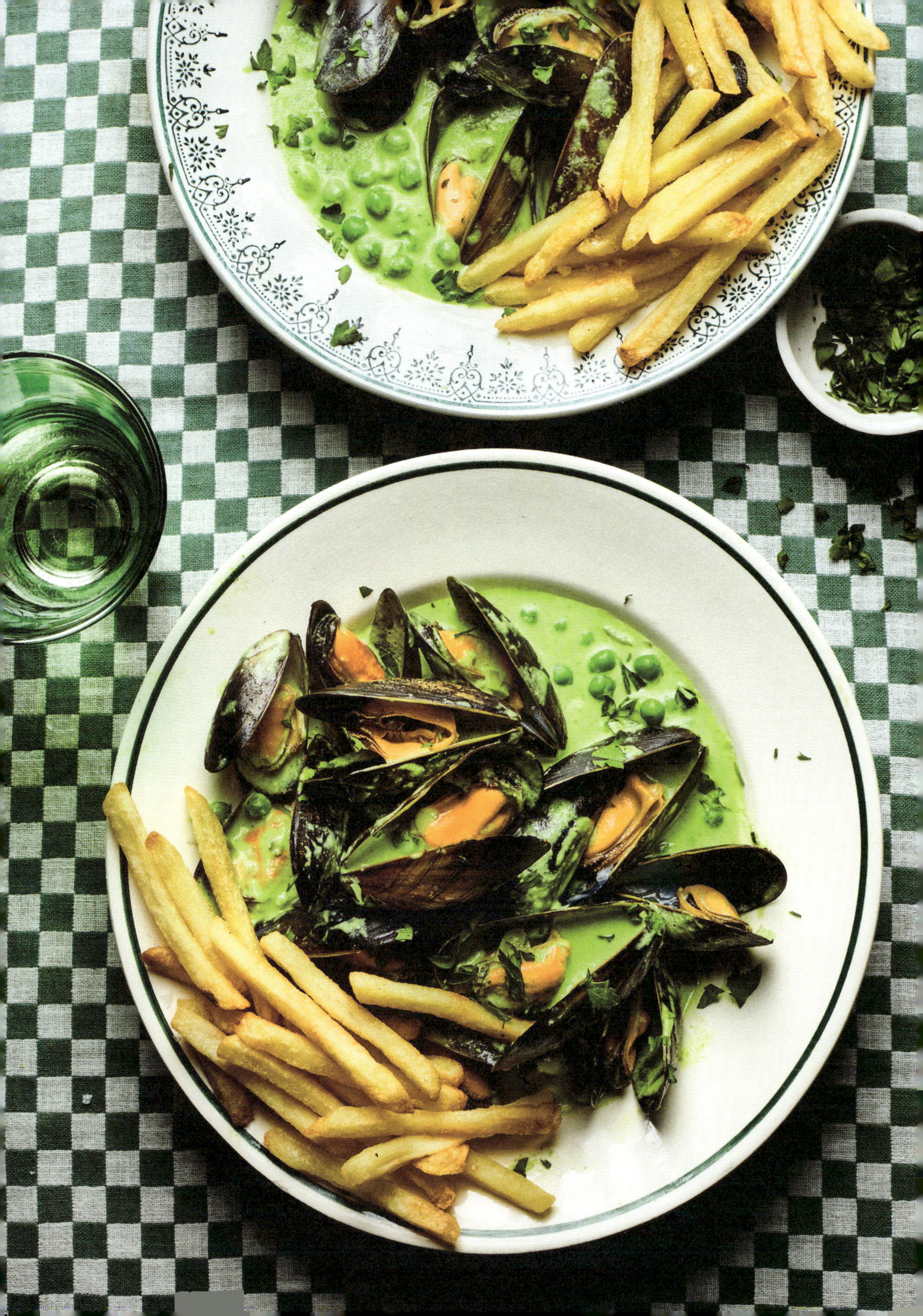

Harissa Chicken and Green Veg Pasta

There's always the need for a quick and easy pasta dish. I love the flavour of harissa and enjoy the contrast in taste and colour of the peas in this one-pot dish. Here, I cook the pasta first and then add it back in a bit later. I often make quick pasta dishes this way because it saves on washing up and I've only got a small kitchen, so it stops everything feeling too overwhelming in there.

SERVES 4

- 400g (14oz) dried pasta (penne and rigatoni work well)
- 2 tablespoons olive oil
- 1 onion, chopped
- 3–4 skinless chicken breasts, sliced or chopped into chunks
- 2 garlic cloves, crushed or finely grated (shredded)
- 3–4 tablespoons harissa paste (depending on how spicy you like it)
- 2 tablespoons tomato paste (concentrated purée)
- 200g (7oz) spinach
- 200g (7oz) kale or cavolo nero
- 200g (7oz) frozen peas

Bring a large pan of salted water to the boil and cook the pasta according to the packet instructions. Drain, reserving a mugful of the pasta cooking water, and set aside.

In the same pan, heat the oil over a gentle heat. Add the onion and fry until soft but not golden, around 8–10 minutes. Stir in the chicken and fry for 4–5 minutes or until beginning to brown and almost cooked through. Tip in the garlic and cook for 1–2 minutes, then stir in the harissa paste and tomato paste and cook for a further 1 minute.

Add the spinach and kale or cavolo nero to the pan with a splash of the reserved pasta cooking water. Stir well and cook until the spinach has wilted. Tip in the frozen peas and pasta along with enough pasta cooking water to create a glossy sauce that coats the pasta. Cook until the peas are warmed through and tender – this should only take just a few minutes. Serve immediately.

Frozen Pea Dal

It's important to note that dal is not only an eaten dish, but it's also named after the ingredient it contains – a split pulse of some kind, usually split lentils or split peas. These are very different to frozen peas and so by adding them, you're not doubling up on a similar ingredient. Instead, you're adding a vibrancy and flavour that complements everything really well.

% ❄ V VG GF DF

SERVES 4

2 tablespoons sunflower oil, vegetable oil or ghee
2 onions, sliced
4 garlic cloves, crushed or finely grated (shredded)
Thumb-sized piece of ginger, grated (shredded) or finely chopped
1 red chilli, finely chopped (optional)
1 teaspoon ground cumin
1 teaspoon ground ginger
1 teaspoon ground turmeric
250g (9oz) yellow split peas or red lentils
1 × 400-ml (14-fl oz) tin coconut milk (or use an extra 400ml/14fl oz stock)
300ml (10fl oz) vegetable stock
6 blocks frozen spinach
350g (12½oz) frozen peas

Heat the oil in a large saucepan over a medium heat. Add the onions and fry until golden, around 6–8 minutes. Stir in the garlic, ginger and chilli, if using, and cook for 1 minute. Stir in the ground cumin, ginger and turmeric and cook for a further 1 minute.

Stir in the split peas or lentils, coconut milk and vegetable stock. Bring to a simmer and cook for 35–45 minutes or until the split peas are tender (red lentils take less time, around 20 minutes). If the dal is looking slightly dry, add a little more stock or water. It should be the consistency of thin porridge.

Tip in the spinach and cook for 3 minutes, then add the frozen peas and cook for a final 2 minutes or until the peas are warmed through and tender.

Serving suggestion Dal goes great with rice, naan breads or roasted vegetables, such as cauliflower or squash. You can top with a scattering of chopped coriander (cilantro) or some yogurt.

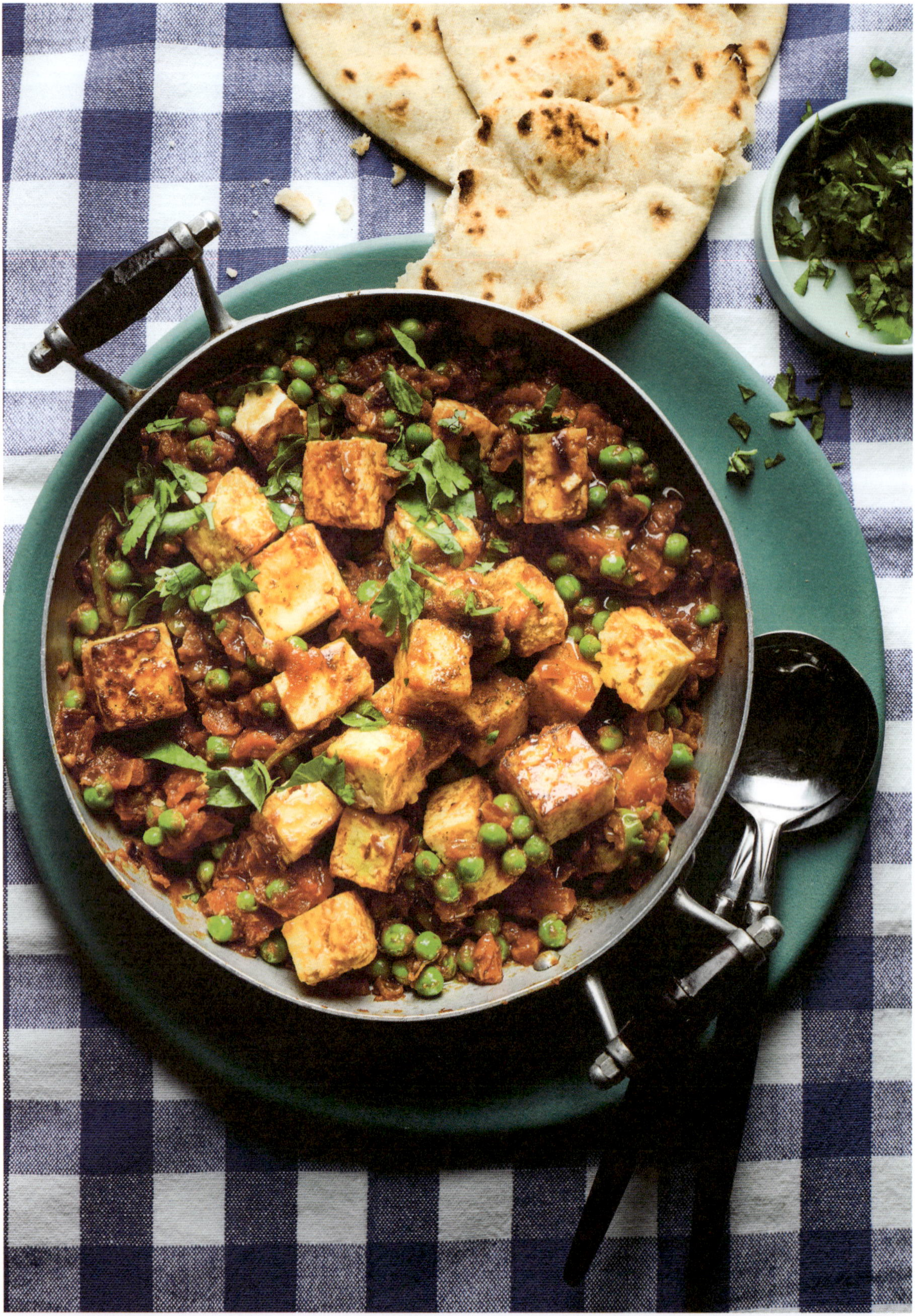

Mattar Paneer

There are a few variations on this dish, as well as spellings, and this is by no means an authentic version. However, it is one that gets as close as possible to the version I like, using what you'll hopefully already have in the storecupboard. Or at least you'll only have to pick up a few bits from the shops. This goes great with naan bread or roti.

SERVES 2–3

- 2 tablespoons vegetable oil
- 200–250g (7–9oz) paneer, depending on pack size, cut into small cubes (around 3cm/1 inch)
- 1 red onion, chopped
- Thumb-sized piece of ginger, grated (shredded)
- 2 garlic cloves, crushed or finely grated (shredded)
- 1 green chilli, deseeded if you like, sliced
- 1 teaspoon cumin seeds
- 1 teaspoon ground coriander
- ½ teaspoon ground turmeric
- ½ teaspoon kasuri methi (optional)
- ½ teaspoon chilli powder (Kashmiri if you have it, optional)
- 1 × 400-g (14-oz) tin chopped tomatoes
- 200g (7oz) frozen peas
- ½ teaspoon garam masala
- Handful of coriander (cilantro), chopped

Heat the oil in a saucepan or frying pan (skillet) over a medium heat. Add the paneer and fry until browned all over. Remove from the pan, leaving the oil behind, and drain on kitchen paper or a clean dish towel.

Stir in the red onion and cook for 6–8 minutes or until golden. Stir in the ginger, garlic and chilli and cook for 1–2 minutes, then stir in the cumin seeds, ground coriander, ground turmeric, kasuri methi and chilli powder, if using. Cook for 1 minute, then tip in the chopped tomatoes and cook for 5–10 minutes or until reduced a little.

Return the fried paneer to the pan and cook for 2–3 minutes until warmed through. Stir in the frozen peas and cook for 2–3 minutes or until they are warmed through and tender.

Spoon into bowl and serve with a pinch of garam masala and a scattering of coriander, if you like.

Chicken and Spring Veg Traybake

There's something very satisfying about a traybake, especially when you don't need to make any sauce or sides to go with it. This all-in-one meal is ideal as a quick Sunday roast or for a relaxed evening dinner. Along with the other spring veg, the peas cheer up any plate.

SERVES 3–4

6–8 chicken thighs, skin-on and bone-in
1 red onion, peeled and cut into 8 wedges
500g (1lb 2oz) baby potatoes, halved or quartered if large
2 tablespoons olive oil
3 leeks, trimmed, halved lengthways and sliced
2 bay leaves
A few thyme or rosemary sprigs
1 lemon, zested and cut into wedges to serve
300ml (10½fl oz) chicken or vegetable stock
300g (10½oz) frozen peas
3 tablespoons crème fraîche or sour cream
2 tablespoons wholegrain mustard
Salt and freshly ground black pepper

Preheat the oven to 220°C/200°C fan/430°F/gas 7.

Put the chicken thighs, red onion and baby potatoes into a large roasting tin (sheet pan) or ovenproof dish. Drizzle over the oil and season well with salt and freshly ground black pepper. Mix everything together.

Roast everything in the hot oven for 15 minutes or until the chicken skin is browning nicely. This is to kickstart the cooking and help the chicken to brown a little.

Lift out the chicken thighs, then add the leeks, bay leaves, thyme or rosemary sprigs, lemon zest and stock to the tin. Mix everything together and then nestle the chicken thighs back on top, skin side up.

Return the tin to the oven and roast everything for a further 30–35 minutes or until the chicken is cooked through, the potatoes are tender and the leeks are soft.

Lift out the chicken thighs again, tip in the frozen peas and spoon in the crème fraîche and mustard. Mix everything together, rest the chicken thighs back on top and then roast for a further 5–8 minutes or until everything is piping hot.

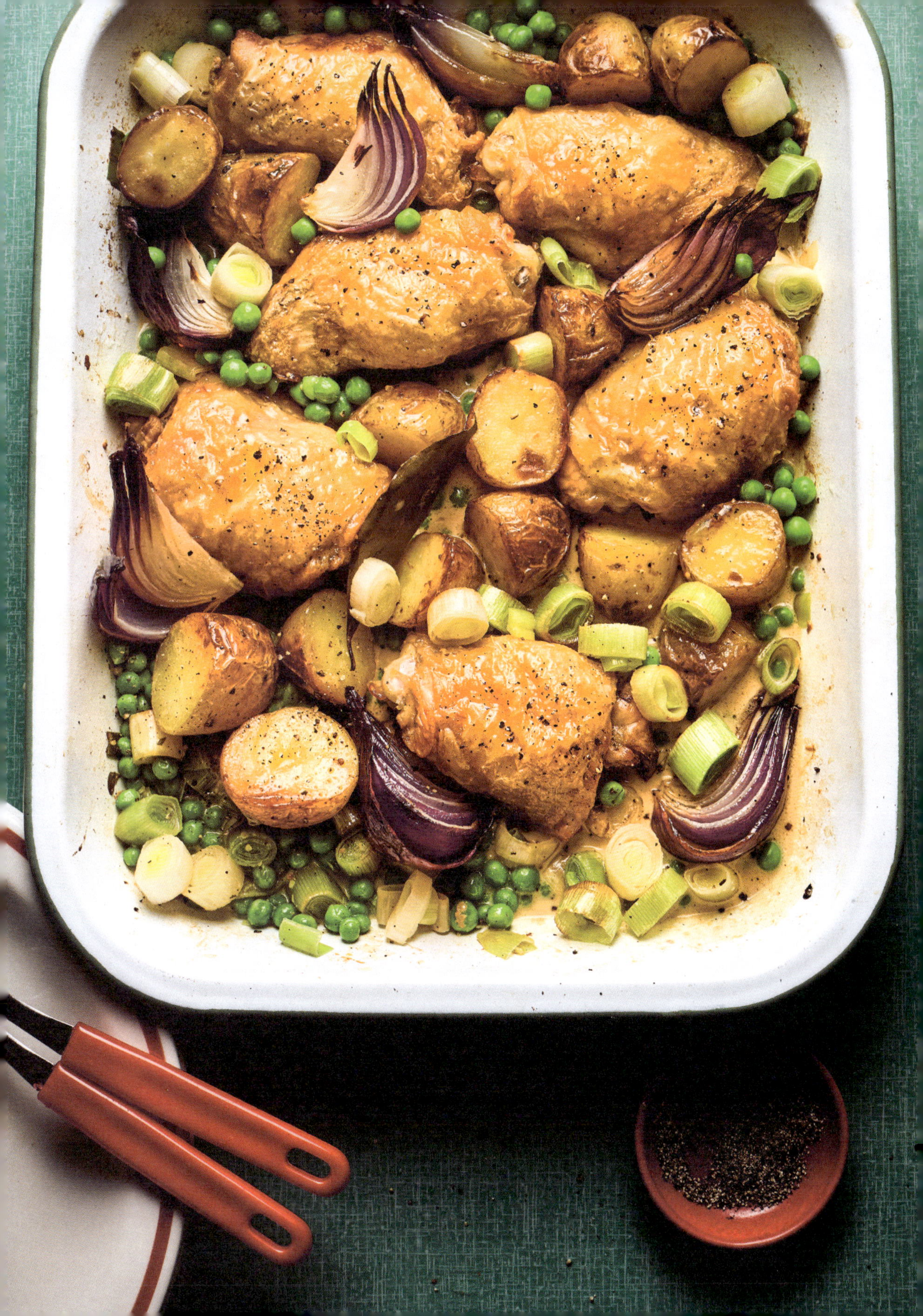

Chicken and Mushroom Pot Pie

I was introduced to chicken and mushrooms in the 1990s via a jar of Chicken Tonight. Who didn't love those adverts? I adore this combo, but the whole thing can look a bit grey. Adding peas adds a pop of colour and some much-needed veg.

SERVES 4–6

- 500g (1lb 2oz) chestnut or button mushrooms, sliced
- 2 tablespoons sunflower or vegetable oil
- 8 boneless, skinless chicken thighs, roughly chopped (or use 4 chicken breasts)
- 1 onion, finely chopped
- 2 carrots, roughly chopped
- 1 celery stick, finely chopped
- 1 tablespoon picked thyme leaves or 1 teaspoon dried mixed herbs
- 30g (1oz) butter
- 30g (1oz) plain (all-purpose) flour
- 350ml (12fl oz) whole (full-fat) milk
- 200g (7oz) frozen peas
- 1 × 320-g (11-oz) packet ready-rolled puff pastry or 500-g (1lb 2-oz) block puff pastry
- 1 egg, beaten

Heat a frying pan (skillet) or saucepan with a lid over a medium heat. Dry fry the mushrooms until they've released their liquid and it has evaporated – this can take 10 minutes. Drizzle in 1 tablespoon of the oil and fry until golden. Remove the mushrooms from the pan, leaving the oil behind.

Add the remaining oil to the pan. Once hot, add the chicken and brown it all over – you can do this in batches if easier. Remove the chicken from the pan, leaving the oil behind.

Tip the onion, carrots, celery and herbs into the pan, reduce the heat to medium-low, and cook with the lid on for 8–10 minutes or until the veg is soft but not golden. Set aside the veggies with the mushrooms and chicken.

Heat the butter in the pan over a medium-low heat. Once melted, add the flour and stir to form a paste. Cook for 1 minute, then gradually add the milk, whisking out any lumps between each addition, until you have a thick sauce.

Tip the mushrooms, chicken, onion, carrot and celery back into the pan along with the peas and cook for 2 minutes. Remove from the heat and scrape everything into a large pie dish.

Unroll the puff pastry and check that it will cover your pie dish. If not, you can roll it out a little further with a rolling pin. Alternatively, roll out the block of puff pastry on a lightly floured work surface until it's around 5mm (¼ inch) thick.

Lay the pastry over the top of the pie dish, then crimp the edges by squeezing the pastry between your thumb and forefinger. If you find it easier, press a fork or knife around the edge. If there are any leftover scraps, use them to decorate the top by sticking them on with beaten egg. Make a few small slits in the pastry top to allow steam to escape.

At this point, you can freeze the pie (providing that your pie dish is freezer-safe) for up to 3 months.

Preheat the oven to 200°C/180°C fan/390°F/gas 6.

Bake the pie in the hot oven for 25–35 minutes or until the pastry is golden and cooked through. If cooking the pie from frozen, bake for slightly longer – around 45 minutes–1 hour.

Toad in the Hole

This British classic is often served with peas on the side, but why give yourself more washing up? It's just as easy to cook it all in one dish. I've also added some leeks because you may as well add as much green veg as you can!

SERVES 4

2 tablespoons sunflower or vegetable oil
12 chipolatas
1 leek, sliced
3 eggs
150g (5½oz) plain (all-purpose) flour
275ml (10fl oz) whole (full-fat) milk
200g (7oz) frozen peas
Salt and freshly ground black pepper

Preheat the oven to 220°C/200°C fan/430°F/gas 7.

Drizzle the oil into a medium roasting tin (sheet pan). It's important the roasting tin is metal otherwise the cooking times will likely be significantly longer. Scatter in the chipolatas and toss to coat in the oil. Put into the hot oven and cook for 5 minutes, then add in the leeks and cook for a further 10–15 minutes or until beginning to brown.

Meanwhile, in a large mixing bowl, combine the eggs, flour and milk. Whisk vigorously to make a smooth batter.

Scatter the frozen peas into the roasting tin and season everything well with plenty of salt and freshly ground black pepper. Mix everything around then pop the tin back in the oven for 2 minutes to get everything hot.

Remove the tin from the oven and pour over the batter. Return the tin to the oven and cook for 30–35 minutes until the batter has risen and turned golden. Depending on the size of your tin, the batter may not puff up around the edges – but that's fine, it'll still be delicious.

Serving suggestion As you've got everything you need in the roasting tin (sheet pan), this really just needs a sauce of your choice. That can be good old-fashioned gravy or a classic ketchup. If I'm honest, I often use gravy granules or ready-made gravy, especially for dishes like this where there are no natural juices being created.

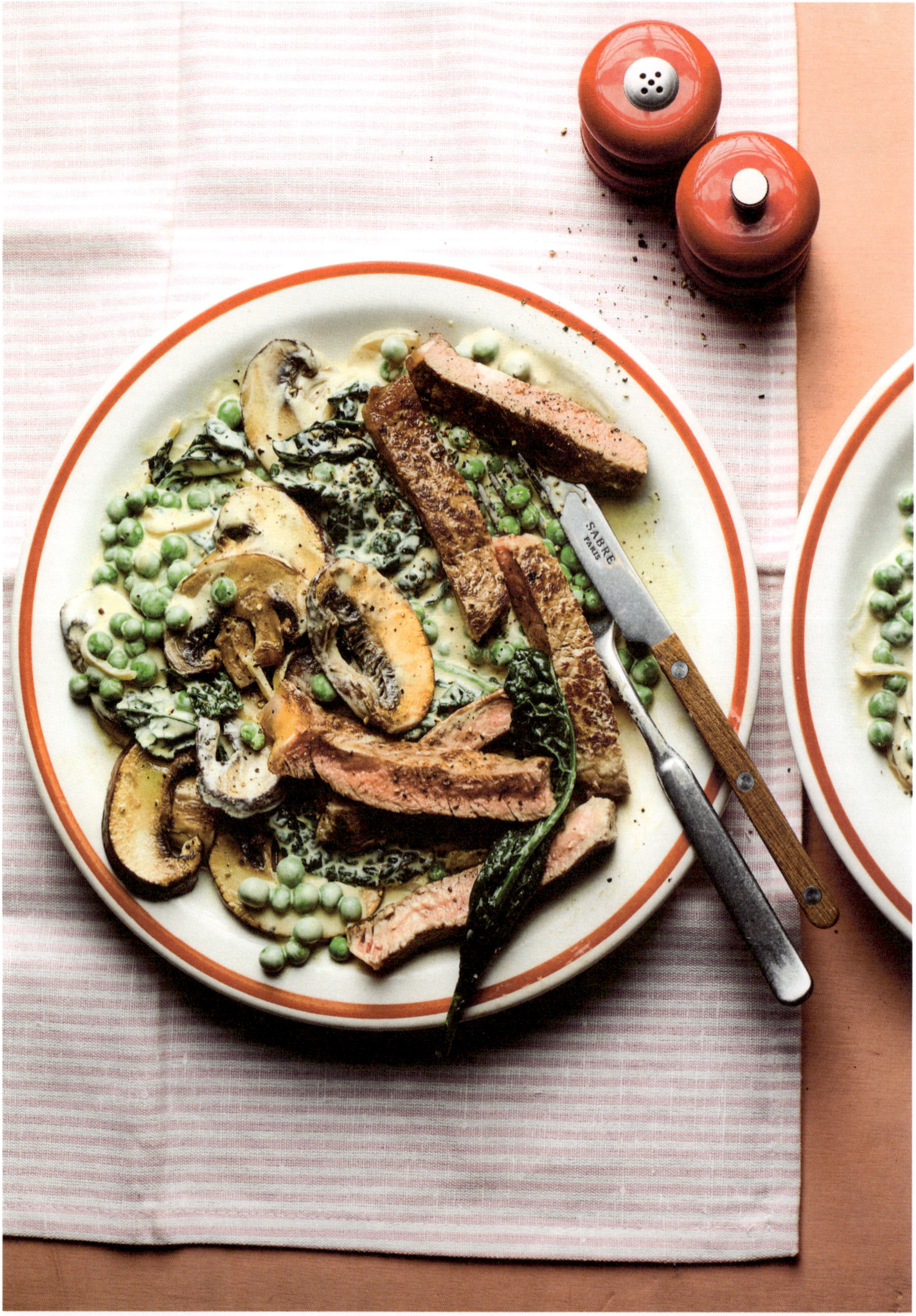
SABRE
PARIS

One-Pan Steak with Mushrooms, Peas and Greens

Steak can feel like quite the luxury, so I love it when it's on special offer and I can make a relaxed dinner that still feels special. While I'm not against the steak-and-chips combo, the colour of the peas here along with the other green veg helps to lift the sauce of crème fraîche and mustard – along with the natural juices, they make a ready-made sauce with minimal effort.

SERVES 2

400g (14oz) steak (sirloin, ribeye or hanger/skirt all work well)
2 tablespoons olive oil
500g (1lb 2oz) chestnut mushrooms, sliced
1 onion, sliced
250g (9oz) cavolo nero, spring greens or kale, shredded
250g (9oz) frozen peas
1 tablespoon Dijon mustard
200–300ml (7–10fl oz) crème fraîche
Handful of chopped parsley, to garnish (optional)
Salt and freshly ground black pepper

Rub the steak all over with ½ tablespoon of the oil and then season with salt and freshly ground black pepper. Set aside.

Dry fry the mushrooms in a large frying pan (skillet) until they've released their liquid and it has evaporated. Drizzle in 1 tablespoon of the oil and continue to fry the mushrooms until browned a little. Remove the mushrooms from the pan, leaving behind as much of the oil as possible.

Fry the steak in the pan, cooking it for 2–3 minutes on each side, depending on how well cooked you like it. Remove the steak from the pan and leave to rest.

Add the remaining oil to the pan, then stir in the onion and fry for 6–8 minutes or until beginning to brown.

Stir the greens into the pan with the mushrooms along with 75ml (2½fl oz) water. Fry for 3–4 minutes or until the greens have started to wilt. Next, mix in the frozen peas and cook for 1 minute to start to thaw them.

Slice the steak into strips and add to the pan with the mushrooms along with any liquid released. Stir in the mustard and enough crème fraîche to make a thick sauce, then season with salt and pepper. Mix everything together and cook for 2–3 minutes to warm everything through. Scatter with parsley, if using.

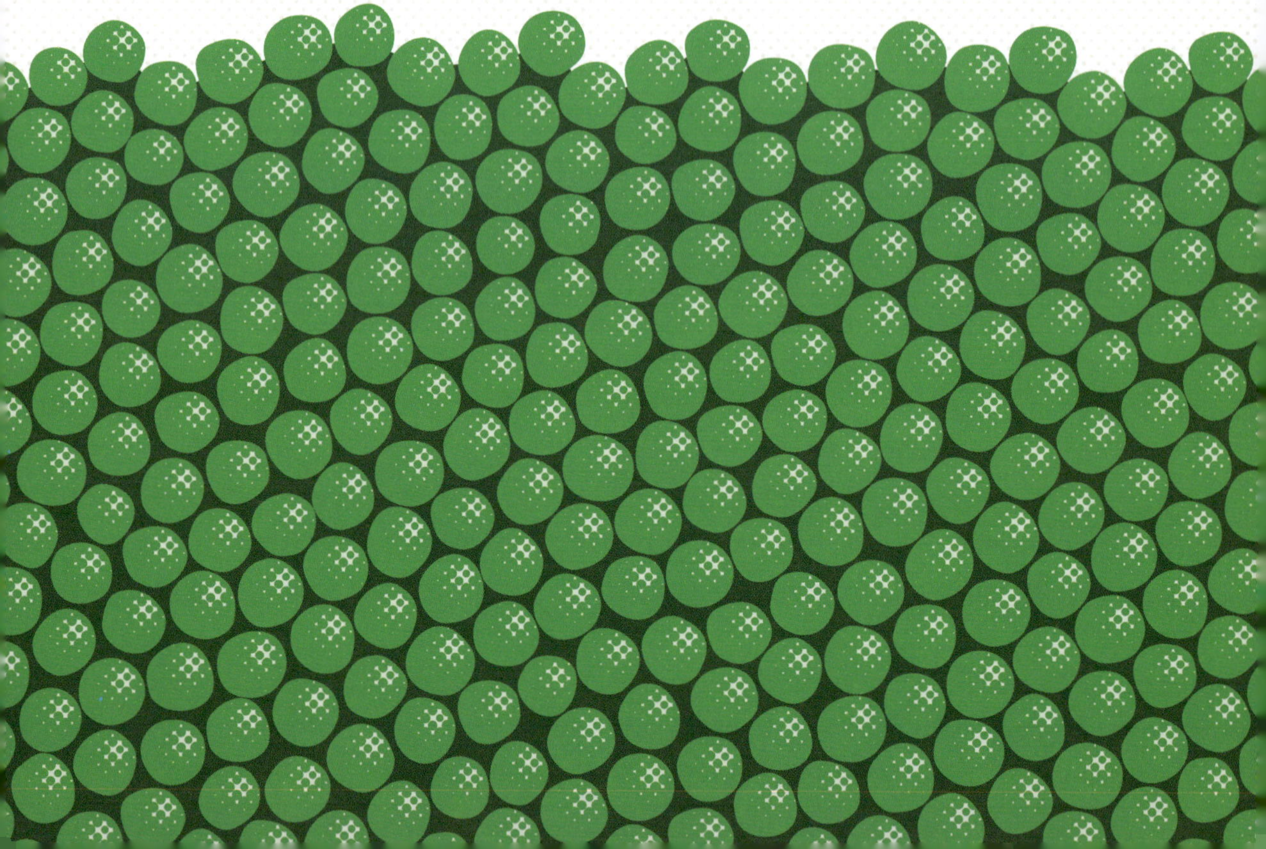

Family Feasts

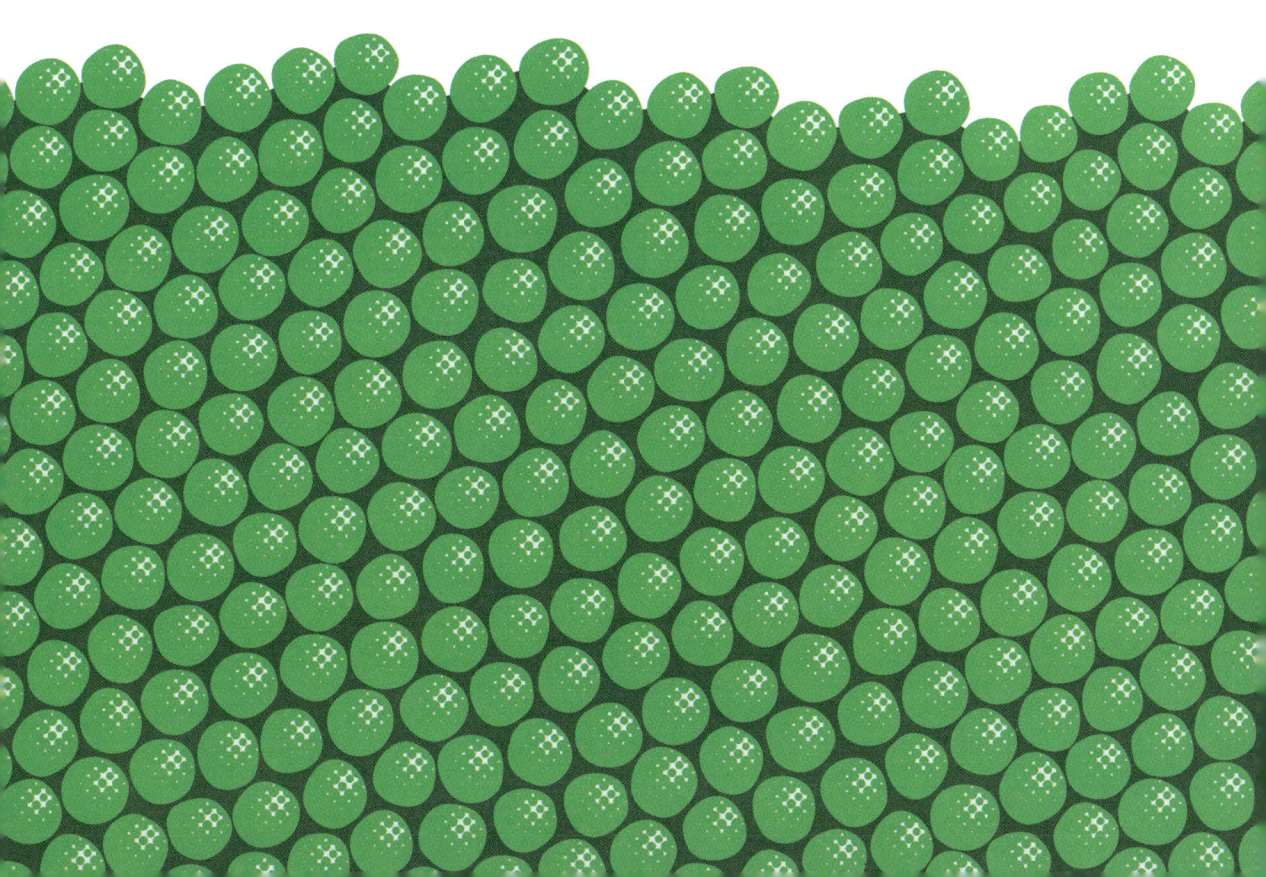

Lamb Kofta with Pea Tabbouleh

There's something very comforting about kofta. I think it's the combination of the fatty lamb and the warming spices. Serving them alongside the pea tabbouleh allows for a simple side that provides a little colour for the otherwise quite brown kofta.

SERVES 4

FOR THE KOFTA
500g (1lb 2oz) minced (ground) lamb
½ teaspoon ground cumin
½ teaspoon ground turmeric
½ teaspoon ground coriander
½ teaspoon chilli powder (optional)
1 garlic clove, crushed or finely grated (shredded)
Handful of coriander (cilantro), finely chopped

FOR THE TABBOULEH
3 tablespoons olive oil
175g (6oz) medium bulgur wheat
350ml (12fl oz) vegetable or chicken stock
Zest and juice of ½ lemon
275g (9½oz) frozen peas
Half a bunch of parsley, finely chopped
A few mint sprigs, leaves picked and chopped
½ cucumber, finely chopped
Yogurt, to serve (see tip below)

Combine the minced (ground) lamb, ground spices, chilli powder, garlic and coriander in a bowl and mix everything really well. It helps to squeeze it with your fingers to get everything nicely mixed together. Divide into 4 large or 8 small sausage shapes and chill.

Heat 2 tablespoons of the oil in a large frying pan (skillet) and fry the bulgur wheat for a couple of minutes until beginning to toast. Pour in the stock and stir in the lemon zest, then cook for 10–15 minutes or until the bulgur wheat is tender and the stock has been absorbed. Add a dash of water, if you need to.

While the bulgur wheat is cooking, defrost the frozen peas in a heatproof bowl by covering them in boiling water and leaving them for 2 minutes. Drain and then stir into the bulgur wheat when it's cooked. Mix in the lemon juice, parsley, mint and cucumber and season well with salt and pepper. Set aside while you cook the kofta.

You can thread the koftas onto skewers, however I find it easier to cook them in a pan without skewering them first. (Unless you cook the kofta in the oven, which you can do at 200°C/180°C fan/390°F/gas 6 for around 20–30 minutes.) Heat the remaining oil in a frying pan (skillet) and cook the kofta all over for 10–15 minutes or until cooked through and browned. Serve with the tabbouleh and spoonfuls of yogurt.

> **Cook's tip** This dish is already packed with flavour, but if you want to ramp up your yogurt, you could stir through some chopped mint or a crushed garlic clove and dust it with a little ground cumin before serving. These are also great served with pitta breads, to stuff everything into.

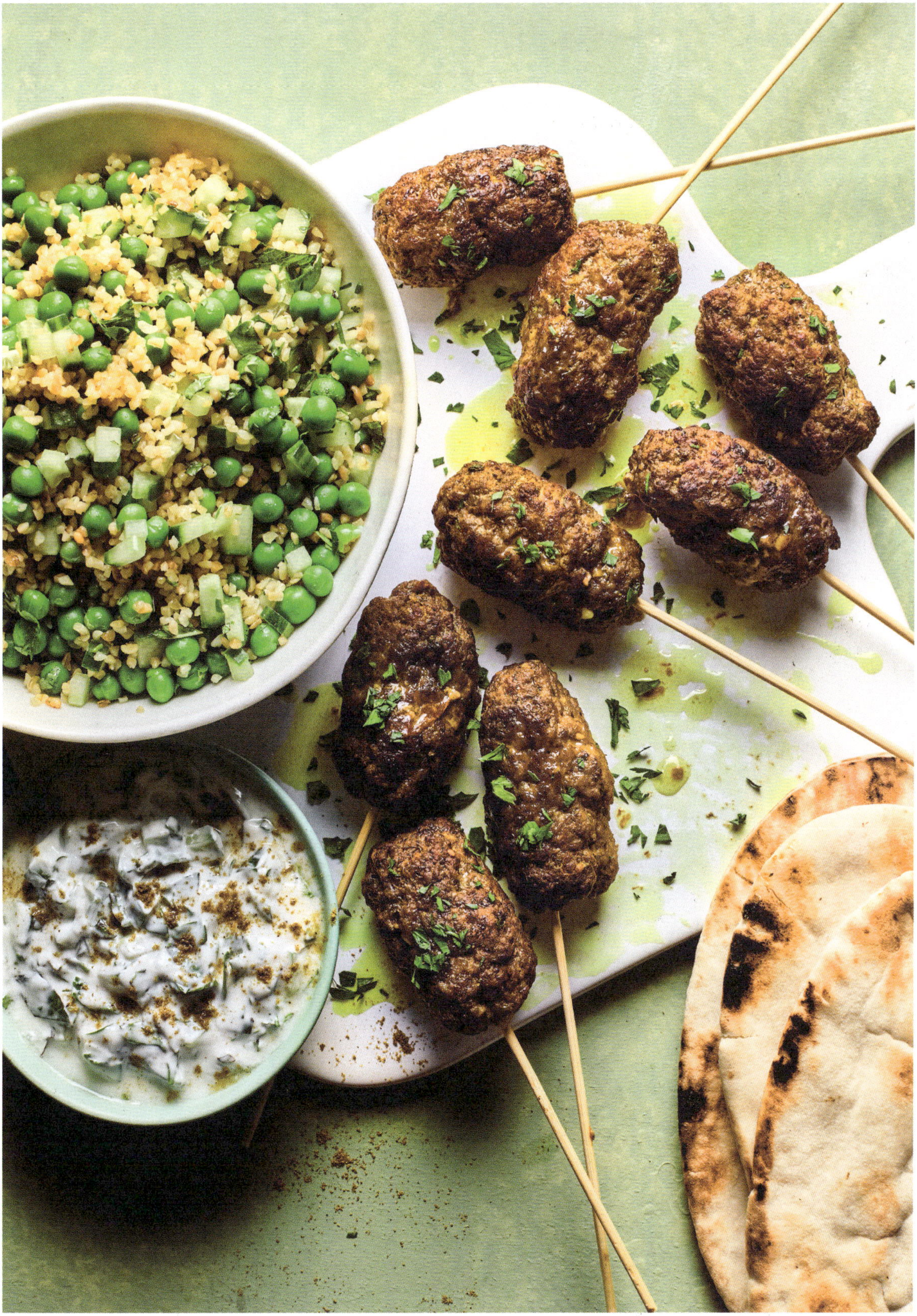

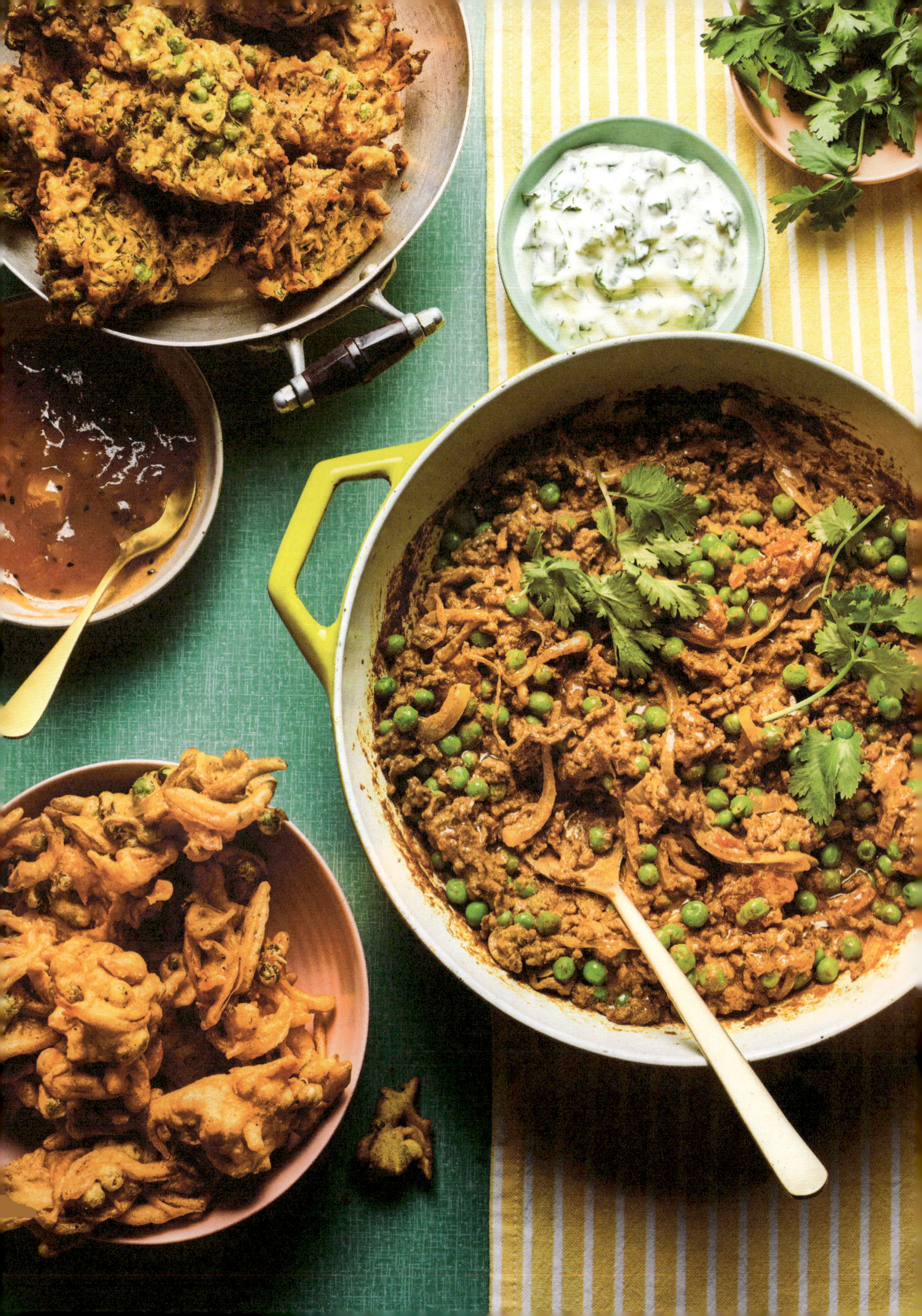

Keema Curry

I love a keema curry. It gives me the vibe of an Indian-inspired shepherd's pie, which is no bad thing. It's also why I've given an option below for turning the curry into a pie. The keema curry is shown opposite with the Pea and Onion Bhaji and the Courgette and Pea Pakora from pages 86–87, along with a raita and mango chutney, but you can serve it with any of your favourite sides.

SERVES 4

- 2 tablespoons sunflower or vegetable oil
- 2 onions, sliced
- 2 garlic cloves, crushed or finely grated (shredded)
- Thumb-sized piece (about 25g/ ¾oz) of fresh root ginger, finely chopped or grated (shredded)
- 500g (1lb 2oz) minced (ground) beef or lamb
- 1 teaspoon ground turmeric
- 2 teaspoons ground cumin
- 2½ teaspoons ground coriander
- 1 green chilli, sliced, plus extra to garnish (optional)
- 4 tablespoons natural yogurt
- 1 × 400-g (14-oz) tin chopped tomatoes
- 250g (9oz) frozen peas
- Handful of coriander (cilantro), chopped, to garnish

Heat the oil in a large frying pan (skillet) or saucepan over a medium heat. Add the onions and fry for 6–8 minutes or until golden. Stir in the garlic and ginger and cook for a further 2 minutes before stirring in the minced (ground) beef or lamb. Fry for 5 minutes, until browned.

Stir in the spices and the chilli and fry for a few minutes until fragrant. Stir in the yogurt and cook for a minute to absorb and then stir in the tinned tomatoes. Cook for 10–15 minutes or until the sauce is slightly drier. Mix in the frozen peas and cook for a few minutes until warmed through and tender.

Serve with a scattering of chopped coriander and sliced green chilli, if you like.

Variation: Keema curry pie Make the keema curry as above then boil 500g (1lb 2oz) chopped sweet potatoes and 500g (1lb 2oz) chopped white potatoes (such as Maris Piper or King Edwards) until tender. Mash the potatoes together with 75g (2½oz) butter, 2 tablespoons milk and then stir in 75g (2½oz) grated (shredded) Cheddar cheese. Put the keema curry in an ovenproof dish and top with the cheesy mashed potato. Scatter over a further 50g (1¾oz) grated (shredded) Cheddar cheese then bake for 30–40 minutes in an oven preheated to 200°C/180°C fan/390°F/gas 6.

Pea and Onion Bhaji

These are a great accompaniment to any curry, especially when you want to serve that curry at a celebration or more special meal. They're also a great option for a sharing dish as part of a buffet. (Shown on page 84.)

MAKES 6–8

1 onion, thinly sliced
100g (3½oz) gram (chickpea) flour
2 teaspoons curry powder
1 green chilli, finely chopped
100g (3½oz) frozen peas, defrosted according to the packet instructions
Sunflower or vegetable oil, for frying
Chutneys of your choice, to serve

FOR THE RAITA

250g (9oz) natural yogurt
Handful of mint leaves, chopped
Handful of parsley, chopped
¼ cucumber, finely diced (seeds removed, if you like)
½ teaspoon garam masala

Combine all the ingredients for the raita in a bowl, then chill in the fridge until needed. (You can make this raita the day before, if you like.)

Pour freshly boiled water over the onions in a bowl, then leave for 20 minutes. Drain and dry well either by leaving in a colander for 30 minutes or using a clean dish towel.

Meanwhile, combine the gram flour, curry powder and a good pinch of salt. Pour in enough water to create a thick batter, around 100ml (3½fl oz).

Tip the onions, chilli and peas into a bowl and mix well to combine. Pour over the batter and give everything a really good mix — you can do this with your hands if you like.

Fill a heavy-based pan one-third full with oil and heat until a drop of batter begins to sizzle and brown. Carefully drop spoonfuls of the bhaji mix into the hot oil and cook for 3–5 minutes, turning halfway through, until golden brown and crisp all over. Remove to a plate lined with kitchen paper or a clean dish towel to drain off a little oil. You can keep them warm in an oven on its lowest setting, if you like.

Serve the bhaji with the raita alongside any chutneys of your choice.

Pea and Courgette Pakora

I learnt a great pakora tip involving courgettes (zucchini) from my friend Chetna Makan (you can also find it on her YouTube channel: Cook with Chetna). Because courgettes have a high water content, you don't need to add any extra water to this pakora batter. You will definitely get your hands messy.

% ❄ V VG GF DF

MAKES ABOUT 12

1 courgette (zucchini), (around 300g/10½oz), coarsely grated (shredded)
1 shallot, finely grated (shredded)
200g (7oz) frozen peas, defrosted according to the packet instructions and mashed a little
150g (5½oz) gram (chickpea) flour
1 tablespoon curry powder (hot or mild)
1 red or green chilli, finely chopped (seeds removed, if you like)
Handful of fresh coriander (cilantro), finely chopped
Sunflower or vegetable oil, to serve
Salt
Chutneys of your choice, to serve

Combine the courgette, shallot, peas, flour, curry powder, chilli and coriander in a large mixing bowl with a good pinch of salt. Get your hands in and mash everything together in between your fingers so that it all combines well and the liquid starts to release from the courgette. You might need to do this for a good few minutes to achieve a sticky mixture. If for any reason your courgettes release less water than usual and the mixture still feels quite dry, you can add ½ teaspoon water at a time, although you don't want the mixture to be wet.

Fill a pan a one-third full of oil and heat until a pinch of the mixture sizzles and turns golden brown in about 5–10 seconds. Carefully drop spoonfuls of the mixture into the pan and cook for 3–4 minutes, turning halfway, until golden brown and crisp. You can always cut one open to check it's cooked through. If they start going dark brown too quickly, turn down the heat. Remove to a plate lined with kitchen paper or a clean dish towel.

Serve the pakora with your choice of chutneys.

Roast Chicken with Cabbage and Peas

I get really excited about a roast chicken; not only is it one of my fave meats for a Sunday roast, but there are inevitably leftovers that you can use later in the week. And if there's not, then you've still got the carcass to make stock from. I sometimes roast a few potatoes to go with this, however in the warmer weather I often don't because this feels enough. The peas with the cabbage are a hearty side but the crème fraîche, somehow, always gives me sunnier vibes.

SERVES 4–6

1 whole chicken (around 1.5kg/3lb 5oz)
2 red onions, cut into wedges
½ bunch of thyme sprigs
4 garlic cloves, bashed
2–3 tablespoons vegetable oil
250ml (9fl oz) chicken stock
175ml (6fl oz) white wine
1 cabbage, sliced
250g (9oz) frozen peas
100g (3½oz) crème fraîche

Preheat the oven to 220°C/200°C fan/430°F/gas 7.

Place the chicken in a large roasting tin (sheet pan), then scatter around 1½ of the red onions. Stuff the remaining onion inside the cavity of the bird. Put a few thyme sprigs in the cavity with the onion and scatter the remaining thyme around the chicken in the tin. Put 2 garlic cloves in the cavity and the other two around the chicken.

Rub the oil into the chicken skin, then season it well with salt and freshly ground black pepper. Pour half of the stock and the wine into the pan around the chicken.

Roast the chicken in the hot oven for 20 minutes – the chicken should be starting to brown nicely at this point. Turn down the heat to 180°C/160°C fan/350°F/gas 4 and roast for a further 40–50 minutes or until the chicken is almost done. A temperature probe should reach around 65°C/150°F at this point.

Carefully lift the chicken out of the tin then mix the cabbage into the onion mixture and pour in the remaining stock. Put the chicken back on top and cook for a further 20 minutes. Check the chicken and, if it's cooked, remove it and rest it. The juices should run clear and a temperature probe should read over 70°C/160°F.

Stir the frozen peas and crème fraîche into the cabbage mixture and cook for a further 5–10 minutes or until the peas are warmed through and tender and the cabbage and chicken are cooked, too.

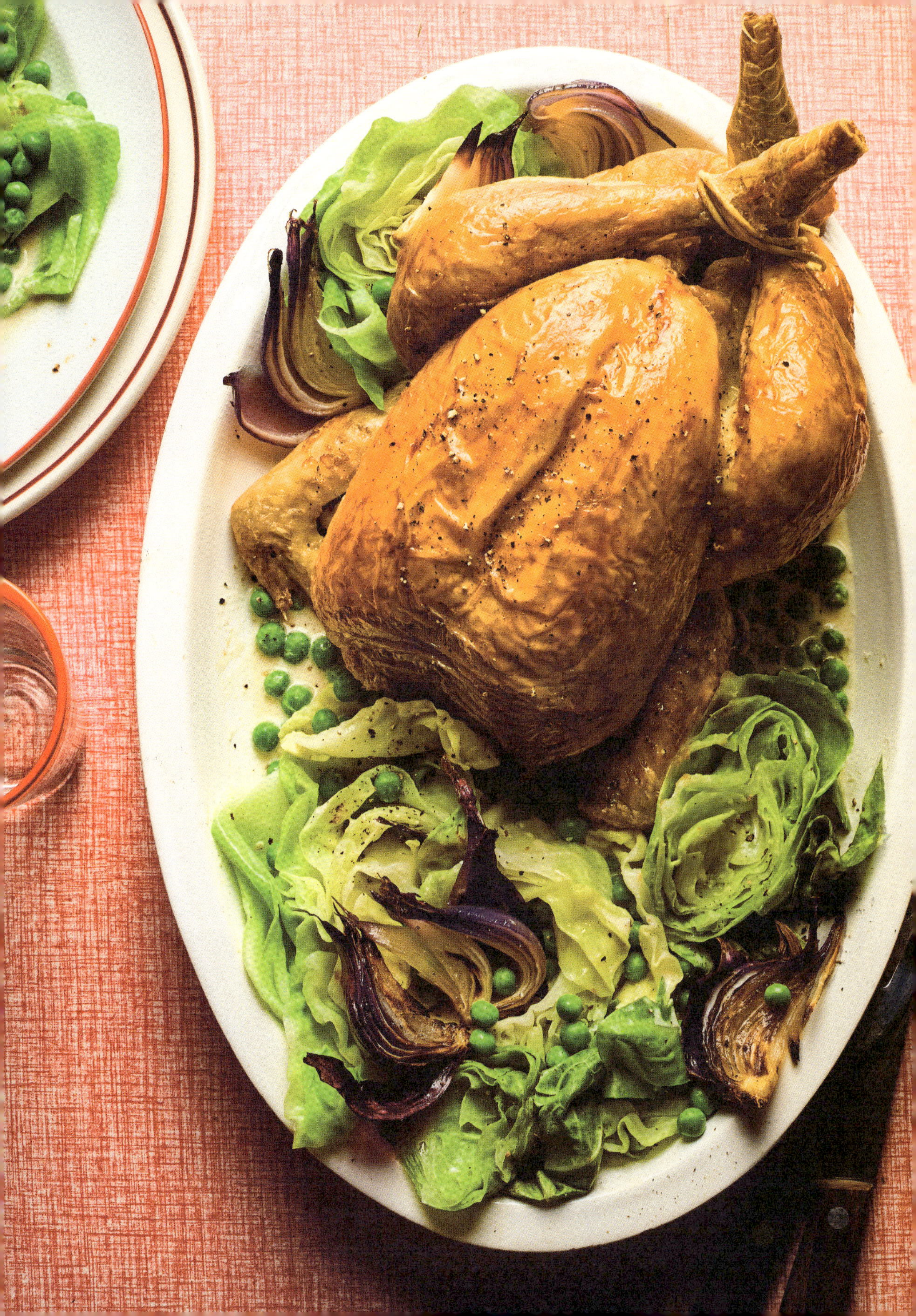

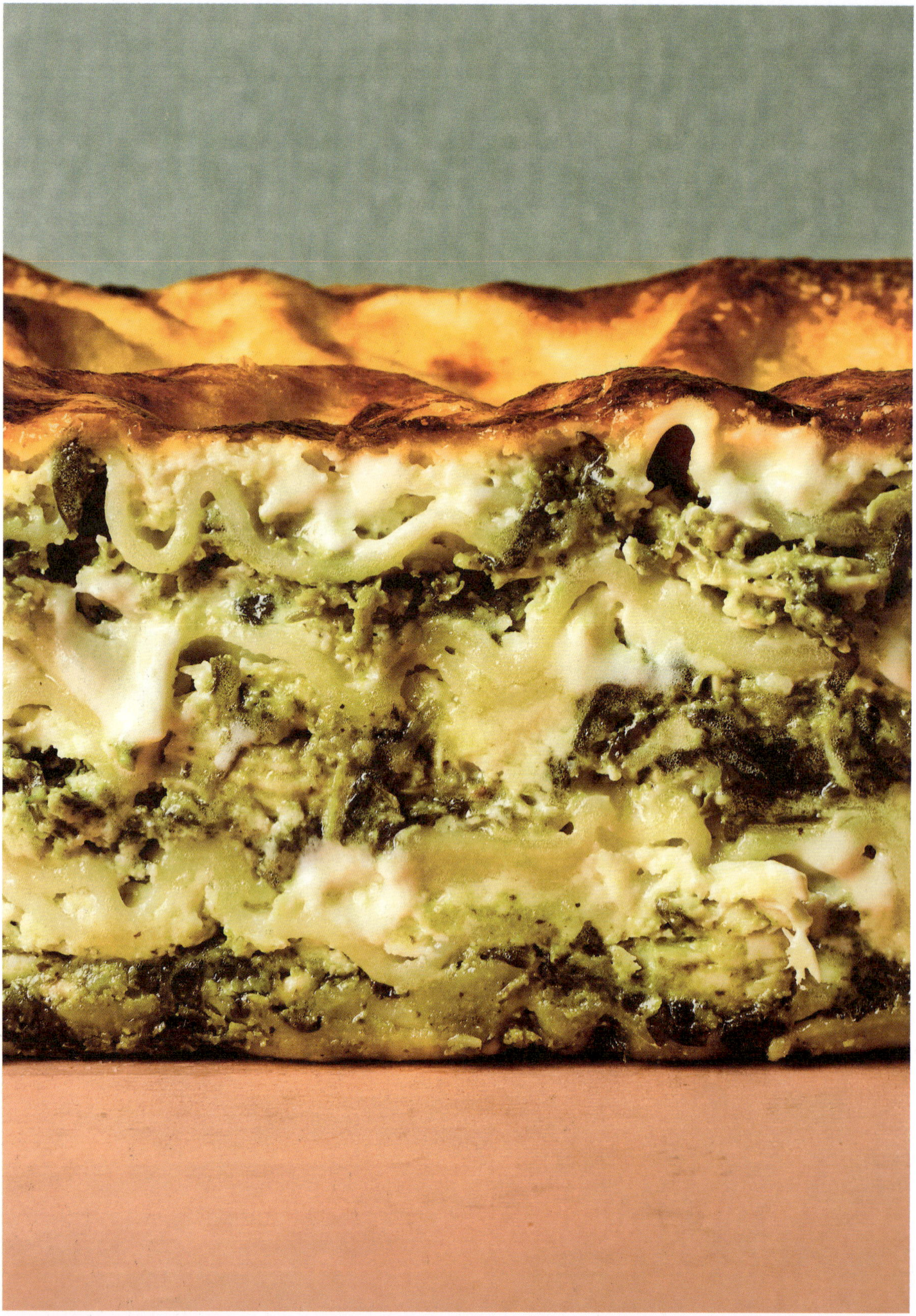

Chicken, Pea and Pesto Lasagne

Pesto pasta is a favourite meal in most households. This lasagne is a way of giving it an upgrade for family gatherings, but safe in the knowledge that the kids will still eat it (and fussy grown-ups, too). I find lasagne is a crowd pleaser, and great for prepping ahead, too. Serve with a leafy salad or, if you're feeling in need of real comfort, some fries and garlic bread.

SERVES 6–8

2 tablespoons olive oil
1 onion, finely diced
250g (9oz) frozen peas
500g (1lb 2oz) skinless chicken breast, sliced
1 × 190-g (7-oz) jar Genovese basil pesto (or see pages 144–146 for homemade)
6 blocks frozen spinach
500g (1lb 2oz) mascarpone
125–175ml (4–6fl oz) whole (full-fat) milk
50g (1¾oz) Parmesan, grated (shredded)
75g (2½oz) mature Cheddar cheese, grated (shredded)
12–15 dried lasagne sheets
Salt and freshly ground black pepper

Cook's tip The instructions above are for a three-layer lasagne, but you may find your ovenproof dish is too large for three layers. When you start spooning over the first layer of pesto chicken filling, if you need around half the mixture to cover the lasagne sheets then go for a two-layer lasagne. Simply use half the mascarpone mixture and half the pesto chicken mixture for each layer and add three layers of lasagne sheets (bottom, middle and top).

Heat half the oil in a frying pan (skillet) or saucepan over a medium heat. Add the onion and fry for 6–8 minutes or until golden. Stir in the frozen peas and cook for a few minutes until warmed through and tender.

Tip the onion and peas into a food processor and blitz or use a handheld stick (immersion) blender. (This is an optional step, you can just tip the onion and peas into a bowl and continue, but I love the vibrancy this gives.)

Preheat the oven to 200°C/180°C fan/390°F/gas 6.

In the same pan, heat the remaining oil and fry the chicken until browned. Stir in the pesto and frozen spinach, then cook for 5–8 minutes or until the spinach has defrosted. Stir in the onion and pea mixture, season with salt and pepper, then fold in 5 tablespoons of the mascarpone. Set aside.

Combine the remaining mascarpone with enough milk to create a white sauce consistency, then mix in two-thirds of the Parmesan and Cheddar cheese. Season well with plenty of salt and pepper. Set aside.

Before assembling the lasagne, see the cook's tip. Lay 3–4 lasagne sheets over the bottom of an 18-cm (7-inch) square ovenproof dish or tin, ensuring they don't overlap too much. To make the first layer, spoon over one-third of the pesto chicken mixture followed by a further 3–4 lasagne sheets and one-third of the mascarpone sauce. Follow with a further two layers, ending with the final batch of mascarpone sauce. Scatter over the remaining cheese.

At this point, you can chill the uncooked lasagne for up to 24 hours or freeze it for up to 3 months.

Bake the lasagne in the preheated oven for 35–40 minutes or until the pasta sheets are tender and the sauce is bubbling. If cooking from chilled, it will take longer. If cooking from frozen, it's worth either defrosting fully first or covering the top with foil to stop it burning.

Chicken and Ham Pie

For me, nothing beats a pie when hosting a gathering of friends or family. There's something both special and effortless about a pie, and it's ideal for making in advance. I appreciate they're not really effortless, but compared to cooking a full roast dinner, it's not so bad. I usually serve a pie with buttery mash, which is why the sauce here is not super thick. If you prefer a thicker sauce, you can add an extra 1–2 tablespoons flour or use 150ml (5fl oz) less stock.

SERVES 4–6

- 2 tablespoons sunflower or vegetable oil
- 8 boneless, skinless chicken thighs, chopped into bite-sized pieces
- 1 onion, chopped
- 2 carrots, chopped
- 2 tablespoons plain (all-purpose) flour
- 150ml (5fl oz) white wine
- 350ml (12fl oz) chicken stock
- 150ml (5fl oz) whole (full-fat) milk
- 200g (7oz) ham, chopped
- 200g (7oz) frozen peas
- A few thyme sprigs
- 1 × 320-g (11-oz) packet ready-rolled puff pastry (or roll out a 500g/1lb 2oz block to 5mm/¼ inch thickness)
- 1 egg, beaten

Heat 1 tablespoon of the oil in a saucepan over a medium heat. Add the chicken and fry until beginning to brown, around 6–8 minutes. Remove the chicken from the pan and add the onions and carrots. Turn down the heat, cover and cook for 8–10 minutes or until softened.

Add the chicken back into the pan and stir in the flour to coat everything, then pour in the wine and cook for 1 minute. Stir in the stock and milk, bring to a simmer and add the ham, frozen peas and thyme. Cook for 2 minutes, then remove the pan from the heat and transfer the contents into a large ovenproof pie dish.

Preheat the oven to 200°C/180°C fan/390°F/gas 6.

Unroll the pastry and check the size is large enough to cover your pie dish. If not, you can roll it out a little on a floured work surface. Lay the pastry over the pie dish and use your finger and thumb to crimp the pastry around the edge of the dish. At this point you can score a pattern into the pie (a criss-cross design or similar), then cover and chill or freeze. When frozen, the pie will keep well for 3 months.

To continue, glaze the pastry top with beaten egg and bake in the hot oven for 30–40 minutes or until the pastry is golden and risen.

When cooking from frozen, lower the oven temperature to 180°C/160°C fan/350°F/gas 4 and bake for 45 minutes– 1 hour, covering the pastry top with foil if it begins to brown too quickly.

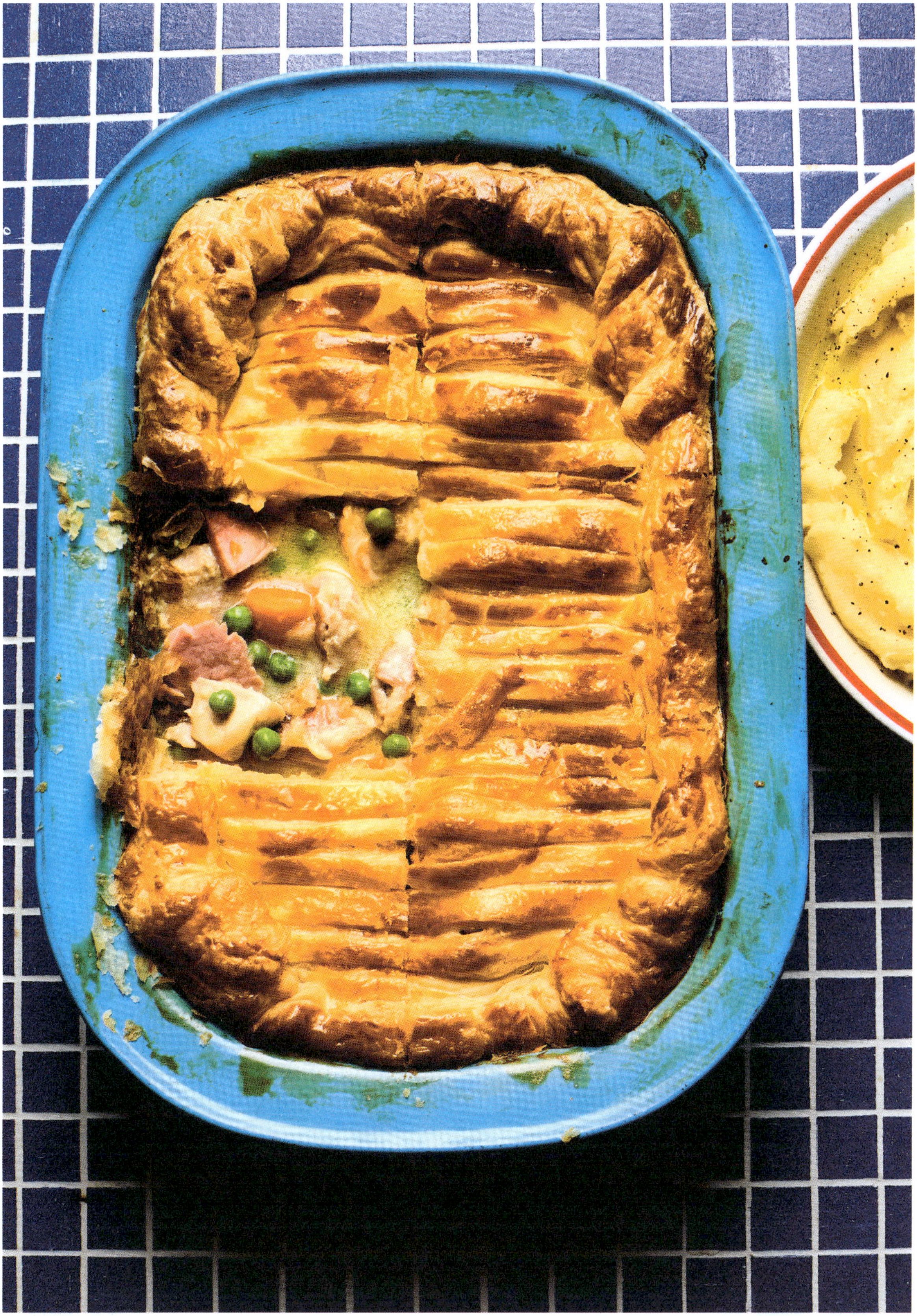

Creamy Chicken, Tarragon and Peas with Cheesy Polenta

I'm going to lay my cards on the table straight away. This is a rich dish, but sometimes you just need a full-smack-in-the-face piece of comfort, and this is it. The peas keep things a little brighter and allow you to feel like you're being good. And if you're not keen on polenta, you can always serve this on a bed of rice or tossed through tagliatelle.

SERVES 4

½ tablespoon sunflower or vegetable oil
1 red onion, thinly sliced
350g (12½oz) skinless chicken breast, sliced
150g (5½oz) garlic and herb soft cheese (I use Boursin)
75ml (2½fl oz) whole (full-fat) milk
Small handful of fresh tarragon leaves, roughly chopped
200g (7oz) frozen peas

FOR THE CHEESY POLENTA

450ml (15fl oz) whole (full-fat) milk
150g (5½oz) quick-cook polenta
40g (1½oz) Parmesan, finely grated (shredded)
40g (1½oz) butter
Salt and freshly ground black pepper

Heat the oil in a frying pan (skillet) over a medium heat. Add the red onion to the pan and fry for 6–8 minutes or until softened but not coloured.

Add the chicken to the pan and fry on all sides until there are no pink bits remaining. Stir in the soft cheese and milk, then cook until the cheese has formed a sauce. Remove the pan from the heat.

To make the polenta, pour the milk into a saucepan with 350ml (12fl oz) water. Bring to a simmer then gradually sprinkle in the polenta, whisking continuously to ensure it doesn't go lumpy. Season heavily with salt and freshly ground black pepper. Cook for up to 5 minutes (or according to the packet instructions) until thickened. Scatter in the Parmesan, tip in the butter and mix everything to combine until the butter and cheese have both melted and the polenta is creamy. If the polenta is looking too thick, add a splash of hot water. Remove the pan from the heat and put the lid on.

Put the frying pan with the chicken back on the heat, stir in the chopped tarragon and frozen peas, season well and cook for a few minutes until the peas are warmed through and tender.

Serve the creamy chicken, tarragon and peas over the polenta.

Blue Cheese and Pea Tart

For a couple of years, I worked as a sous chef alongside food writer and author Orlando Murrin. We cooked this tart more times than I can remember. It's great because you can make it the day before and then bring it up to room temperature before serving. Or you can make a batch to freeze ahead. It's a great base for other flavour tarts, one of my favourites being a trout version.

SERVES 8–10

1 × 500-g (18-oz) block shortcrust pastry
Flour, for rolling out
200g (7oz) frozen peas
200g (7oz) mascarpone
100g (3½oz) blue cheese
300ml (10fl oz) double (heavy) cream
1 tablespoon melted butter
3 eggs
Half bunch of fresh chives (around 5g/⅙oz), finely chopped
Salt and freshly ground black pepper

Preheat the oven to 180°C/160°C fan/350°F/gas 4.

On a lightly floured work surface, roll out the pastry to a 5mm (¼ inch) thickness. Line a 23-cm (9-inch) tart tin with the pastry. Don't worry if there are any rips, you can patch these up. Prick the pastry base all over with a fork, cover with parchment paper and tip some baking beans or dried pulses on top of the paper.

Bake the pastry case in the hot oven for 10–15 minutes or until a light shortbread colour. Remove the baking beans and parchment paper, then bake the case uncovered for a further 5–10 minutes or until lightly golden.

Meanwhile, place the frozen peas in a heatproof bowl and cover them with freshly boiled water to defrost. Leave for a few minutes and then drain. Set aside.

Put the mascarpone, blue cheese, cream and butter in a food processor and blitz together or use a handheld stick (immersion) blender. Pour the mixture into a large bowl or jug (pitcher) and beat in the eggs, then mix in the peas and chives. Season well with salt and pepper.

Once the tart pastry case is ready, carefully pour in the filling. Bake the tart in the hot oven for a further 25–35 minutes or until the filling is golden, it may puff up slightly. Leave the tart to cool a little before removing it from the tin. You can leave the tart to cool completely before slicing and serving, however I think it is best a little warm.

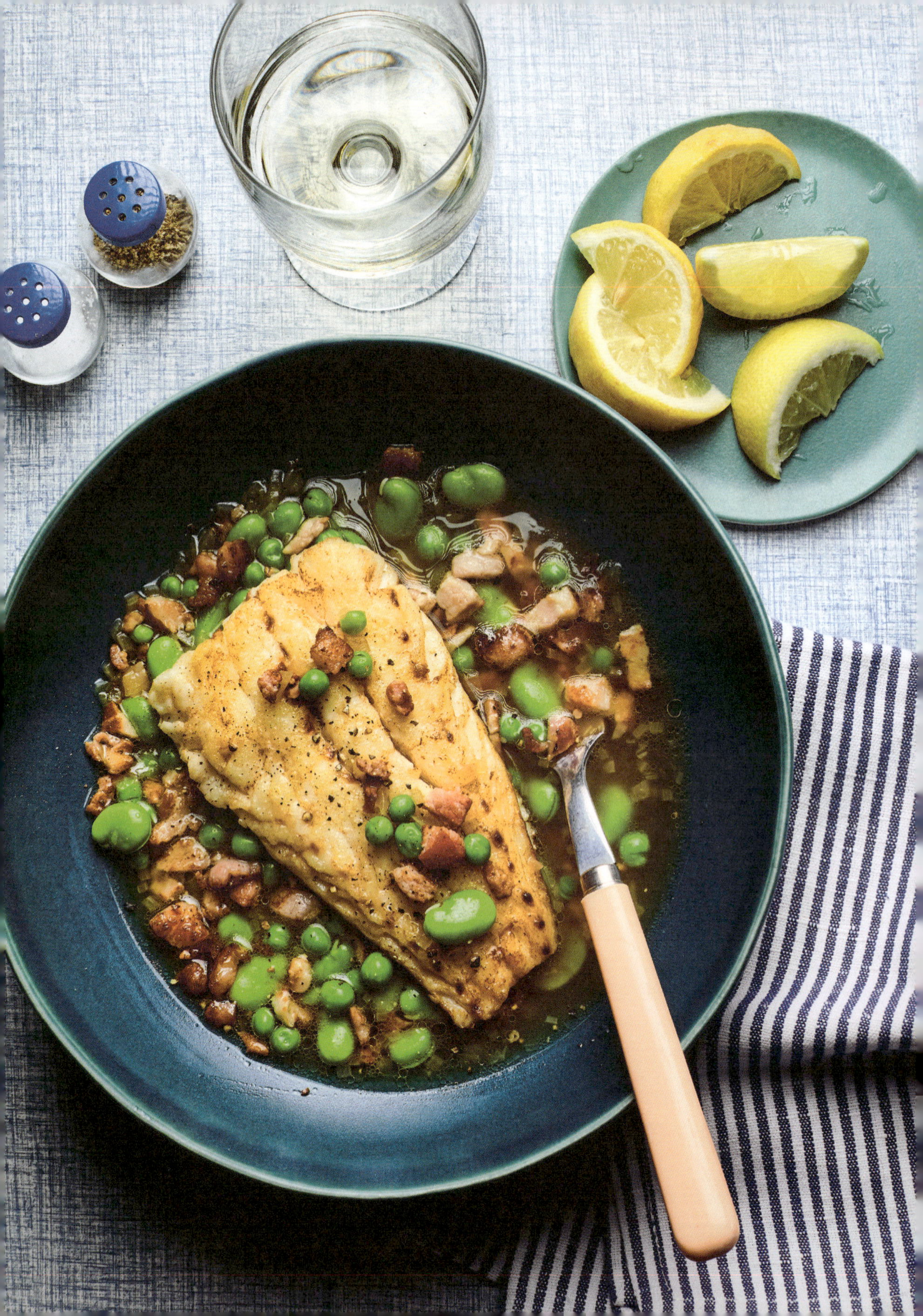

Hake with Braised Peas, Broad Beans and Pancetta

White fish is great with peas – both are reasonably delicate in flavour, so neither are fighting for your taste buds. I like to use hake both because of its mild flavour and the fact it's currently a sustainable fish, but any other fish with firm white flesh will work nicely. If you can, try to buy a sustainable cut (look for the MSC label). I know it's not always possible, but you don't have to spend a fortune to get a piece of fish that's not over-fished.

SERVES 2

- 150g (5½oz) frozen broad (fava) beans (see tip below)
- 1 tablespoon olive oil
- 1 shallot, finely chopped
- 150g (5½oz) diced pancetta
- 150ml (5fl oz) chicken stock
- 1 tablespoon butter
- 2 hake portions (around 300g/10½oz in total)
- 200g (7oz) frozen peas
- 1 lemon, cut into wedges

Bring a saucepan of salted water to the boil. Add the broad beans and cook for 3–4 minutes, then drain and immediately plunge the beans into ice-cold water. Pop the broad beans out of their tough skins, then put the bright green beans in a bowl and set aside.

Heat half the oil in a small saucepan with a lid over a medium heat. Fry the shallot for 4–5 minutes or until softened and beginning to turn golden. Stir in the pancetta and fry for a few minutes until beginning to brown. Pour in the chicken stock, put the lid on and simmer gently while you tend to the fish.

Heat the remaining oil and the butter in a frying pan (skillet). Lay the hake in the pan (if there's skin on the fish then place it skin-side down first), season the top of the fish and cook for 3–4 minutes until cooked roughly halfway through and golden underneath.

While the hake is cooking, add the broad beans and frozen peas to the pan with the stock and continue to simmer.

Turn the hake over, season the top of the fish and cook for a further 3–4 minutes.

Spoon the braised peas and broad beans into deep bowls, then lay the hake on top and serve with lemon wedges.

Cook's tip You don't *have* to peel the broad (fava) beans, but you will get a much better result if you do. My suggestion is to use an extra 150g (5½oz) frozen peas if you can't take the time to peel the broad beans.

Tomato and Pea Galette

There's something satisfying about a galette; it's much simpler to make than a regular pastry tart as there's no lining of tins or blind baking. Galettes are a bit rough around the edges, but that is all part of their charm. I love how the peas are hidden here until you cut through and see the lovely contrast between the green and the red.

V

SERVES 4

350g (12½oz) ripe tomatoes, halved if small or sliced if large (a mix of sizes and colours is nice)
Handful of basil leaves, torn, plus a few extra to garnish
1 garlic clove, crushed or finely grated (shredded)
1 teaspoon salt
1 × 500-g (18-oz) block shortcrust pastry
100g (3½oz) frozen peas, defrosted according to the packet instructions
40g (1½oz) Gruyère, Manchego or other vegetarian hard cheese, finely grated (shredded)
1 teaspoon olive oil
1 egg, beaten
2–3 tablespoons pea pesto (see page 144) or vegetarian basil pesto (optional)
Freshly ground black pepper

Combine the sliced tomatoes with the torn basil, garlic and 1 teaspoon salt. Tip everything into a colander set over a bowl, then leave for 30 minutes to allow the juices to drain.

Meanwhile, preheat the oven to 220°C/200°C fan/430°F/gas 7.

On a lightly floured work surface, roll out the pastry into a round 6mm (¼ inch) thick which is slightly larger than 30cm (12 inches). Using a large dinner plate as a template, cut out a large circle, around 30cm (12 inches) in diameter. Transfer the pastry circle to a lined baking tray.

Blitz the peas, cheese, olive oil and a good grinding of black pepper until the peas are roughly chopped. Spread this mixture over the base of the pastry, keeping a clear border around the edges as you'll be folding the sides of the galette up and over the filling.

Lay the tomato mixture on top of the peas so that the tomato slices are flat, then fold the edges up and over the filling to create a border around 4–5cm (1½–2 inches) wide. Glaze the exposed pastry with the beaten egg and drizzle over a little pesto, if you like.

Bake the galette in the hot oven for 10 minutes. Turn down the oven temperature to 200°C/180°C fan/390°F/gas 6 and bake for a further 30–40 minutes or until the pastry is golden and the tomatoes have softened.

Scatter over a few extra basil leaves immediately before slicing and serving.

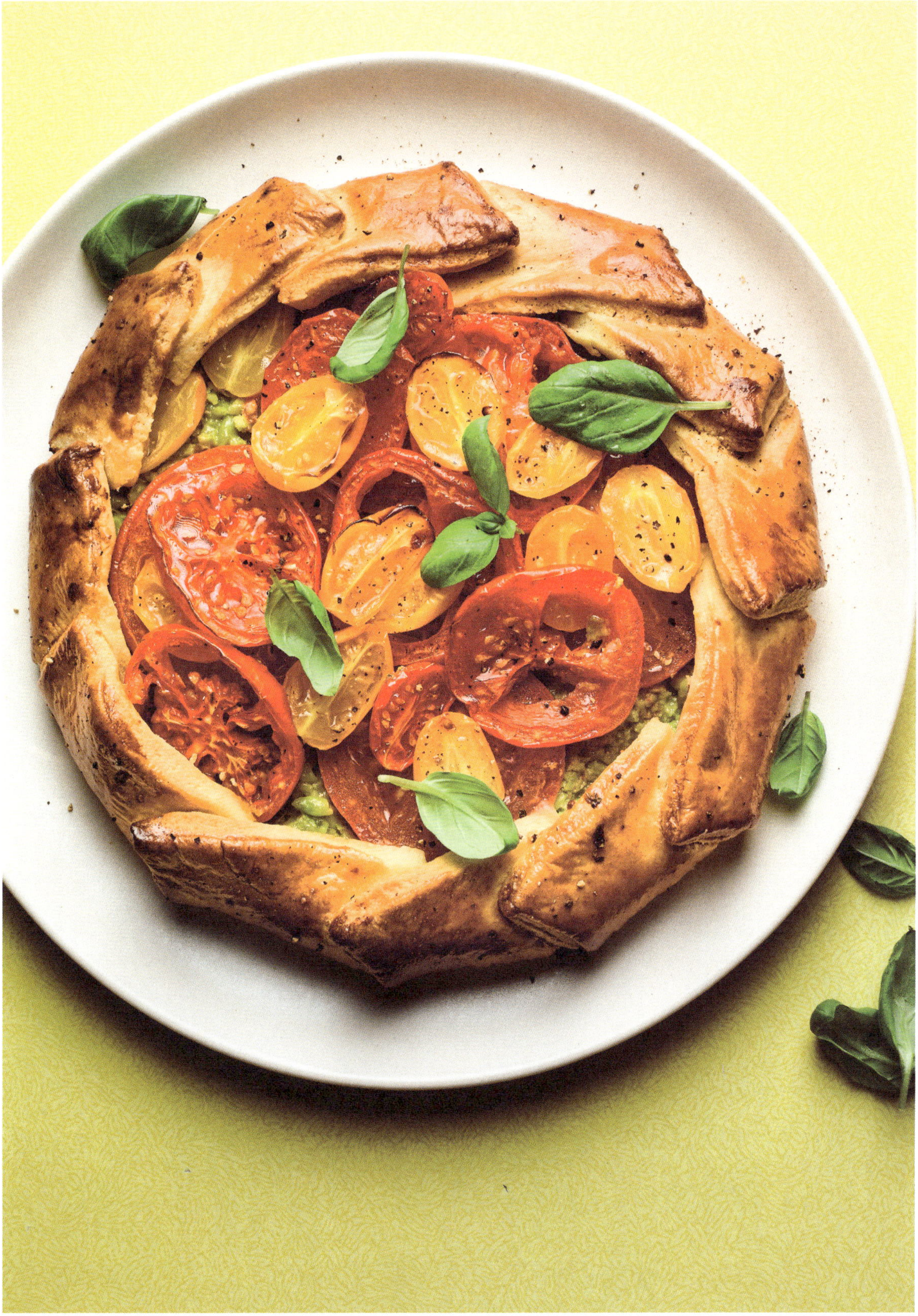

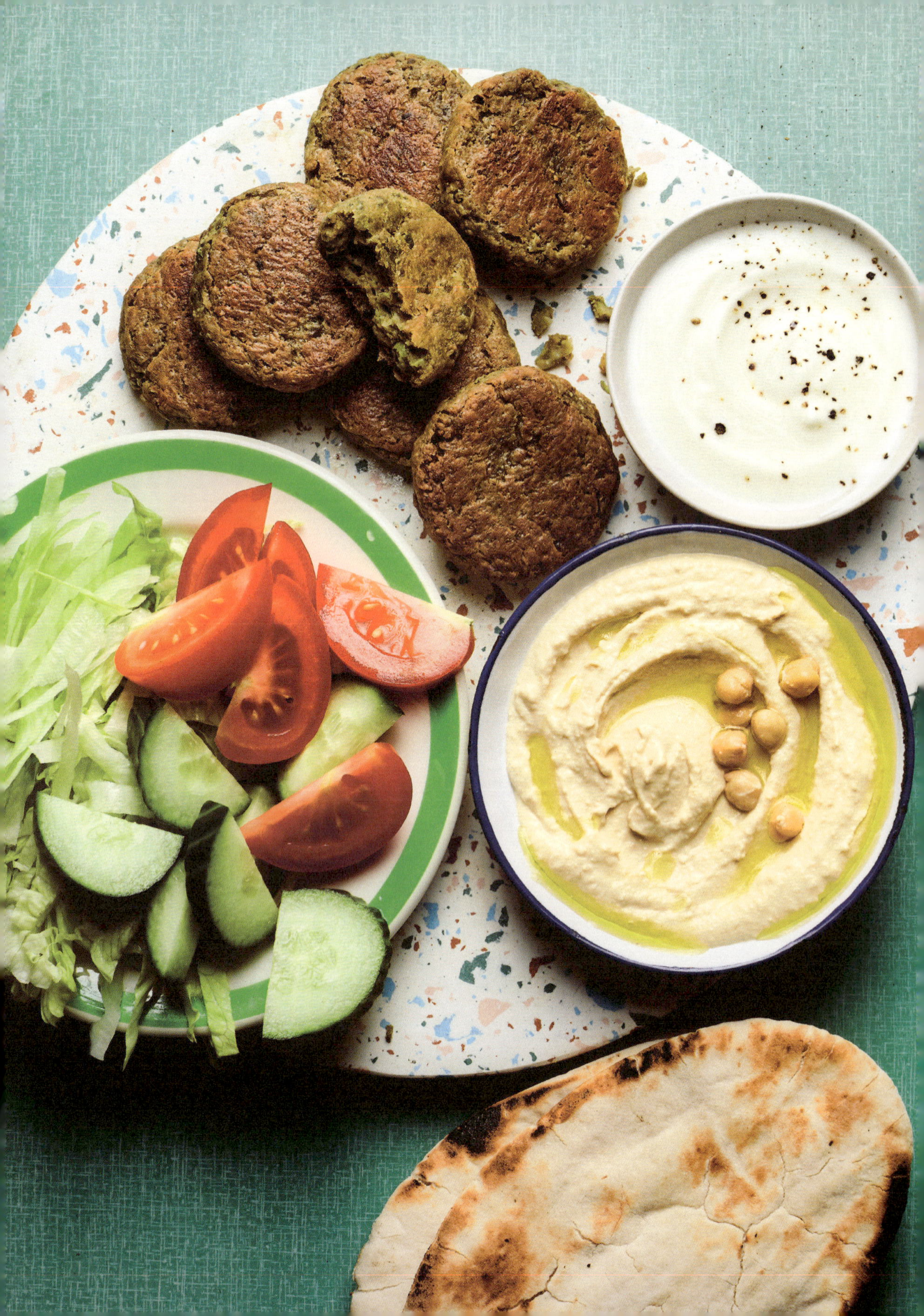

Pea Falafel Pittas

Falafel pittas are a great 'build your own' dinner, perfect for a relaxed gathering. These falafels can be made in batches and frozen, so you'll only need to defrost them before cooking. Freeze them on a tray until the outside is frozen (about 30 minutes) then transfer to a freezer bag or storage container to fully freeze and store. The quantities below make 12 falafel, so depending on whether you're serving 4 or 6 people, each person gets 3 or 4 falafel.

SERVES 4–6

FOR THE FALAFEL
- 250g (9oz) frozen peas
- 1 × 400-g (14-oz) tin chickpeas (garbanzo beans), drained
- 2 spring onions (scallions), sliced
- 3 garlic cloves, crushed or finely grated (shredded)
- 1½ teaspoons ground cumin
- ½ teaspoon ground coriander
- ½ teaspoon chilli powder (optional)
- Handful of coriander (cilantro), roughly chopped
- Handful of parsley, roughly chopped
- 3 tablespoons tahini
- 2½ tablespoons plain (all-purpose) flour, plus extra for dusting
- 2–3 tablespoons olive oil

TO SERVE
- 4–6 pitta breads
- 4–6 tablespoons hummus (shop-bought or homemade, see page 150)
- 4–6 tablespoons natural yogurt or plant-based yogurt alternative
- Your choice of lettuce, cucumber, tomato and lemon wedges, to serve

Place the frozen peas in a heatproof bowl and cover them with freshly boiled water to defrost. Leave for a few minutes and then drain. Tip the peas into the food processor along with all the remaining ingredients for the falafel (except the oil). Blitz to a thick paste – you may need to add a drizzle of water. It should be a soft mixture.

Tip the mixture into a bowl or onto a clean work surface, then shape the mixture into 12 balls, roughly the size of a large walnut. Flatten the balls slightly and dust them with a little flour. Chill in the fridge for 20–30 minutes.

If you want to bake the falafel, preheat the oven to 200°C/180°C fan/390°F/gas 6. Bake in the preheated oven for around 30 minutes, turning halfway. You can also cook them in the air fryer at 180°C/390°F for around 15–20 minutes. To fry in a frying pan (skillet), heat 1 tablespoon of oil over a medium heat and fry the falafel, adding more oil as necessary, for around 4 minutes on each side or until golden and cooked through – you may need to do this in batches.

Serve the falafel tucked into the pitta breads with spoonfuls of hummus and yogurt, and with plenty of salad.

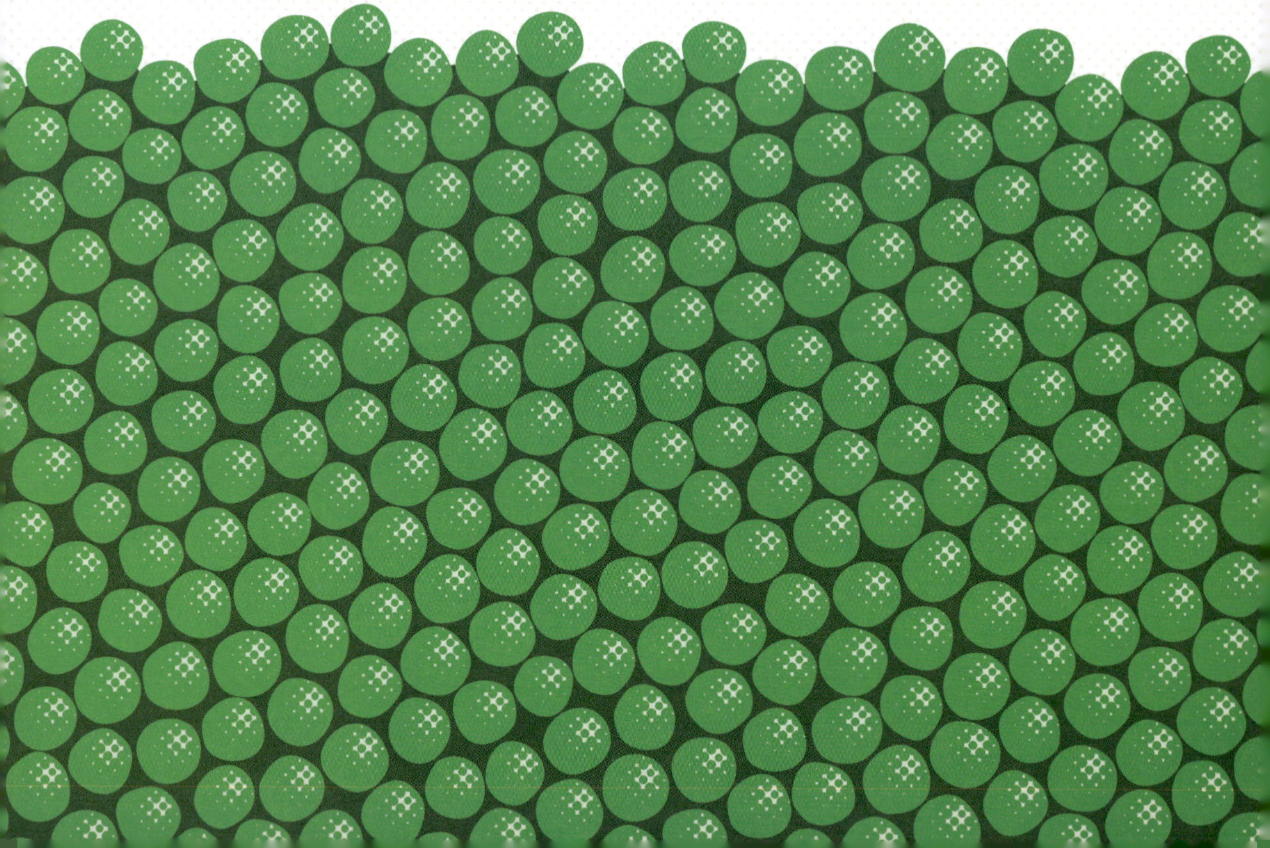

Midweek Meals

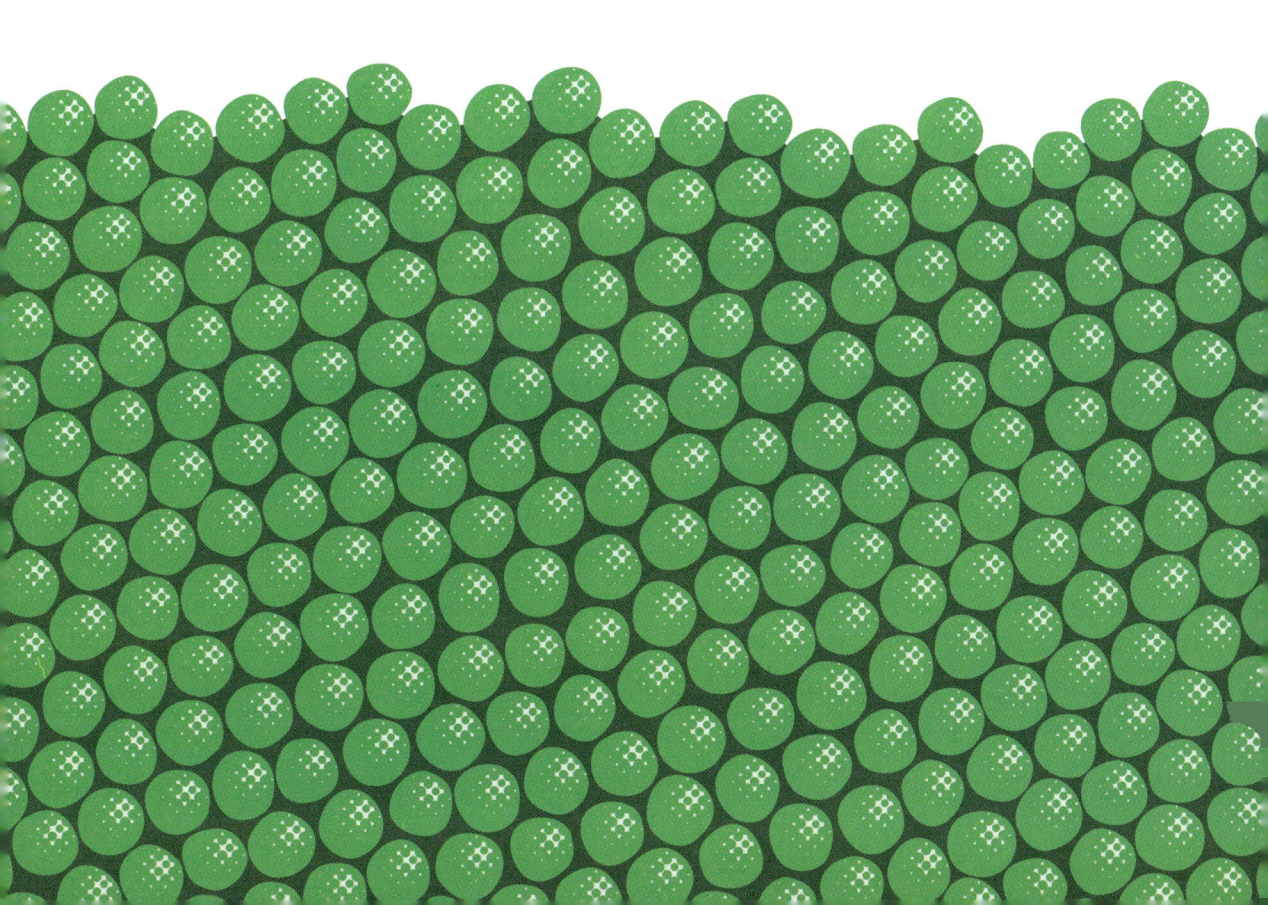

Chicken Peasar Salad

Sometimes you just have to jump all in and embrace the pun, but that doesn't mean this spin on the classic Caesar salad isn't a serious recipe. Oh no, the peas bring another level to this gastro-pub favourite. I scatter in the whole peas and also use some to create a vibrant dressing so you're using all of the pea's natural strengths.

SERVES 4–6

- 4 thick slices of white bread from a loaf, cut into chunks
- 3–4 tablespoons olive oil
- 2 skinless chicken breasts
- 2 Romaine heart lettuce
- 250g (9oz) frozen peas
- 1 garlic clove, crushed or finely grated (shredded)
- 4 anchovies from a tin
- 4 tablespoons mayonnaise
- ½ tablespoon extra virgin olive oil
- Zest and juice of 1 lemon
- 15g (½oz) Parmesan, grated (shredded), plus optional extra for shavings
- Salt and freshly ground black pepper

Preheat the oven to 200°C/180°C fan/390°F/gas 6.

Scatter the bread chunks over a baking tray then drizzle with enough oil so that they are well coated. Season with a little salt and freshly ground black pepper then bake in the hot oven, tossing every now and then, for 10–15 minutes or until golden and crisp. Set aside.

Season the chicken generously all over with salt and pepper then fry in a frying pan (skillet) over a medium heat for 10–15 minutes or until lightly browned and cooked through. (At this point you can either continue to fry until cooked through or pop in the oven seeing as it's already on and bake until cooked through, this will take a little longer but might save a little energy.) Set aside once cooked.

Break the lettuces apart and separate them into single leaves. Either place the lettuce leaves on a serving platter or in a large salad bowl, ready to toss together with everything else.

Place the frozen peas in a heatproof bowl and cover them with freshly boiled water to defrost. Leave for a few minutes and then drain. Place 175g (6oz) of the peas in with the lettuce and put the rest of the peas in a food processor.

Add the garlic, anchovies, mayonnaise, extra virgin olive oil, lemon zest and juice and the grated (shredded) Parmesan to the processor, then blitz to a smooth, thin dressing. If you need to thin the dressing down a bit, add a splash of water or more extra virgin olive oil. Taste for seasoning then adjust with more salt and pepper to taste.

Pour the dressing over the lettuce leaves and peas, then toss in the croutons. Chop or shred the chicken and add that in too, then toss everything together.

Serve the salad on a large serving platter with some extra Parmesan shavings, if you like.

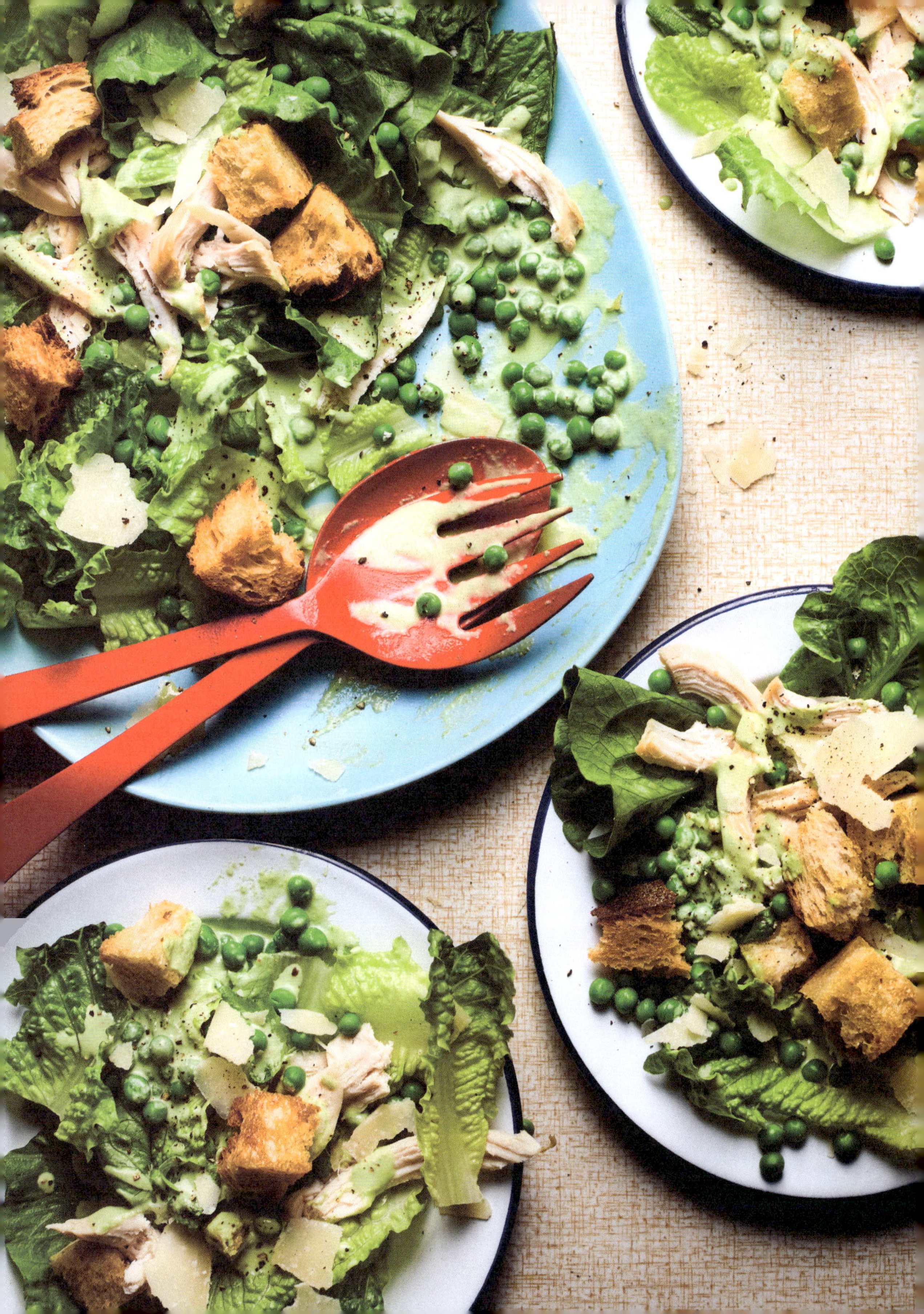

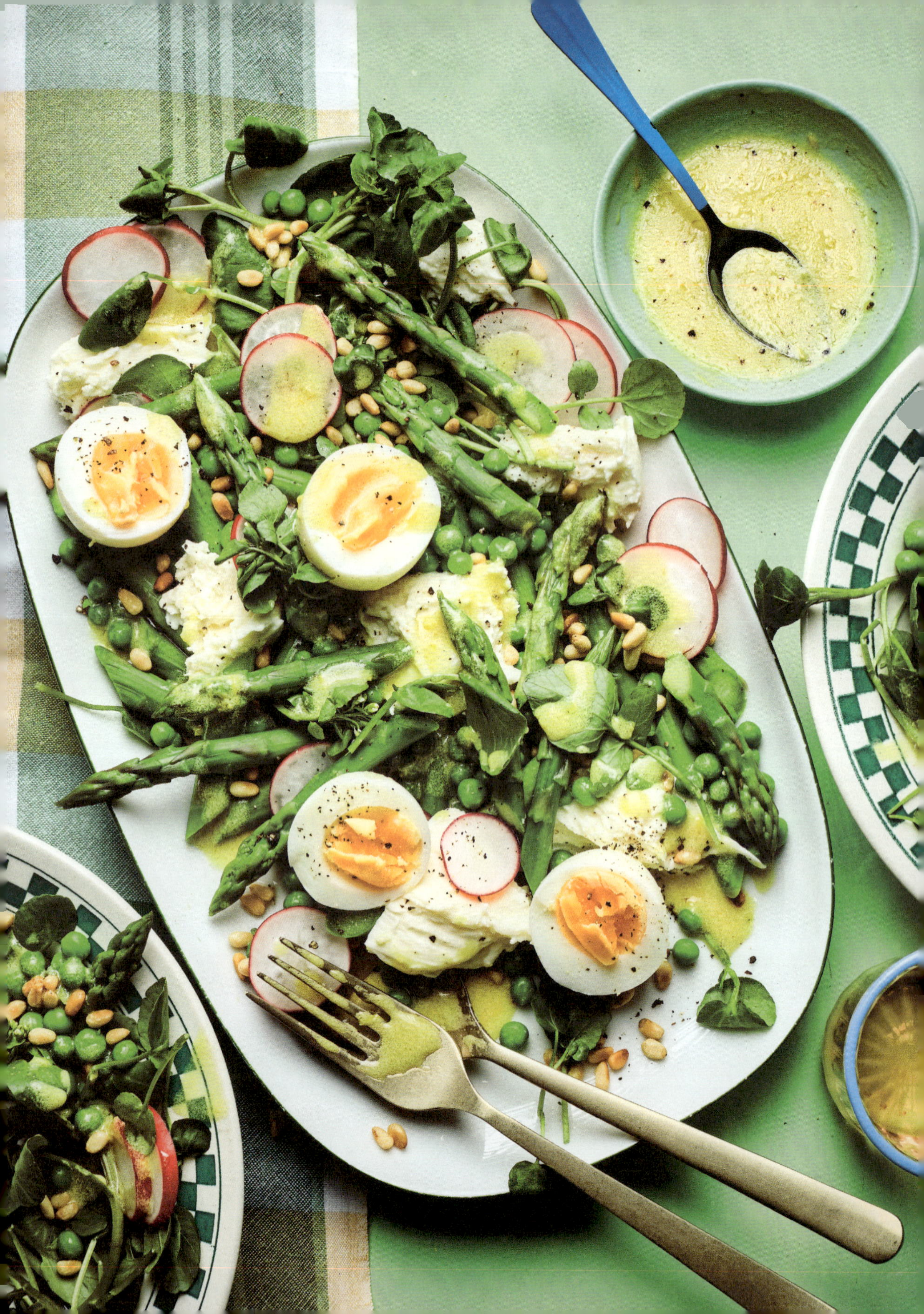

Asparagus, Pea and Mozzarella Salad

The perfect salad for asparagus season. Even though fresh peas can sometimes coincide with the asparagus season around June, unless I've picked them immediately before serving (which never happens on my tiny balcony), I still use frozen peas because I think the flavour is better. Plus it saves time. There's something about an egg on a salad that I love. I think it's because it makes it feel more substantial and the yolks add a lovely colour. I also sometimes swap out the torn mozzarella for Parmesan shavings.

% V GF

SERVES 2

2 eggs
200g (7oz) asparagus spears, trimmed and cut into bite-sized pieces
200g (7oz) frozen peas
100g (3½oz) watercress
30g (1oz) toasted pine nuts
4 radishes, thinly sliced
125g (4½oz) mozzarella ball, drained

FOR THE DRESSING

1 tablespoon extra virgin olive oil
Juice and zest ½ lemon
1 teaspoon Dijon mustard
Salt and freshly ground black pepper

Bring a pan of water to the boil and gently lower the eggs into the water. Cook for 7 minutes then lift the eggs out of the water and plunge into iced cold water. Leave to cool then bash a little and peel the shell from the egg. Set aside.

In the same water, add the asparagus spears and frozen peas and cook for 2–3 minutes or until just tender. Drain and plunge into cold water. Leave for a few minutes then drain. Combine the asparagus and peas with the watercress.

Combine all the ingredients for the dressing with a good pinch of salt and freshly ground black pepper. Pour the dressing over the asparagus, peas and watercress. Toss to coat the salad.

Arrange the dressed asparagus salad over a serving platter, then scatter over the pine nuts and place the radish slices all over. Tear the mozzarella and dot around the top of the salad. Cut the eggs in half and place on top of the salad, season the yolk with a little pepper before serving.

Harissa Couscous Salad with Goats' Cheese

On the first day I started recipe testing for my friend Xanthe Clay, she asked me to add collecting harissa to the list of things we needed to do that day. Considering how much I use it now, I am mildly ashamed to say I thought that meant collecting her daughter from school. It was, in fact, to make a version of this salad, which I adored the moment I tasted it. I've added the stock cube, peas and lime – although it's Xanthe's love of lime that has also influenced mine.

**SERVES 2 AS A MAIN OR
4 AS A LIGHT LUNCH OR SIDE**

225g (8oz) couscous
Zest and juice of 1 lime
1 vegetable stock cube
150g (5½oz) frozen peas
1 tablespoon rose harissa (or slightly less if using a spicy harissa)
1 tablespoon tomato paste (concentrated purée)
60g (2oz) wild rocket (arugula)
150g (5½oz) goats' cheese (the softer variety, and vegetarian, if necessary), cut into chunks
Salt and freshly ground black pepper

Tip the couscous into a heatproof bowl with the lime zest. Squeeze the lime juice into a jug (pitcher), then add the stock cube and add enough boiling water to make it up to 250ml (9fl oz). Pour this stock over the couscous and leave for 5 minutes or until the couscous has absorbed the water. Fluff up the couscous with a fork.

Place the frozen peas in a heatproof bowl and cover them with freshly boiled water to defrost. Leave for a few minutes or until fully thawed. Drain the peas, then fold them through the couscous.

In a small bowl, combine the harissa and tomato paste with a teaspoon of water, then season with a good pinch each of salt and freshly ground black pepper. Fold this paste through the couscous and peas until everything is well coated.

Arrange the rocket over a serving platter, cover the leaves with the couscous and peas, then scatter over the chunks of goats' cheese.

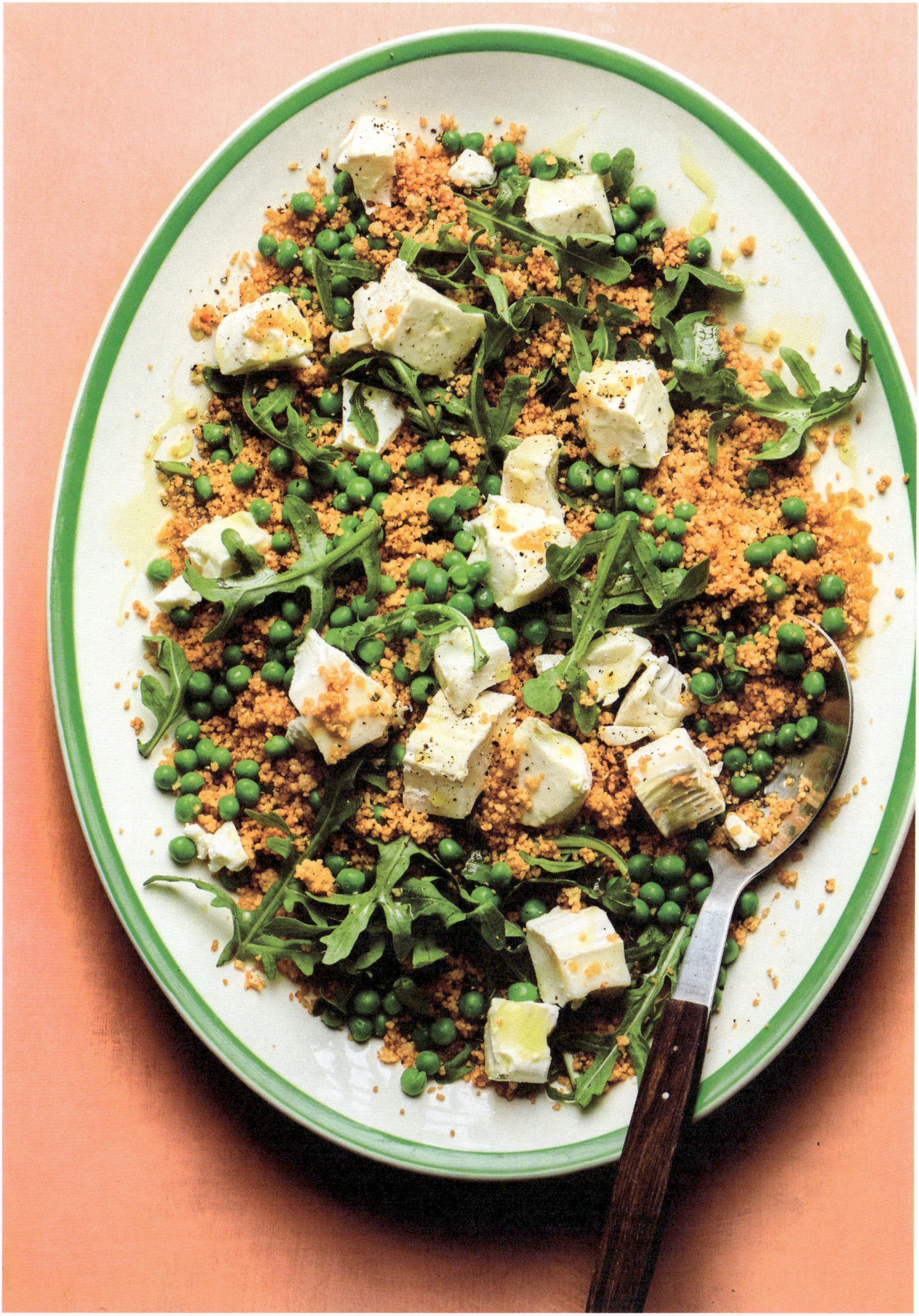

MIDWEEK MEALS

Green Goddess Salad

I find TikTok trends can be a bit hit and miss. (Someone once told me about a viral biryani covered in chocolate sauce?!) This one, however, makes sense. I think it's probably come from the increasing interest in wellness recipes as it uses a variety of green vegetables that pack a punch when it comes to vitamins and minerals. I use the peas both in the salad and in the dressing. It is called 'green goddess' after all.

% V GF

SERVES 4–6

FOR THE SALAD
2 eggs
150g (5½oz) frozen peas
2 Little Gem lettuces, leaves separated
1 celery stick, sliced
1 green apple, cored and finely sliced
½ cucumber, finely chopped
1 avocado, roughly chopped
Handful of pumpkin seeds (pepitas) or chopped pistachios

FOR THE DRESSING
2 tablespoons olive oil
75g (2½oz) frozen peas
Zest and juice of 1 lime
Handful of chopped chives
Handful of chopped parsley
50g (1¾oz) natural yogurt
1 garlic clove, crushed or finely grated (shredded)

Lower the eggs into a saucepan of boiling water and cook for 7 minutes. Using a slotted spoon, remove the boiled eggs from the pan and plunge them straight into a bowl of iced water to stop them cooking further. When cool enough to handle, peel the eggs, cut them into wedges and set aside.

Using either the egg cooking water or some freshly boiled water, defrost the frozen peas in a heatproof bowl by covering them with boiling water and leaving for 3 minutes. Drain, then set aside.

Put all the dressing ingredients into a blender or food processor and blitz until smooth.

Arrange the lettuce, celery, apple, cucumber and avocado on a serving platter, pour over the dressing, then scatter over the pumpkin seeds or pistachios and top with the boiled egg wedges.

Added extras I've gone with the purely green version (other than the eggs) here, but some shredded chicken, quinoa and couscous all work nicely in this salad.

Loaded Jackets

Who knew baked potatoes could get even better? Sure, you could cover them in beans and cheese (and in a way, you'd be mad not to) or spoon in some tuna mayo, but this recipe takes them to the next level. What I also like about serving jackets this way is that it's easier to serve them with something alongside, like a salad or some roasted veg. Of course, you're welcome to mix it up a bit and go back to the classic baked potato once in a while... I'll forgive you.

SERVES 4

4 baking potatoes
2 teaspoons olive oil
100–150g (3½–5½oz) sour cream or soft cheese
4 spring onions (scallions), finely sliced
150g (5½oz) frozen peas
Handful of parsley or chives, finely chopped
75g (2½oz) mature Cheddar cheese, grated (shredded)
Salt and freshly ground black pepper

Preheat the oven to 220°C/200°C fan/430°F/gas 7.

Using a fork, prick the potatoes all over and rub the oil into their skins. Season well with salt and pepper and place on a baking tray. Bake the potatoes in the hot oven for 1 hour–1 hour 15 minutes or until the potato skins have crisped up and they are tender in the middle. (You could also microwave the potatoes for around 10 minutes, then bake them in the air fryer for around 20–30 minutes.)

Once cooked, turn off the oven, cut the potatoes in half and leave to cool for around 30–40 minutes. (If you don't have time to wait, put on some clean kitchen gloves to protect your hands from the heat and continue.)

Turn on the oven once more and preheat it to 200°C/180°C fan/390°F/gas 6.

Leaving a thin layer just inside the skins, scoop out the potato into a bowl. Add the sour cream or soft cheese, spring onions, frozen peas, chopped herbs and half of the Cheddar cheese to the bowl and mix everything together. Spoon the potato filling back into the potato skins, heaping the mixture, then scatter over the remaining cheese. Bake in the hot oven for 20–30 minutes or until golden.

Cook's tip The cooking time for the baked potatoes will very much depend on the variety and size of the potato as well as your oven. I've given a guide cooking time, but you may need to bake your potatoes for longer. Regardless of whether you're cooking them in the oven or air fryer, I very much recommend giving them a blast in the microwave for 10 minutes before baking as it speeds things along.

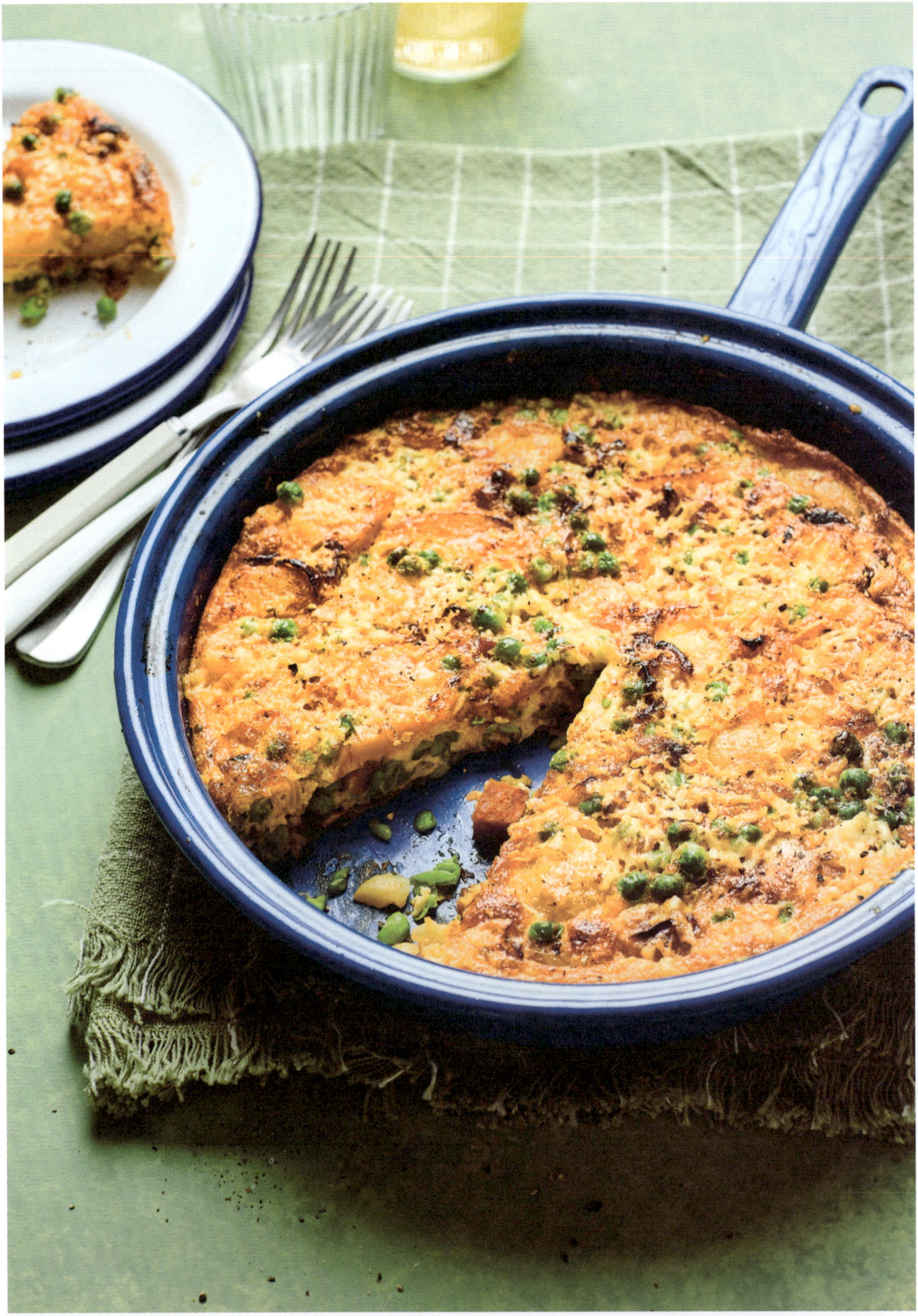

MIDWEEK MEALS

Chorizo, Potato and Pea Frittata

When tinned potatoes started to make a comeback, I wasn't entirely convinced. However, once I understood how versatile they are and how they speed up cooking times, I realised it was time to jump on the band wagon. Plus I found out that Nadiya Hussain is a big fan, so they must be great. I think they're perfect for a frittata because you don't have to boil them separately first, and I'm always concerned they'll be a little too hard if I don't. They're also fantastic with peas and so it really is a win-win all round.

SERVES 4–6

2 tablespoons sunflower, vegetable or olive oil
1 large onion, sliced
1 teaspoon smoked paprika
100g (3½oz) chorizo, roughly chopped
1 x 400-g (14-oz) tin potatoes, drained and cut in half
150g (5½oz) frozen peas
6 eggs
50g (1¾oz) mature Cheddar cheese, grated (shredded)
Salt and freshly ground black pepper

Heat the oil in an ovenproof frying pan (skillet) over a medium heat. Add the onion and fry until golden, around 8 minutes. Stir in the paprika and cook for a further 1 minute.

Stir in the chorizo and cook for a few minutes or until it's starting to brown and the oil has been released. Add the potatoes, mix together and then cook for 3–4 minutes to brown a little. Stir in the frozen peas and season with salt and pepper, then cook for a few minutes to thaw slightly.

Beat the eggs together with a good crack of black pepper, then mix in half of the cheese. Pour this egg mixture over the potato and peas in the pan. Cook the frittata over a medium heat for about 10 minutes or until the egg has set underneath and around the edges.

Meanwhile, turn the grill on to its hottest setting.

Scatter the remaining cheese over the frittata and put the pan under the hot grill for 5–10 minutes or until the eggs have set and the frittata is golden. It may puff up a little, which is absolutely fine.

Once cooked, leave the frittata for a few minutes before slicing and serving. It is equally good eaten warm or cold.

Variation: Red bell pepper and pea frittata This frittata is also great with a few roasted red bell peppers from a jar. You can either replace the tinned potatoes with jarred bell peppers or halve the quantity of potatoes and add two chopped roasted red bell peppers when you add the potatoes.

Variation: Leek and feta frittata Omit the onion, paprika and chorizo and instead slice and fry a leek in the oil, stir in the potatoes, followed by the peas and then replace the grated (shredded) Cheddar cheese with crumbled feta. This is also lovely with some fresh green herbs, such as parsley, dill or tarragon.

Pea Fritters, Three Ways

If there's one thing I can't refrain from ordering at brunch, it's a fritter; pea or sweetcorn, preferably. That, and a cocktail, something fizz-based. Anyway, I digress. The fritter is the king of brunch, especially when topped with a poached egg and accompanied by a zingy dip – I recommend something with harissa. Not only do I love the flavour and colour of a pea fritter, I love folding in some whole peas for a little crunch. Here are three ways I like to make mine.

Pea Fritters

MAKES 10–12

200g (7oz) frozen peas
4 spring onions (scallions), finely sliced
2 tablespoons chopped mint, dill or parsley
100g (3½oz) self-raising flour
2 eggs
1 tablespoon milk
1 tablespoon mayonnaise
Oil, for frying
Salt and freshly ground black pepper

Place the peas in a heatproof bowl and cover with freshly boiled water to defrost. Leave them for a few minutes, then drain. Leave the peas to dry for 5 minutes.

Remove a handful of peas and set aside, then roughly chop the rest before putting them in a bowl with the spring onions and herbs.

In a separate bowl, beat together the flour, eggs, milk and mayonnaise to make a smooth batter. Season well with plenty of salt and pepper. Fold this into the pea mixture along with the reserved whole peas.

Form the pea mixture into 10–12 fritters and chill in the fridge for 20 minutes.

Heat 1 tablespoon of oil in a large frying pan (skillet) over a low heat. Add the fritters and fry for 3–5 minutes on each side until golden and cooked through. (I prefer to cook over a low heat to ensure they don't burn on the outside.) You may need to cook the fritters in batches; if so, add a little more oil after each batch, if necessary.

Serving suggestion Pea fritters go well with poached eggs, spiced yogurt (mixed with ground spices, harissa or chilli sauce), guacamole, salsa, a light salad and lime wedges, to name but a few accompaniments.

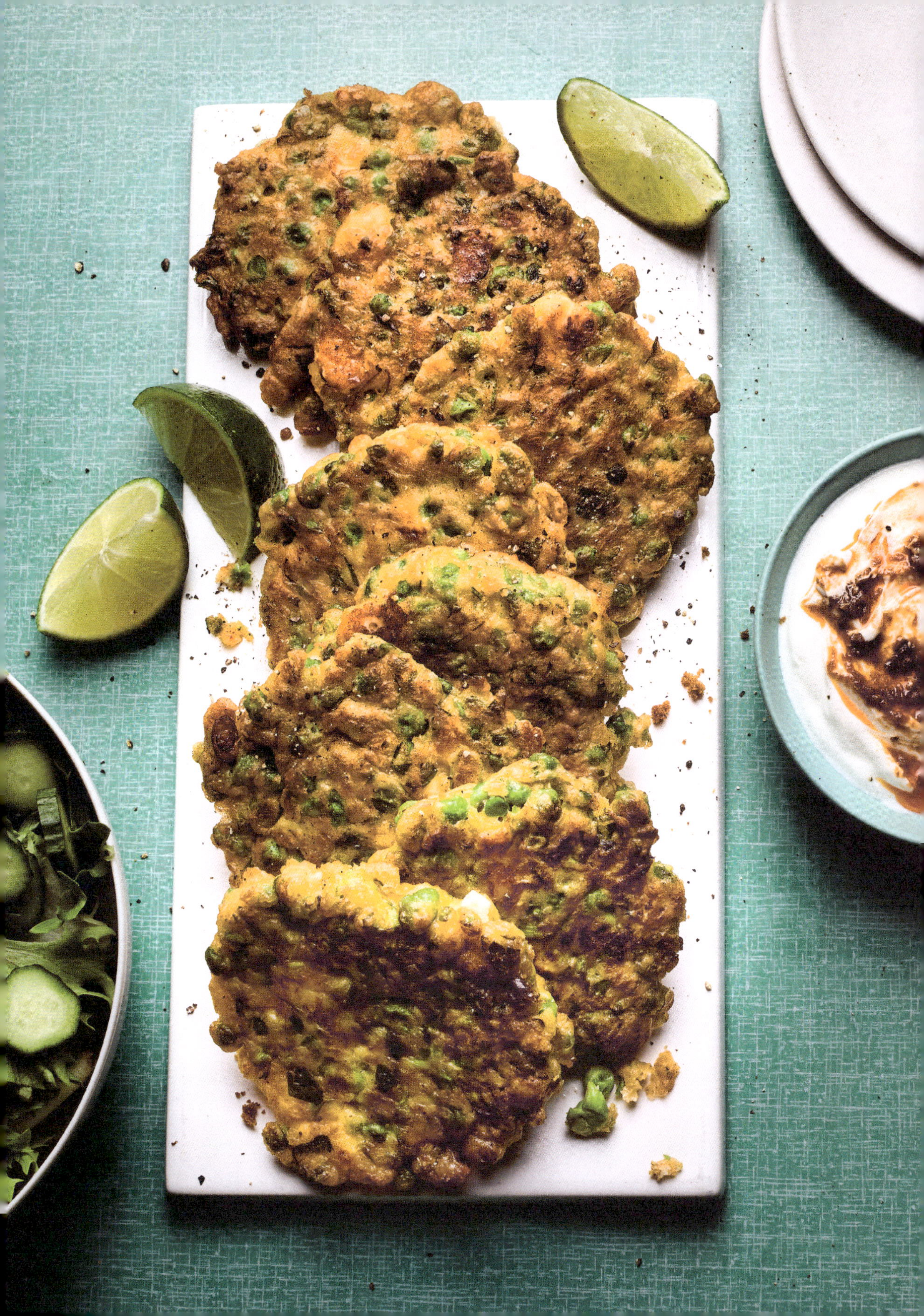

Pea, Feta and Harissa Fritters

MAKES 8

200g (7oz) frozen peas
1 garlic clove, crushed or finely grated (shredded)
2 spring onions (scallions), finely sliced
2 tablespoons chopped parsley
75g (2½oz) feta (vegetarian, if necessary), crumbled
75g (2½oz) self-raising flour
Zest of ½ lemon
2 eggs
1 tablespoon harissa (as hot as you like it)
1 tablespoon milk
Oil, for frying

Place the peas in a heatproof bowl and cover with freshly boiled water to defrost. Leave them for a few minutes, then drain. Leave the peas to dry for 5 minutes.

Roughly chop the peas and tip them into a large bowl with the garlic, spring onions, parsley and feta.

In a separate bowl, beat together the flour, lemon zest, eggs, harissa and milk until smooth. Season well with plenty of salt and pepper. Fold the pea mixture into the batter.

Heat 1 tablespoon of oil in a large frying pan (skillet) over a low heat. Drop an eighth of the mixture into the pan to make a fritter. Continue adding more mixture, leaving 3cm (1 inch) between each fritter, until the frying pan is full. Cook the fritters for 4–5 minutes on each side, turning carefully with a fish slice, until golden, cooked through and puffed up a little. You may need to cook the fritters in batches.

Pea, Sweetcorn and Halloumi Fritters

MAKES 10–12

100g (3½oz) frozen peas
100g (3½oz) frozen sweetcorn
1 x 225-g (8-oz) block halloumi, coarsely grated (shredded)
1 garlic clove, crushed or finely grated (shredded)
Half bunch of chives, finely sliced
½ red chilli, finely chopped (optional)
100g (3½oz) self-raising flour
Zest of ½ lemon
2 eggs
3 tablespoons milk
Oil, for frying
Guacamole, salsa, harissa yogurt or sriracha mayonnaise, to serve

Place the peas and sweetcorn in a heatproof bowl and cover with freshly boiled water to defrost. Leave them for a few minutes, then drain. Leave the peas and sweetcorn to dry for 5 minutes.

Remove a couple of handfuls of the peas and sweetcorn and set aside, then roughly chop the rest before putting them in a large bowl with the halloumi, garlic, chives and red chilli, if using.

In a separate bowl, beat together the flour, lemon zest, eggs and milk until smooth. Season well with plenty of salt and pepper. Fold the pea and sweetcorn mixture into the batter.

Heat 1 tablespoon of oil in a large frying pan (skillet) over a low heat. Working in batches, drop large spoonfuls of the mixture into the pan to make the fritters. Continue adding more mixture, leaving 3cm (1 inch) between each fritter, until the frying pan is full. Cook the fritters for 4–5 minutes on each side, turning carefully with a fish slice, until golden, cooked through and puffed up a little. You may need to add a little more oil after each batch, if necessary.

Chicken and Squash Curry

A curry is a great dish for when you've got a group of hungry mouths to feed. This one serves 8–10 people, but if you're serving fewer, it's easier to halve the quantities or freeze the leftovers for a midweek meal or an emergency supper. I love the way the peas lend a touch of colour, but I also adore the sweetness they bring, which pairs really nicely with the spice.

SERVES 6–8

- 2 tablespoons sunflower or vegetable oil
- 2 onions, sliced
- 10–12 boneless, skinless chicken thighs, roughly chopped
- 4 garlic cloves, crushed or finely grated (shredded)
- Thumb-sized piece of ginger, finely grated (shredded)
- 1 butternut squash (around 750g/1lb 10oz), peeled, deseeded and cut into bite-sized pieces
- 1 x 280-g (10-oz) jar curry paste (I use korma or tikka masala, but use your favourite)
- 2 x 400-g (14-oz) tins chopped tomatoes
- 1 x 400-ml (14-fl oz) tin coconut milk
- 6 blocks frozen spinach
- 250g (9oz) frozen peas
- Cooked rice, to serve
- Coriander (cilantro) leaves, chopped, to serve (optional)

Heat the oil in a large saucepan with a lid over a medium heat. Add the onions and fry for 6–8 minutes or until beginning to brown.

Stir in the chicken and fry until the meat is no longer raw and there are brown spots, then add in the garlic and ginger and cook for a few minutes.

Stir in the squash until everything is mixed well, then spoon in the curry paste and stir so everything is well coated.

Pour in the tomatoes and coconut milk, then bring to a simmer and cook, with the lid on, for about 15 minutes or until the squash is almost cooked (a knife should go through easily).

Tip in the frozen spinach and stir. If the sauce is still a little liquid, leave the lid off. Cook for 2–3 minutes or until the spinach has pretty much thawed, then tip in the frozen peas and cook for a further 2 minutes or until the peas are warmed through and tender.

Serve with some cooked rice and a scattering of coriander (cilantro), if you like.

Pan-fried Gnocchi with Peas in a Creamy Tarragon Sauce

Tarragon and peas is a great combination. A quick and easy way to add a hit of flavour, tarragon is a herb that can overpower dishes and so I've not used too much of it here. I suggest adding just a single tablespoon first, especially if you're relatively new to it, and then you can always stir through a little more.

SERVES 2–4

½ tablespoon oil
1 onion, chopped
200g (7oz) unsmoked or smoked bacon lardons
1 x 500-g (1lb 2-oz) packets ready-made gnocchi
150ml (5fl oz) vegetable or chicken stock
150ml (5fl oz) double (heavy) cream
2 tablespoons chopped tarragon
200g (7oz) frozen peas
Salt and freshly ground black pepper

Heat the oil in a large frying pan (skillet) over a medium heat. Add the onion and fry for 5 minutes or until softened and beginning to brown.

Stir in the bacon and fry for 5–6 minutes or until golden, crisp and the fat has been released.

Tip the gnocchi into the pan and fry for 2–3 minutes or until starting to brown a little, stirring them carefully to ensure they don't break up. Transfer the cooked gnocchi to a plate and set aside.

Combine the stock and cream in a jug (pitcher) and pour the mixture into the pan. Season well with salt and pepper, then bring to a simmer and cook for 1 minute. Stir in the chopped tarragon and frozen peas, then cook for a further 2 minutes or until the peas are warmed through and tender.

Return the gnocchi to the pan, gently stir into the sauce and cook for 1–2 minutes or until the gnocchi are warmed through. Serve immediately.

Cook's tip You can make this dish vegetarian by omitting the bacon, although you may want to add a little saltiness by grating (shredding) over some vegetarian Italian hard cheese just before serving.

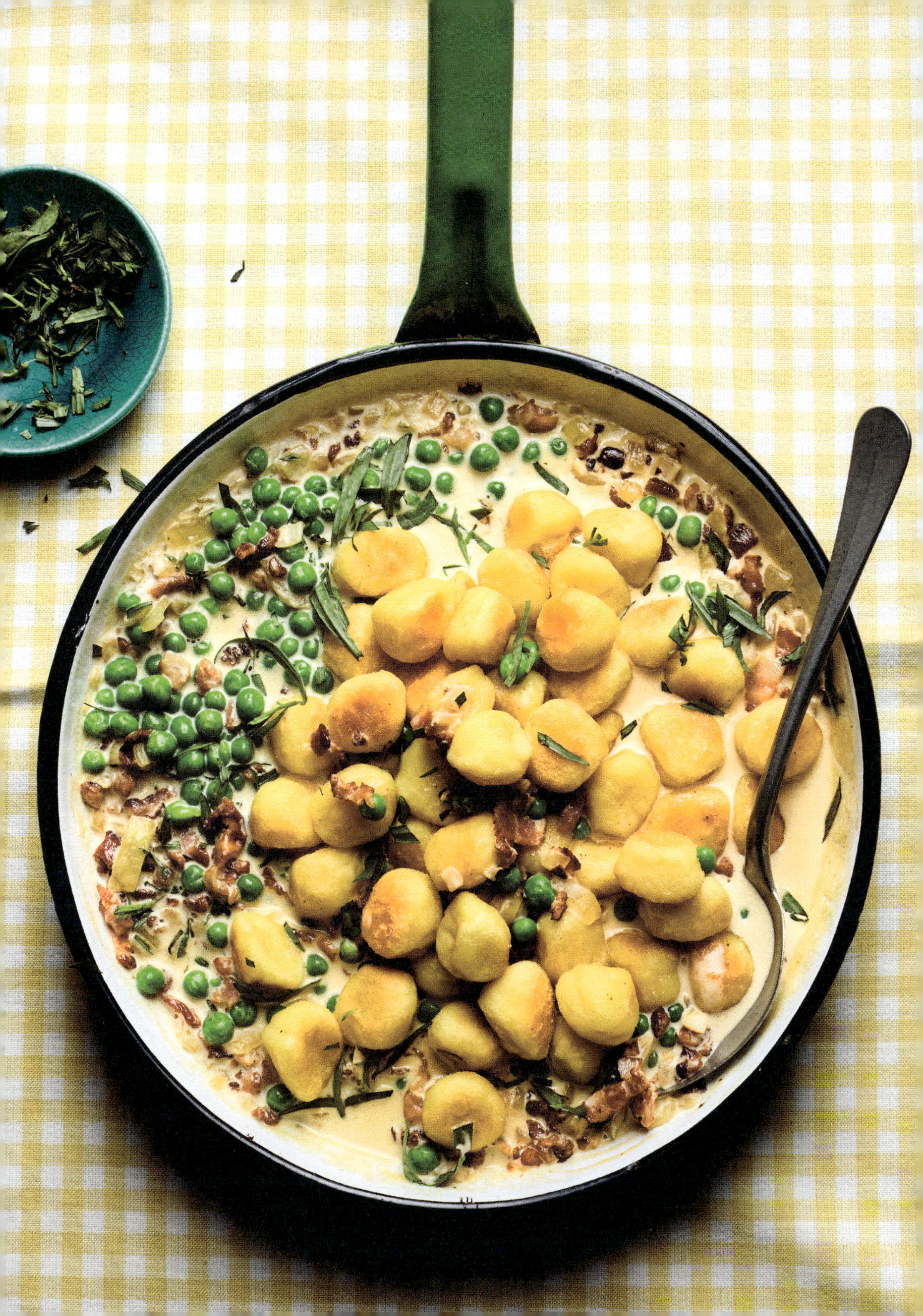

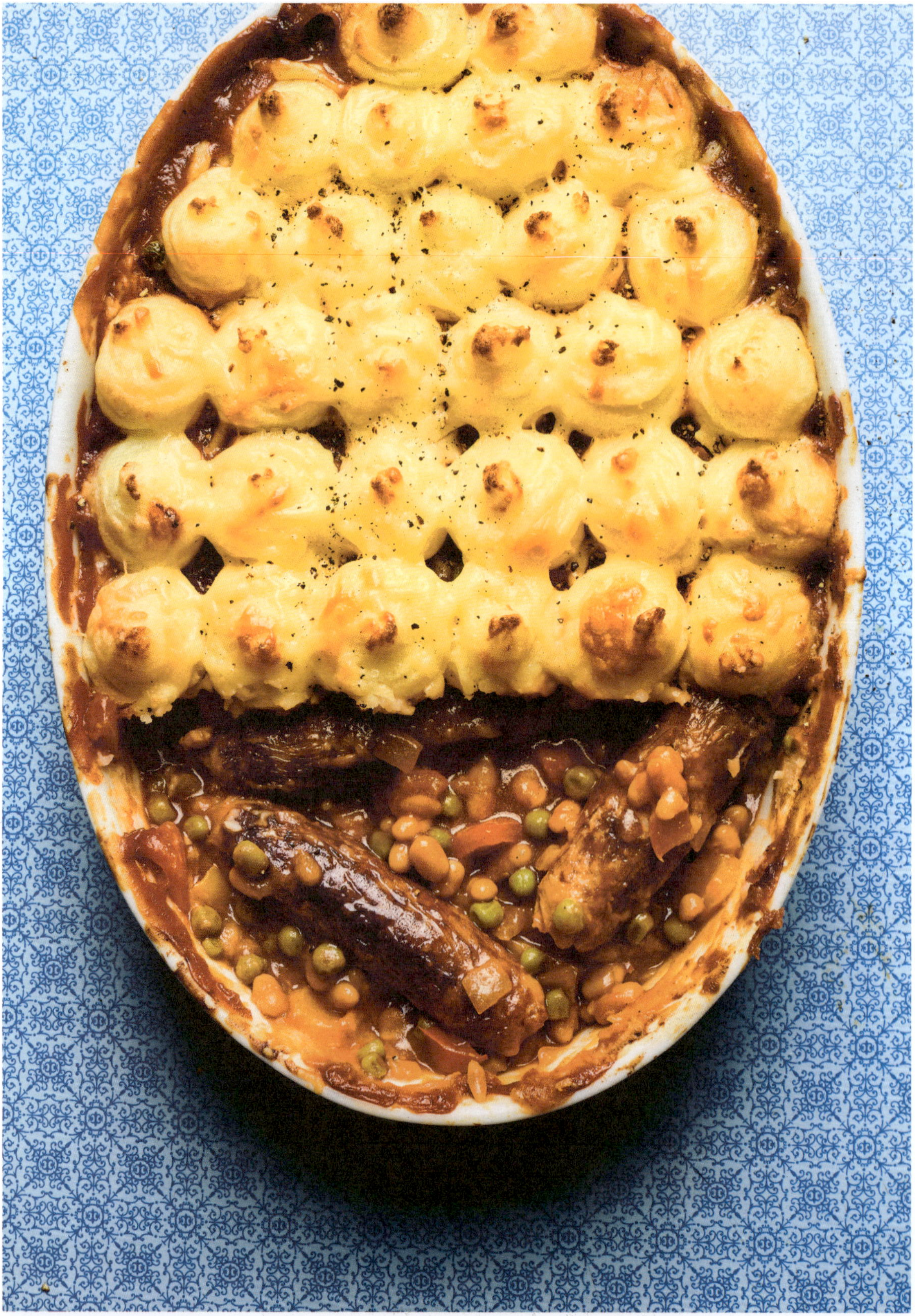

Rhinestone Cowboy Pie

When we were at uni together, my friend Bex made a dish that was basically fancy baked beans; she'd lace a tin of beans with onion and pepper before adorning her toast with them and crowning the dish with a good scattering of cheese. I've taken her dish and crossed it with a cowboy pie to create this bejewelled version. I find this way I don't need any sides but, of course, you can serve it however you like.

SERVES 4–6

1½ tablespoons sunflower or vegetable oil
6–8 sausages (vegetarian, if you prefer)
1 onion, chopped
1 red bell pepper, chopped
1 yellow bell pepper, chopped
1 teaspoon paprika
2 x 400-g (14-oz) tins baked beans
2 tablespoons barbecue sauce
200g (7oz) frozen peas

FOR THE POTATO TOPPING

1kg (2lb 4oz) potatoes, peeled and chopped
75g (2½oz) butter
3 tablespoons milk
50g (1¾oz) mature Cheddar cheese, grated (shredded)

Heat ½ tablespoon of the oil in a large frying pan (skillet) over a medium heat. Add the sausages and fry for a few minutes or until browned on all sides. Remove from the pan, leaving the oil behind, and place in an ovenproof dish.

Drizzle the remaining oil into the pan and reduce the heat to medium-low. Tip in the onion and bell peppers, then fry for 10–12 minutes or until both have softened.

Stir the paprika into the veg, then once coated stir in the beans and barbecue sauce. Bring everything to a simmer, remove from the heat and then stir in the frozen peas. Tip the baked bean mixture into the ovenproof dish along with the sausages.

Preheat the oven to 200°C/180°C fan/390°F/gas 6.

Put the potatoes in a large pan of salted water. Bring to the boil and cook for 10–15 minutes or until tender. Drain, tip back into the pan and mash with the butter and milk. Spoon the mashed potato on top of the baked bean mixture to cover it, then scatter over the Cheddar cheese.

Bake in the preheated oven for 30–40 minutes or until bubbling and the cheese is golden.

Jerk-Spiced Chicken with Coconut Rice with Peas

There's a time and a place for shop-bought spice blends, whether that's fajita seasoning, Cajun spice blends or, as I am using here, jerk-style seasoning. It's important to note that such blends are incredibly far away from the real thing. For example, jerk chicken is not called so because of the spices used but rather the way it's cooked. That's not to say spice blends are not worth using; you just need to be aware that you aren't getting an authentic experience. When time is of the essence, spice blends add a lot of flavour with minimal effort. I feel the same way about using coconut milk to cook rice and my beloved frozen peas, all of which come together here to create a midweek meal that's full of flavour.

% ❄ GF DF

SERVES 4

- 4 chicken legs or 8 thighs, skin-on and bone-in
- 2–4 teaspoons jerk-style spiced seasoning (see note below)
- 2 tablespoons soy sauce
- 2 tablespoons honey
- 3 tablespoons sunflower or vegetable oil
- Zest and juice of ½ lime, the other half cut into wedges
- 4 spring onions (scallions), finely sliced
- 300g (10½oz) long-grain rice
- 1 onion, finely sliced
- 1 x 400-ml (14-fl oz) tin coconut milk
- 200g (7oz) frozen peas

Note on spice As with most spice blends, they vary depending on the brand. I recommend trying a little first – dab your pinky finger in the spices and bring it to the tip of your tongue – in order to determine how much to use. This is mainly so you don't ruin the dish by making it too spicy for your palate.

Using a sharp knife, score the chicken legs or thighs a few times and put them in a bowl. Add in the jerk-style spiced seasoning, soy sauce, honey, 1 tablespoon of the oil, the lime zest and juice and the spring onions (scallions). Mix everything together and leave to marinate for 20 minutes – you can also do this the day before, if you want to get ahead.

Heat 1 tablespoon of the oil in a frying pan (skillet) or wide saucepan with a lid over a medium heat. Leaving any excess marinade in the bowl, add the chicken to the pan and brown all over, this will take around 5–6 minutes. Reduce the heat to medium-low, pop the lid on the pan and cook the chicken for 15–20 minutes, turning occasionally, until the meat is cooked through – the juices should run clear or a thermometer should read 70°C/160°F.

Meanwhile, rinse the rice under cold running water until it runs almost clear. I do this by putting the rice in a bowl, covering with water and then draining, and repeating this 3 or 4 times. Set aside.

Heat the remaining oil in a saucepan with a lid over a medium heat. Add the onion and cook for 5–6 minutes or until beginning to brown. Stir in the rice, cook for 1 minute, then pour in the coconut milk plus one-third of a tin of water. Bring to a simmer, cover and cook for 10–12 minutes or until almost cooked. If the pan starts to run dry, add more water. Stir the frozen peas into the rice and cook for a further 2–3 minutes or until the peas and rice are tender.

Serve the rice and chicken together with the lime wedges for squeezing over.

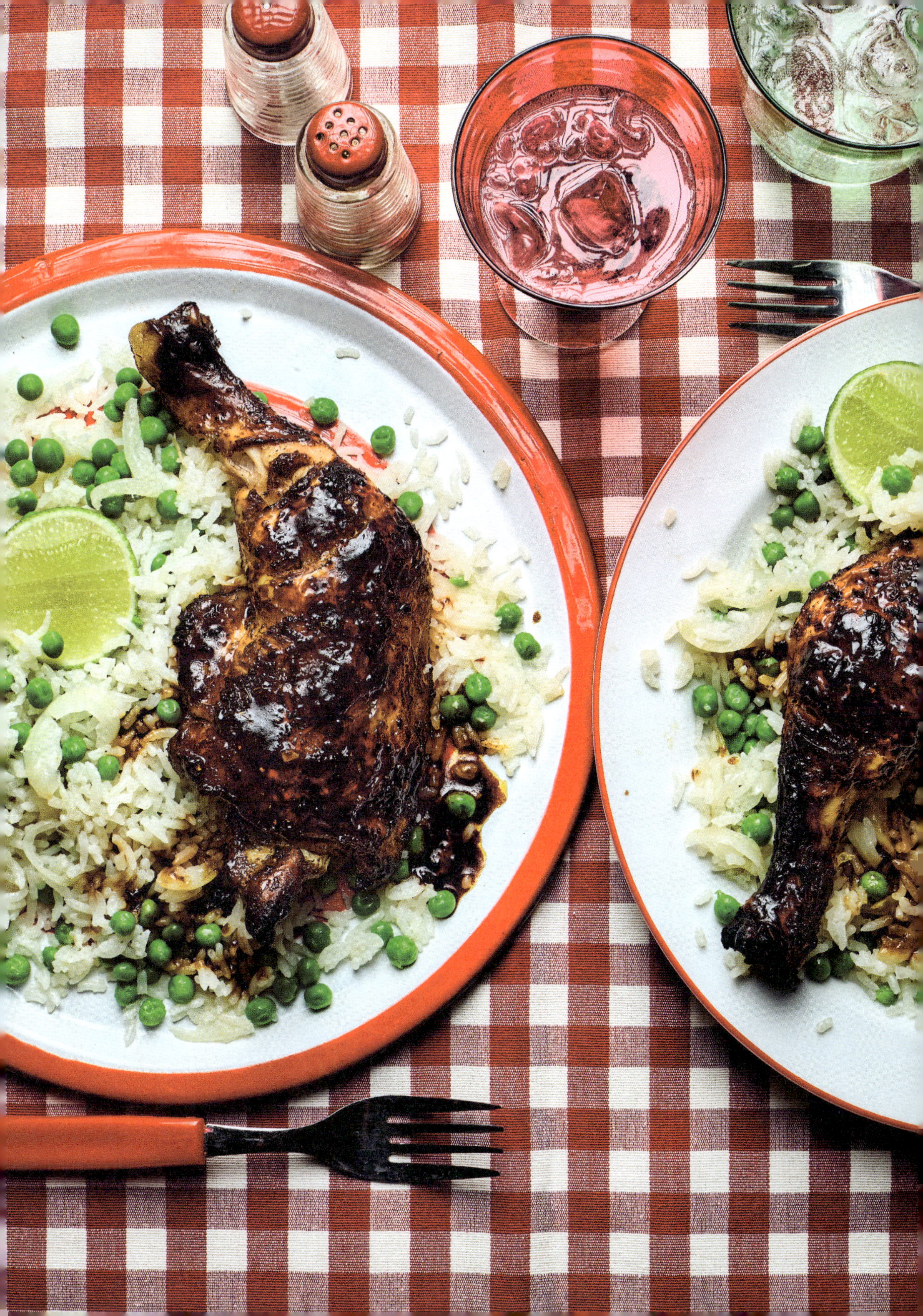

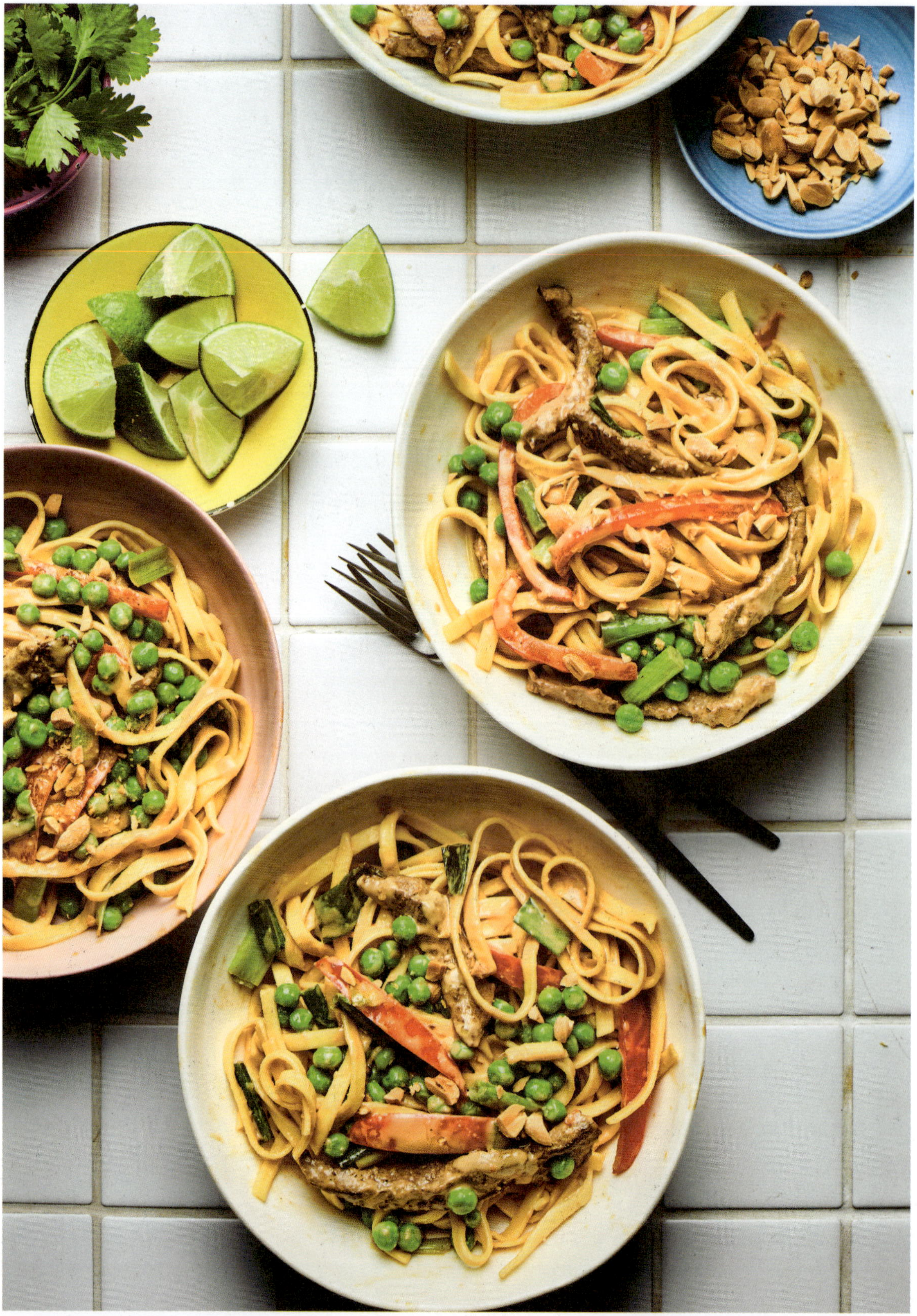

Spiced Beef and Peanut Butter Noodles

This is possibly one of the longest lists of ingredients for any recipe in this book, but I think it's worth it. Most of the ingredients are found hanging around the fridge or storecupboard shelves. As with any stir-fry dish, the key is to prep everything before you start cooking so that nothing burns while you're chopping. Noodles, peanut butter, lime, soy and peas are, for me, real comfort food – salty, sweet, umami and sour all in one mouthful.

SERVES 3–4

250g (9oz) dried medium egg noodles
2 large garlic cloves, crushed or finely grated (shredded)
1 tablespoon lemongrass paste
½ tablespoon ginger paste or grated (shredded) fresh ginger
1 red chilli, finely sliced (seeds removed, if you like, optional)
10g (⅓oz) coriander (cilantro), leaves and stalks separated and both finely sliced
1 teaspoon soy sauce, plus extra to serve
1 teaspoon fish sauce (or an extra 1 teaspoon soy sauce)
2 tablespoons peanut butter (I like to use roasted peanut butter)
Juice of ½–1 lime
2 tablespoons sunflower or vegetable oil
1 red, yellow or orange bell pepper, sliced
6–8 spring onions (scallions), sliced
250g (9oz) beef stir-fry strips
150g (5½oz) frozen peas
Handful of chopped peanuts to garnish (optional)

Bring a saucepan of water to the boil. Plunge the noodles in the water, then immediately remove the pan from the heat and leave for 6 minutes. Alternatively, cook the noodles according to the packet instructions. Drain, reserving a mugful of the noodle cooking water, and set aside.

While the noodles are cooking, combine the garlic, lemongrass, ginger, chilli, if using, and coriander stalks in a small bowl. Mix together the soy sauce, fish sauce (or extra soy sauce), peanut butter, the juice of ½ lime and 2 tablespoons of the noodle cooking water in another bowl. If the noodles aren't yet cooked at this point, firstly, congratulations on your speed and, secondly, just scoop the water straight out of the pan.

Heat the oil in a large frying pan (skillet) or wok over a medium to medium-high heat. Add the peppers and fry for a couple of minutes or until browning, then stir in the spring onions (scallions) and cook for a further 1–2 minutes or until beginning to colour.

Stir in the beef stir-fry strips and cook for a few minutes until browned. Tip in the garlic mixture, cook for 1 minute and then stir in the frozen peas and cook for 2–3 minutes or until the peas are warmed through and any liquid has started to evaporate.

Pour in the soy sauce mixture and stir everything together before adding the cooked noodles and tossing to combine – add some of the reserved noodle cooking water, if you need to loosen it all a little. Serve with a scattering of coriander leaves and chopped peanuts, if you like.

Simple Salmon and Pea Fishcakes

I can't deny that fishcakes sometimes feel like a bit of a faff to make. I've made these ones as simple as possible by leaving off the breadcrumb coating, because I don't think it's necessary (although feel free to coat the fishcakes in beaten egg and then breadcrumbs, if you like). You can also try using tinned potatoes to make things even simpler. If you're frying the fishcakes in a pan, cook them over a lower heat so that you don't burn the outside while the centre remains cold and uncooked.

MAKES 4 LARGE OR 8 SMALL FISHCAKES

2 salmon fillets (around 260g/9½oz) or a similar weight of tinned pink salmon
500g (1lb 2oz) potatoes, cut into chunks
125g (4½oz) frozen peas
Handful of dill, finely chopped (optional)
Handful of parsley, finely chopped
Zest of 1 lemon, plus cut into wedges, to serve
Flour, for dusting
1–2 tablespoons olive oil
Salt and freshly ground black pepper

Cook's tip If you chill the fishcakes first, I recommend baking or air frying them. Bake in a hot oven at 180°C/160°C fan/350°F/gas 4 for around 30 minutes. You can also cook them in an air fryer at 180°C/350°F for 15–20 minutes, turning halfway through.

Bring a large pan of salted water to the boil. If using salmon fillets, poach the fish over a low heat for 6–8 minutes or until the salmon is just cooked. Lift the salmon out, drain and set aside.

In the same water, boil the potatoes (unless using tinned potatoes) for 10–15 minutes or until just tender – a knife should slip easily through the centre. Be careful not to overcook the potatoes and let them go mushy.

Using either the potato cooking water or some freshly boiled water, defrost the frozen peas in a heatproof bowl by covering them with boiling water and leaving for 3 minutes. Drain, then roughly chop or mash the peas.

Mash the cooked potatoes until fluffy then flake in the salmon (if using tinned pink salmon, it'll already be in flakes). Mix in the peas, herbs, lemon zest and a good seasoning of salt and pepper.

Form the mixture into 4 large or 8 small fishcakes. At this point, you can chill the fishcakes in the fridge for up to 24 hours – just allow them to come to room temperature for 30 minutes before cooking.

When ready to cook, dust each fishcake with a little flour. Heat 1 tablespoon of the oil in a frying pan (skillet) over a medium-low heat and fry the cakes for 6–12 minutes on each side, depending on whether you made them small or large, until golden and heated through. Add a little more oil if the cakes absorb too much.

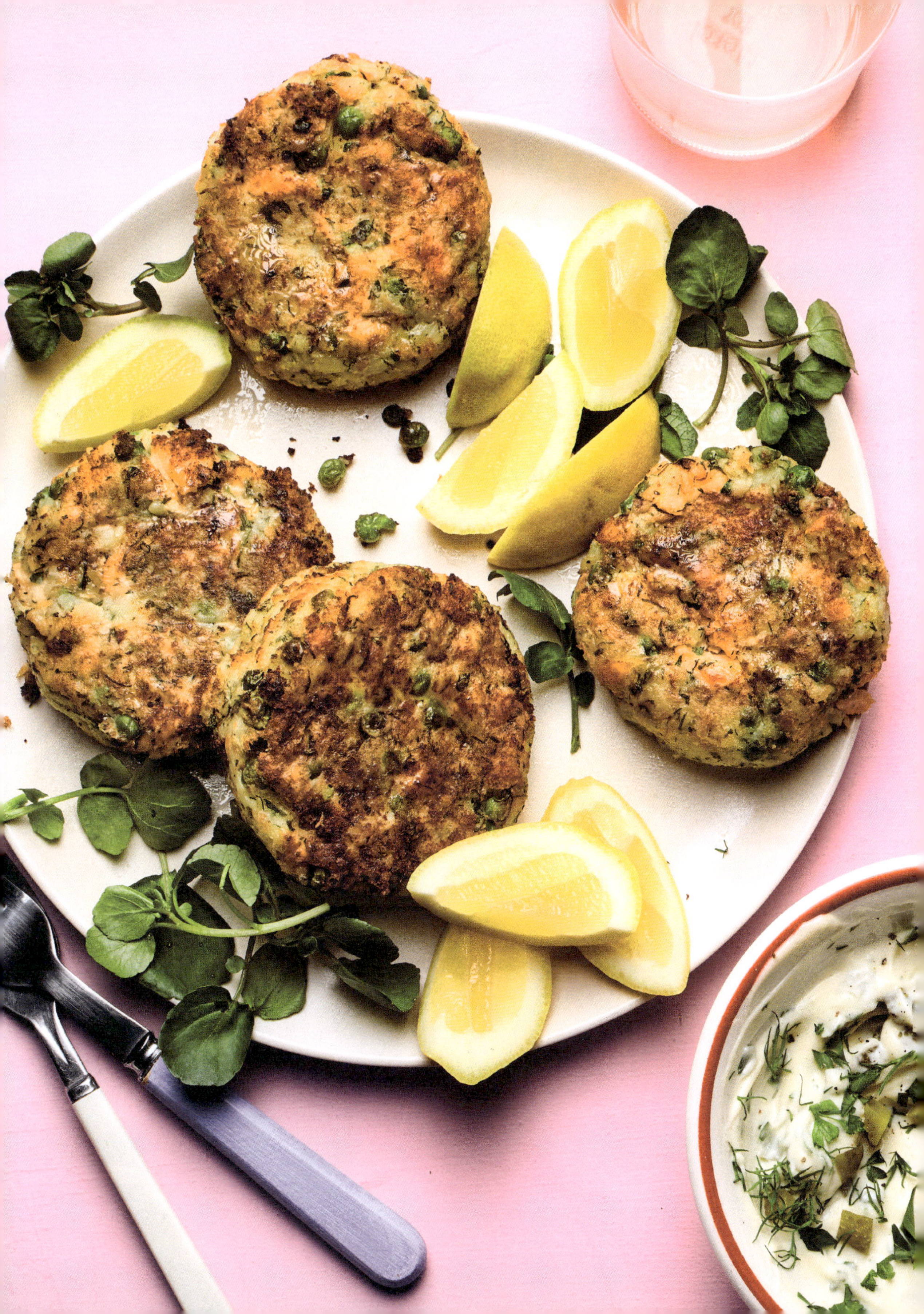

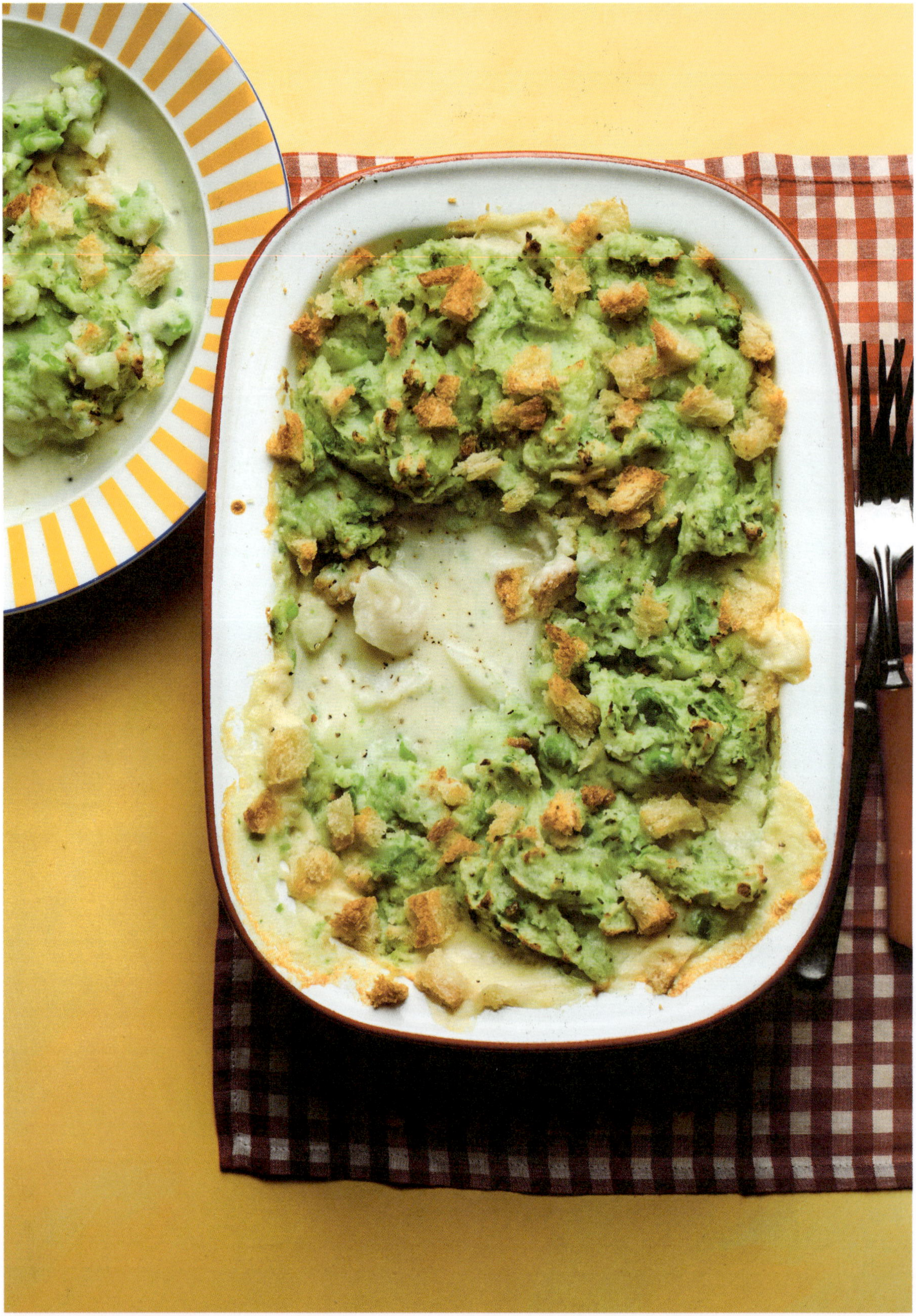

Mash 'n' Pea Fish Pie

Fish pie wouldn't be the same without peas. In this version, shared with me by my friend Lorna, the peas are added to the topping rather than mixed through the sauce. Lorna runs an online Duke of Edinburgh cookery school, which is all about building confidence in young people. Before that, she was the Queen of Canapés, cooking for the stars and writing countless articles and books. There's nothing she doesn't know about cooking, so I practically bit her hand off when she said she had a great fish pie recipe to share.

SERVES 2

- 2 Maris Piper potatoes (around 400g/14oz), peeled and cut into 3-cm (1-inch) cubes
- 40g (1½oz) butter
- 20g (¾oz) plain (all-purpose) flour
- 300ml (10fl oz) whole (full-fat) milk
- 300g (10½oz) skinless sustainable white fish fillet (such as cod, haddock or pollock), cut into 3-cm (1-inch) cubes or use a fish pie mix
- 1 slice white bread
- 1½ tablespoons olive oil
- 150g (5½oz) frozen peas or petits pois
- Salt and freshly ground black pepper

Put the potatoes in a saucepan of salted water. Bring to the boil, then simmer for 10 minutes or until cooked through.

While the potatoes are cooking, make the sauce. Melt half of the butter in a small saucepan over a low heat. Remove the pan from the heat and stir in the flour, mix well. Gradually add the milk, stirring continuously. If there are any lumps, vigorously beat them out with a wooden spoon or whisk.

Put the saucepan back over a medium-low heat, bring to a simmer then cook for 1 minute while stirring. The sauce should lightly coat the back of a spoon. Season well with salt and freshly ground black pepper.

Remove the saucepan from the heat and gently stir in the fish.

Make the crumbs by tearing the bread, including the crust, into very small pieces. Put them in a small mixing bowl with the oil, season well and stir well with a fork to coat in the oil.

Preheat the oven to 220°C/200°C fan/430°F/gas 7.

Once the potatoes are cooked, add the frozen peas and cook for 2 minutes. Drain the potatoes and peas, then return them to the pan. Add the rest of the butter and mash well – you should end up with smooth mash, but you'll only be able to crush the peas, so the mixture will be a combination of rough and smooth. Season well with plenty of salt and pepper.

Spoon the fish and sauce into an ovenproof dish and top with the potato-pea mash, spreading the mixture to the edges of the dish with a fork. Scatter over the crumbs.

Put the dish on a baking tray and place on the middle shelf of the oven. Bake in the hot oven for 20 minutes, or until the fish is cooked through and the crumbs are crisp and golden. Serve on warmed plates.

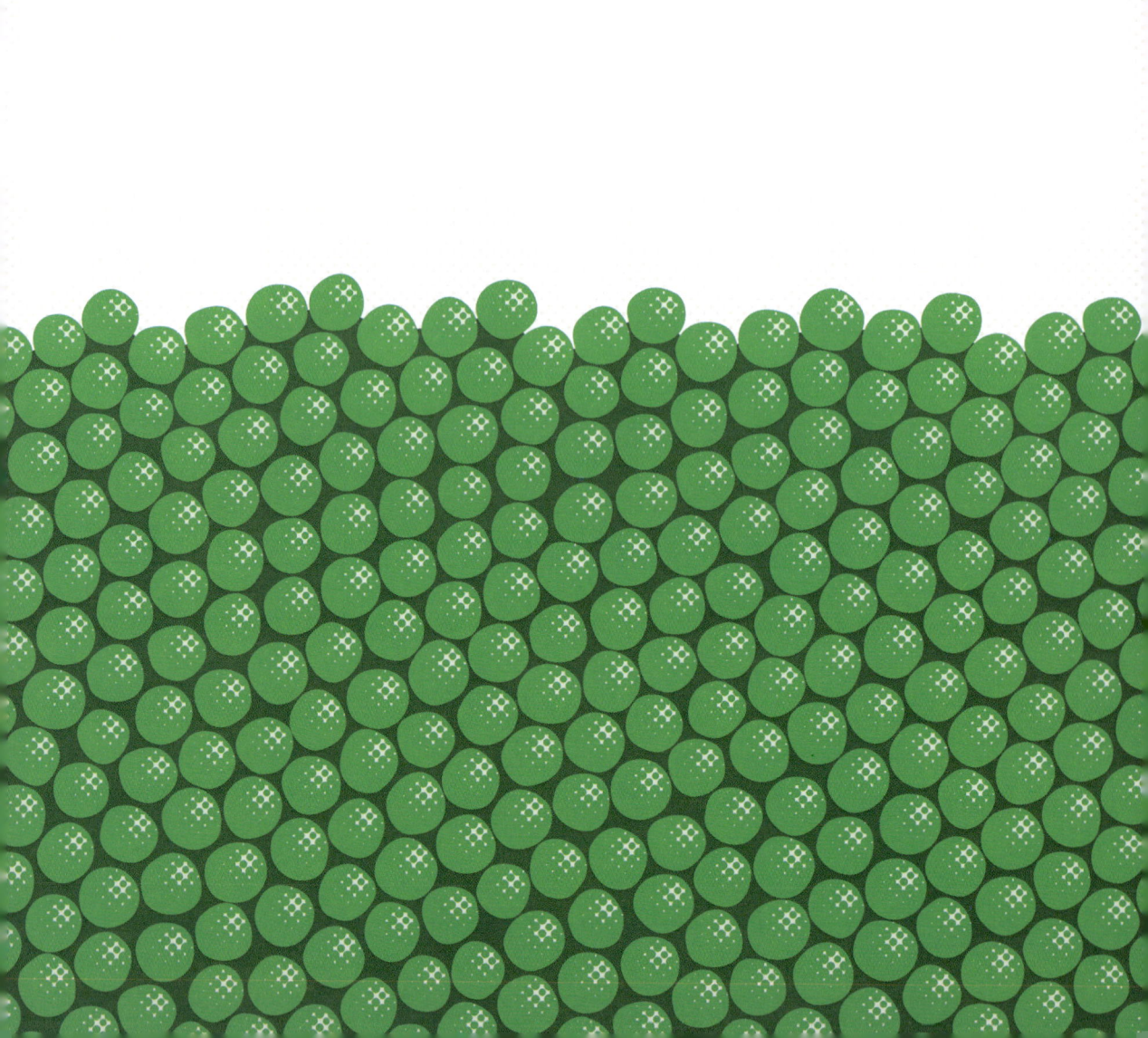

Sides, Sauces and Snacks

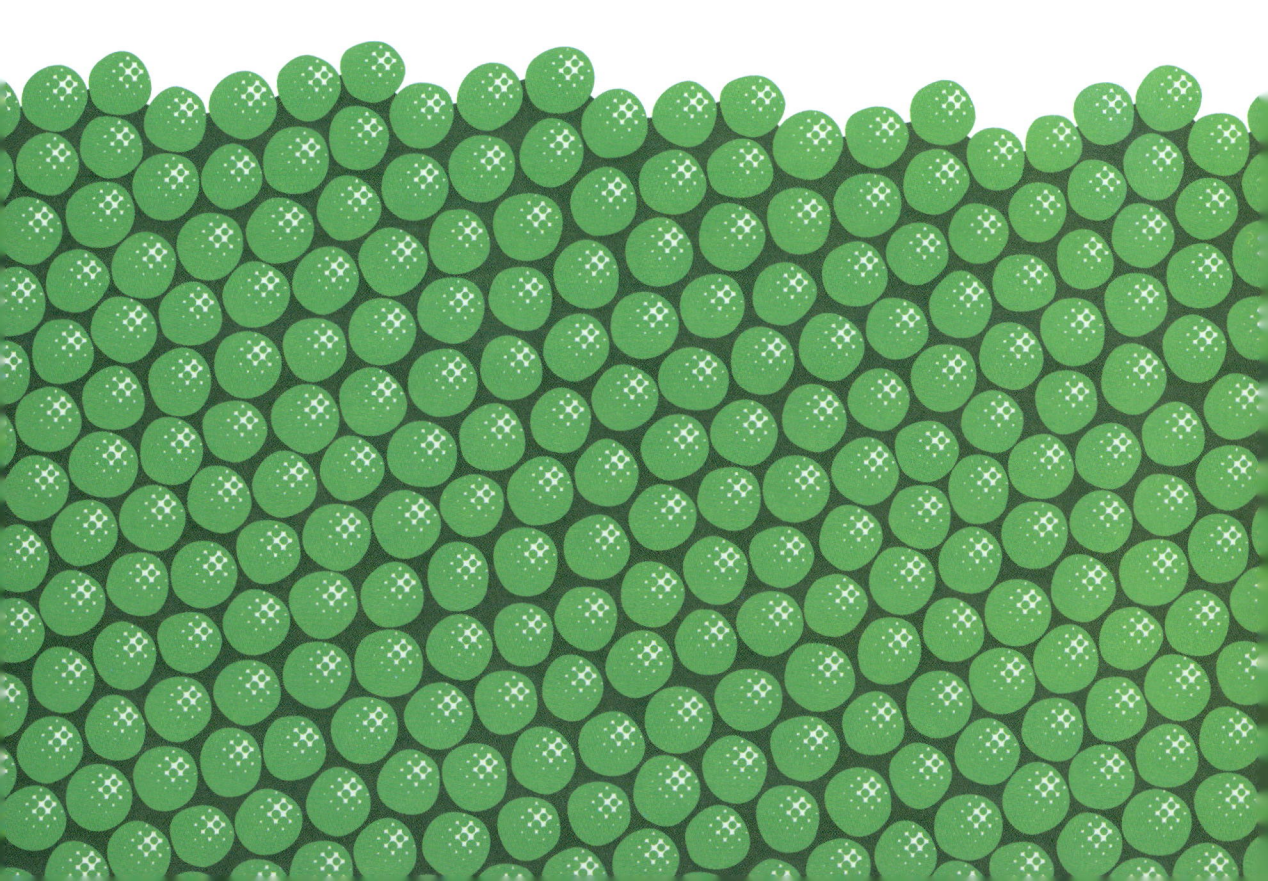

SIDES, SAUCES AND SNACKS

Baked Breakfast Eggs

I'm not one for spending ages cooking at breakfast time – it's usually at least 10am before I can be bothered. I try not to eat sugary cereal, which is the usual quick-and-easy option (no judgement if you do, it's just that I get peckish 30 minutes later, once the sugar rush has subsided), so that's why these baked eggs are perfect. They require minimal effort but make a lovely, tasty breakfast treat. It's important to oil your tin, though, otherwise the difficulty of the washing up negates the ease of cooking. You might not think of peas as traditional breakfast fare, however they add a subtle sweetness to the eggs, as well as brightening up your morning.

% V GF DF

SERVES 2

2 teaspoons olive oil
4 eggs
1 avocado, sliced
8 cherry tomatoes, halved
60g (2oz) frozen peas
½ lime, cut into wedges
Handful of coriander (cilantro) or parsley, chopped
Salt and freshly ground black pepper

Preheat the oven to 220°C/200°C fan/430°F/gas 7.

Grease a small ovenproof dish or pan with the oil, then crack the eggs into the dish.

Arrange the avocado slices around the eggs, tucking them into the whites but being careful not to pop the yolks. Do the same with the cherry tomatoes. Scatter in the frozen peas and season well with salt and freshly ground black pepper.

Bake the eggs in the hot oven for 15–20 minutes or until the whites are set. (Depending on your oven, the eggs can cook much quicker so keep an eye on them from 10 minutes onwards.) If you like a solid yolk, bake the eggs for longer.

Scatter over the coriander or parsley, season with more salt and pepper and serve with lime wedges for squeezing over.

Make it your own If you fancy more of a classic Full English breakfast vibe, tuck in some cooked sausage and hash browns and serve with a squeeze of red or brown sauce. If you want this dish to feel even more special, use individual ovenproof dishes to make single portions; just put half of everything in each one.

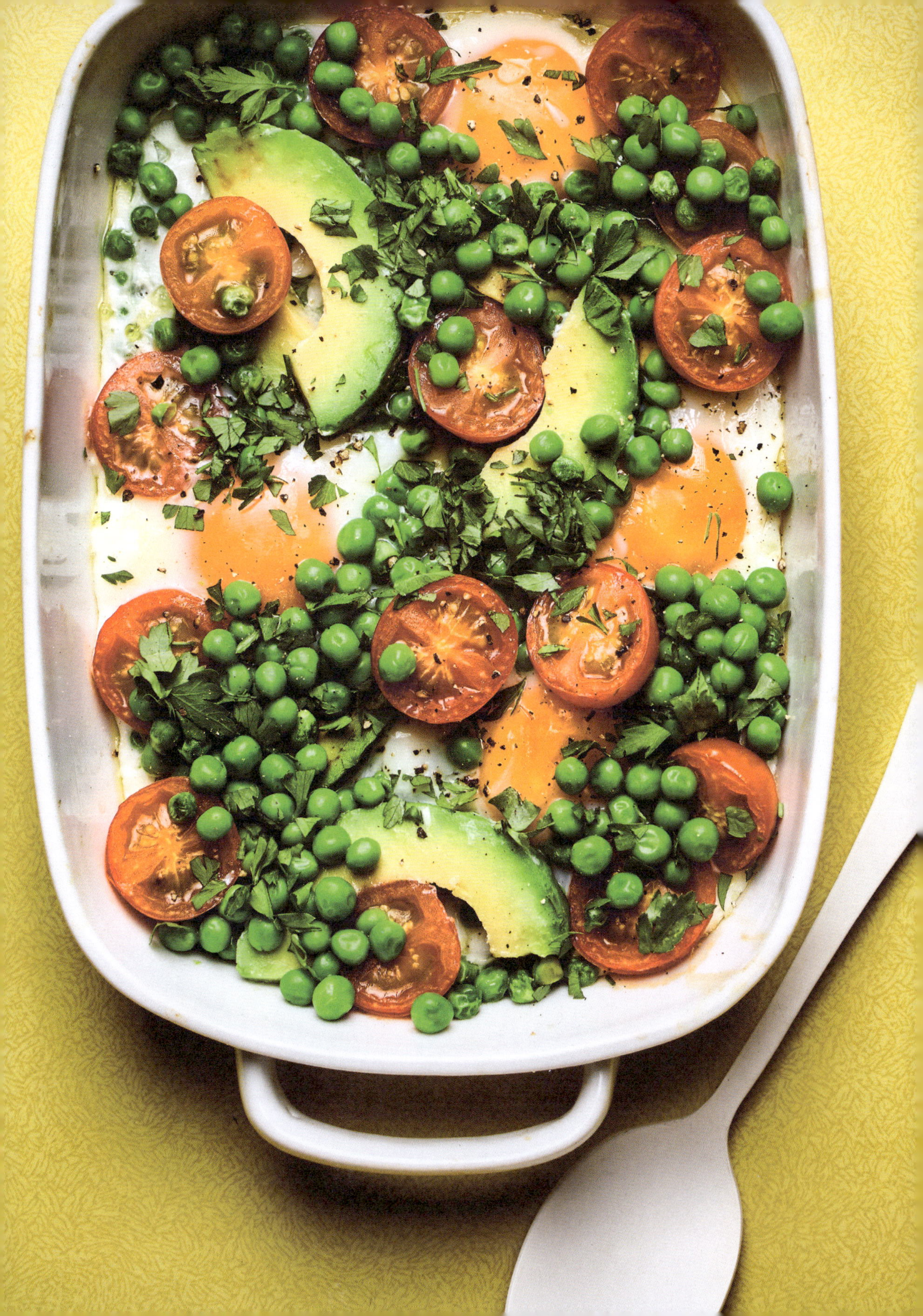

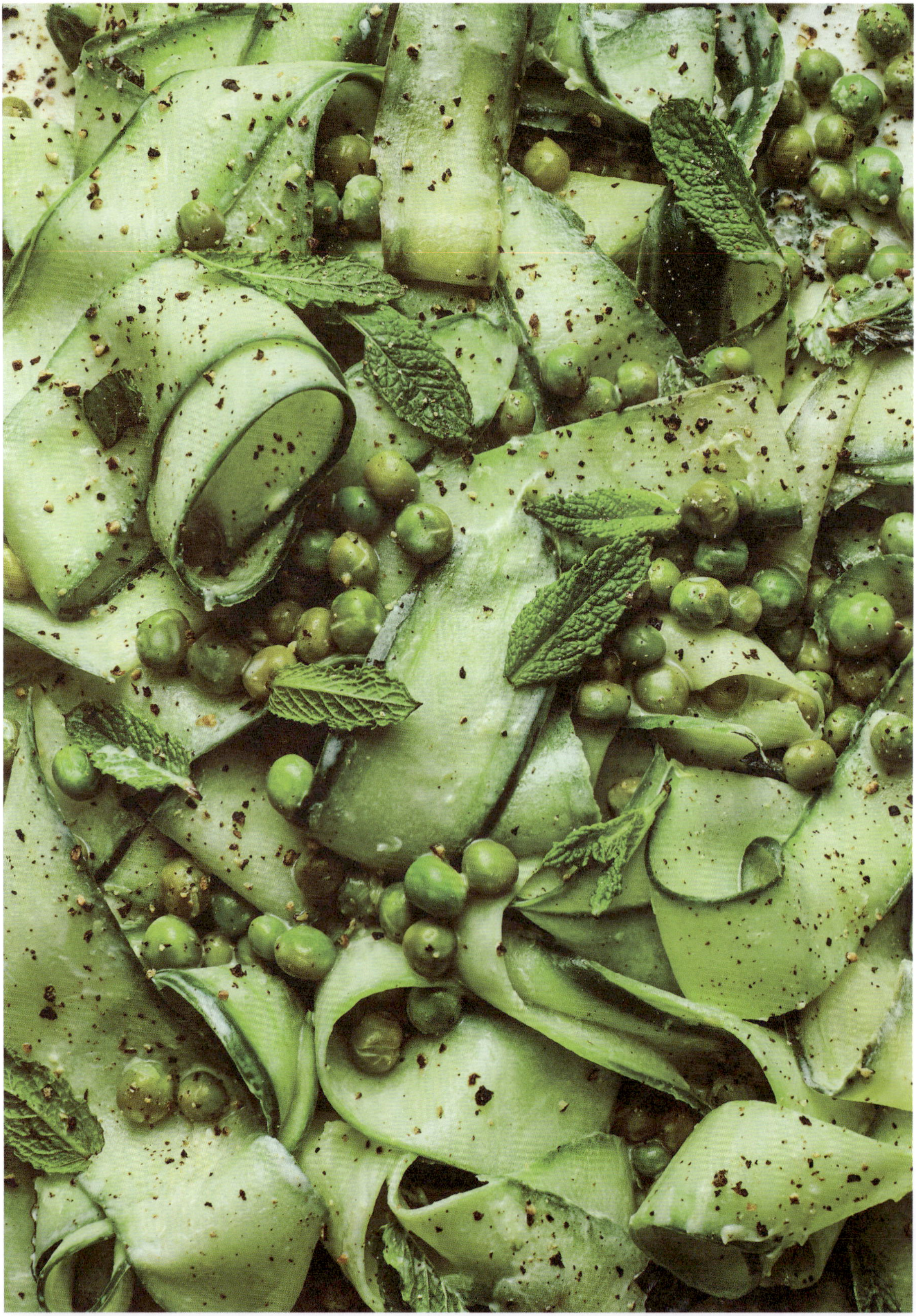

Minty Peas with Warm Cucumber Ribbons

I love how the flavour of cucumbers develops as they're warmed through. Slicing them into ribbons is easier with a Y-style vegetable peeler because they're slightly wider than a standard peeler; you can also use a mandoline.

% V GF

SERVES 4

1 tablespoon olive or rapeseed oil
150g (5½oz) frozen peas
Handful of mint leaves, sliced
2 cucumbers, sliced into thin ribbons using a peeler or mandoline
Zest and juice of ½ lemon
2 tablespoons crème fraîche (optional)

Heat the oil in a large saucepan over a medium heat. Add the frozen peas directly to the pan and cook for a few minutes until defrosted.

Stir the mint into the peas, cook for 1 minute and then add the cucumber ribbons and lemon zest.

Season with salt and pepper and then squeeze in as much lemon juice as you like. Remove the peas from the heat and stir in the crème fraîche, if using.

Petits Pois à la Française

There's something about laying the leaves of the Little Gem lettuce in this dish that I love. It feels intricate and I love to lift them up and peek at the peas before serving. They'll have lost their colour, but it won't matter.

% GF

SERVES 4

150g (5½oz) bacon lardons
8 spring onions (scallions), sliced
400g (14oz) frozen peas
75g (2½oz) butter
100ml (3½fl oz) white wine
Handful of mint leaves, sliced
1 Little Gem lettuce, leaves separated

Tip the bacon lardons into a non-stick saucepan with a lid. Heat over a medium heat until the lardons start to release the fat, then cook until golden. Stir in the spring onions and fry for 2 minutes.

Stir in the frozen peas and butter and cook until the butter has melted. Stir in the wine and mint and cook until the wine begins to simmer then remove the pan from the heat.

Lay the lettuce leaves on top of the peas. Cover the pan with the lid, reduce the heat to low and cook for around 20 minutes or until the peas have soften and the lettuce has wilted – both the peas and lettuce will lose their vibrancy, but this is normal.

Zesty Mashed Peas

A simple way to make your frozen peas a little more special is to give them a mini-twist. I often fall back on frozen peas as a simple side dish and this makes me feel like I've made a little extra effort.

% ❄ V VG GF DF

SERVES 4

400g (14oz) frozen peas
Zest of 1 lemon, juice of ½ lemon
Handful of parsley, finely chopped
Salt and freshly ground black pepper

Bring a saucepan of salted water to the boil. Tip in the frozen peas and cook for 2–3 minutes or until they are fully defrosted and cooked through. Drain, then tip into a bowl.

Mash the peas with a masher (you can also pulse them in a food processor), then stir through the lemon zest and parsley. Season to taste with salt, pepper and a squeeze of lemon juice.

Cheat's Mushy Peas

Mushy peas are not traditionally made with fresh or frozen peas, but rather with dried marrowfat peas. There's not always time to boil dried peas for a simple side so here's an option with frozen peas that will still sit nicely alongside your fish and chips.

% ❄ V GF

SERVES 4

1 tablespoon butter
400g (14oz) frozen peas
125ml (4½fl oz) double (heavy) cream
Juice of ½ lemon (optional)

Heat the butter in a frying pan (skillet). Once sizzling, add the frozen peas, season and cook for 2–3 minutes or until they are fully defrosted and cooked through. Pour in the cream and cook until steaming.

Tip the peas into a food processor or blender, or use a handheld stick (immersion) blender, and pulse until mostly smooth with some chunks of peas. Season to taste with salt, pepper and a squeeze of lemon juice, if you like.

SIDES, SAUCES AND SNACKS

Cheesy Leeks and Peas

Sometimes you just want something different to serve with a Sunday roast, then sometimes you want a big bowl of something super comforting to eat on its own while watching *Grey's Anatomy*. This is a great option for both of those occasions.

SERVES 4-6

1 tablespoon sunflower or vegetable oil
2 leeks (around 300g/10½oz), trimmed, halved lengthways and sliced
2 garlic cloves, crushed or finely grated (shredded), (optional)
300ml (10½fl oz) whole (full-fat) milk
30g (1oz) butter
30g (1oz) plain (all-purpose) flour
75g (2½oz) mature Cheddar cheese, grated (shredded)
15g (½oz) Parmesan or vegetarian hard cheese, grated (shredded)
1 teaspoon English mustard
200g (7oz) frozen peas

OPTIONAL TOPPING FOR BAKING

50g (1¾oz) mature Cheddar cheese, grated (shredded)
25g (¾oz) Parmesan or vegetarian hard cheese, grated (shredded)
50g (1¾oz) panko breadcrumbs

Heat the oil in a saucepan over a medium heat. Add the leeks and fry for 4–5 minutes or until soft. If using the garlic, add and cook for a further 1–2 minutes or until soft. Remove from the pan and set aside.

Warm the milk in the microwave for 2–3 minutes in 30 second blasts (this is optional, but it makes it much easier to make the sauce). Tip the butter into the pan and heat until melted, then stir in the flour and cook for 1–2 minutes or until combined. Add in the milk a ladleful at a time, stirring until the milk is absorbed. Continue until all the milk has been used, then season well and stir, bringing to a simmer. Simmer for 1 minute before removing the pan from the heat and stirring in the Cheddar, Parmesan and mustard. Stir until all the cheeses have melted.

Tip in the frozen peas and stir to warm them through, then mix in the leeks. Return the pan to the heat and bring everything back to a simmer.

At this point, you can serve the dish but if you'd like to bake them then you can tip the leeks into an ovenproof dish and combine the topping ingredients before scattering on top of the cheesy leeks and peas. Bake in a 200°C/180°C fan/390°F/gas 6 oven for 15–20 minutes or until golden on top. The peas will likely dull in colour but they'll still be delicious.

Variation: Blue cheese leeks and peas If you're a blue cheese lover, feel free to swap out 50g (1¾oz) of the Cheddar cheese in the sauce for 50g (1¾oz) blue cheese, such as Stilton. This also works well with 500g (1lb 2oz) mushrooms, fried and then added at the same time as the cooked leeks.

SIDES, SAUCES AND SNACKS

Zesty Pan-Fried Purple Sprouting Broccoli

Purple sprouting broccoli (aka PSB to the superusers) is a useful veg to have in the fridge when in season. It's great with a roast dinner, simply steamed and buttered or, as cooked here, with a zesty twist and coupled with frozen peas.

% V VG GF DF

SERVES 4

3 tablespoons olive oil
2 banana shallots, finely diced
2 garlic cloves, crushed or finely grated (shredded)
Zest and juice of 1 lemon
400g (14oz) purple sprouting broccoli
250g (9oz) frozen peas
Salt and freshly ground black pepper

Heat 2 tablespoons of the oil in a large frying pan (skillet) over a medium-low heat. Add the shallots and cook for 8–10 minutes or until softened but not golden. Stir in the garlic and lemon zest and cook for a further 1 minute.

Tip in the broccoli, season well with salt and freshly ground black pepper and cook for 5 minutes, mixing regularly to fry the broccoli all over.

Add the frozen peas and half the lemon juice to the pan, then cook for 2–3 minutes or until the peas are warmed through and tender. Squeeze over the remaining lemon juice to taste and drizzle in an extra tablespoon of oil, if you like.

Green Beans and Peas with Anchovies

When making side dishes, I often find I need a little inspiration but don't want to drown out the flavours of the main dish. The anchovies add a saltiness that compliments the sweetness of the peas without being so overpowering that you won't taste what you're serving alongside.

% GF DF

SERVES 4–6

2 tablespoons olive oil
1 shallot or small red onion, finely chopped
6 anchovies, chopped (the type in oil)
2 garlic cloves, crushed or finely grated (shredded)
300g (10½oz) green beans
200g (7oz) frozen peas

Heat the oil in a frying pan (skillet) or saucepan over a medium heat. Fry the shallot for 4–5 minutes or until soft and turning golden. Mix in the anchovies and garlic and cook for a further 2 minutes until the anchovies start to dissolve – do not burn the garlic, lower the temperature a little if this helps. Remove the pan from the heat and set aside.

Bring a saucepan of salted water to the boil. Cook the beans for 2 minutes. Add the frozen peas, bring everything back to a simmer and cook for 2 minutes or until the beans are cooked and peas are warmed through and tender. Drain, leave for 1–2 minutes to dry off, then toss in the pan with the anchovies. Season before serving.

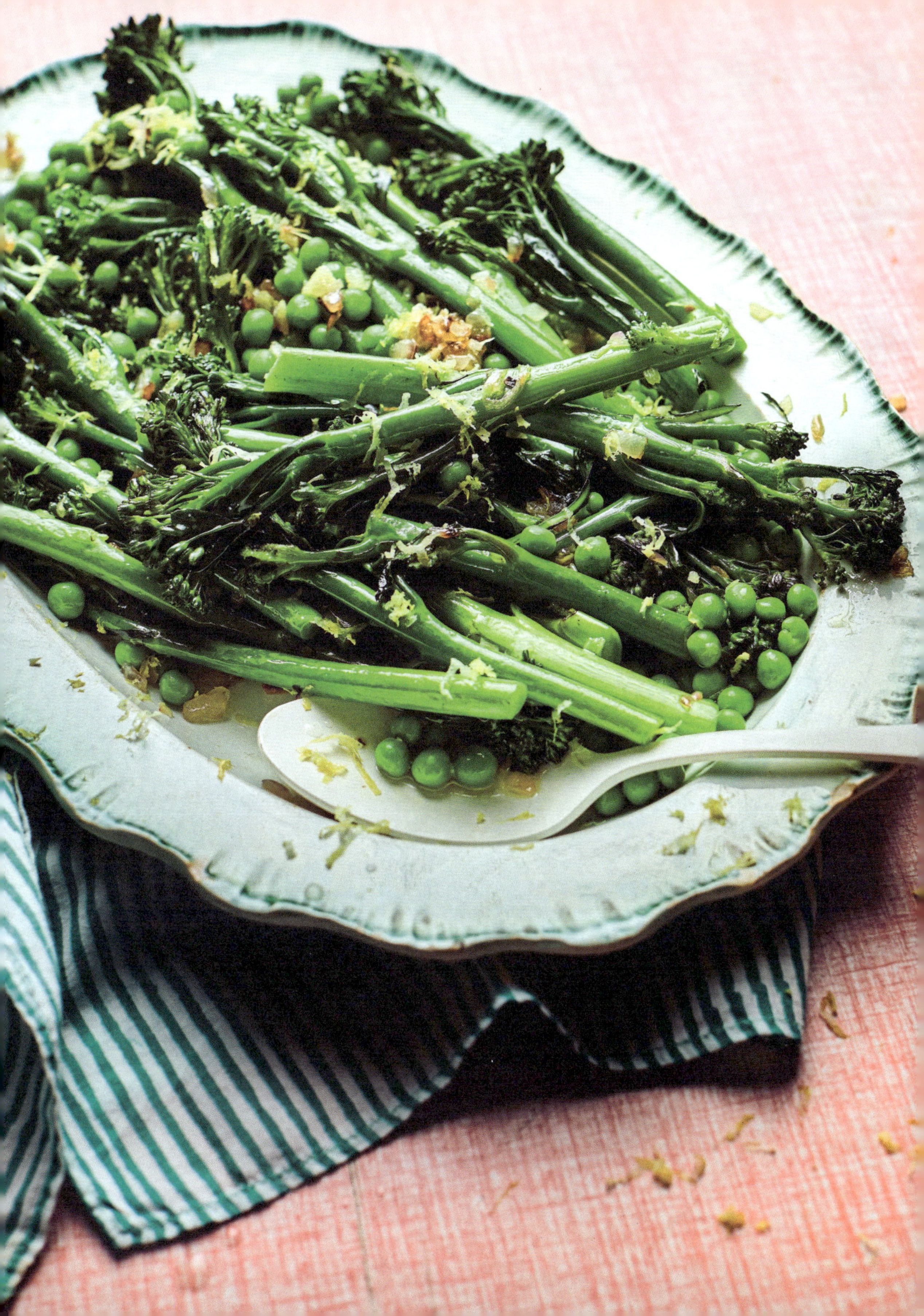

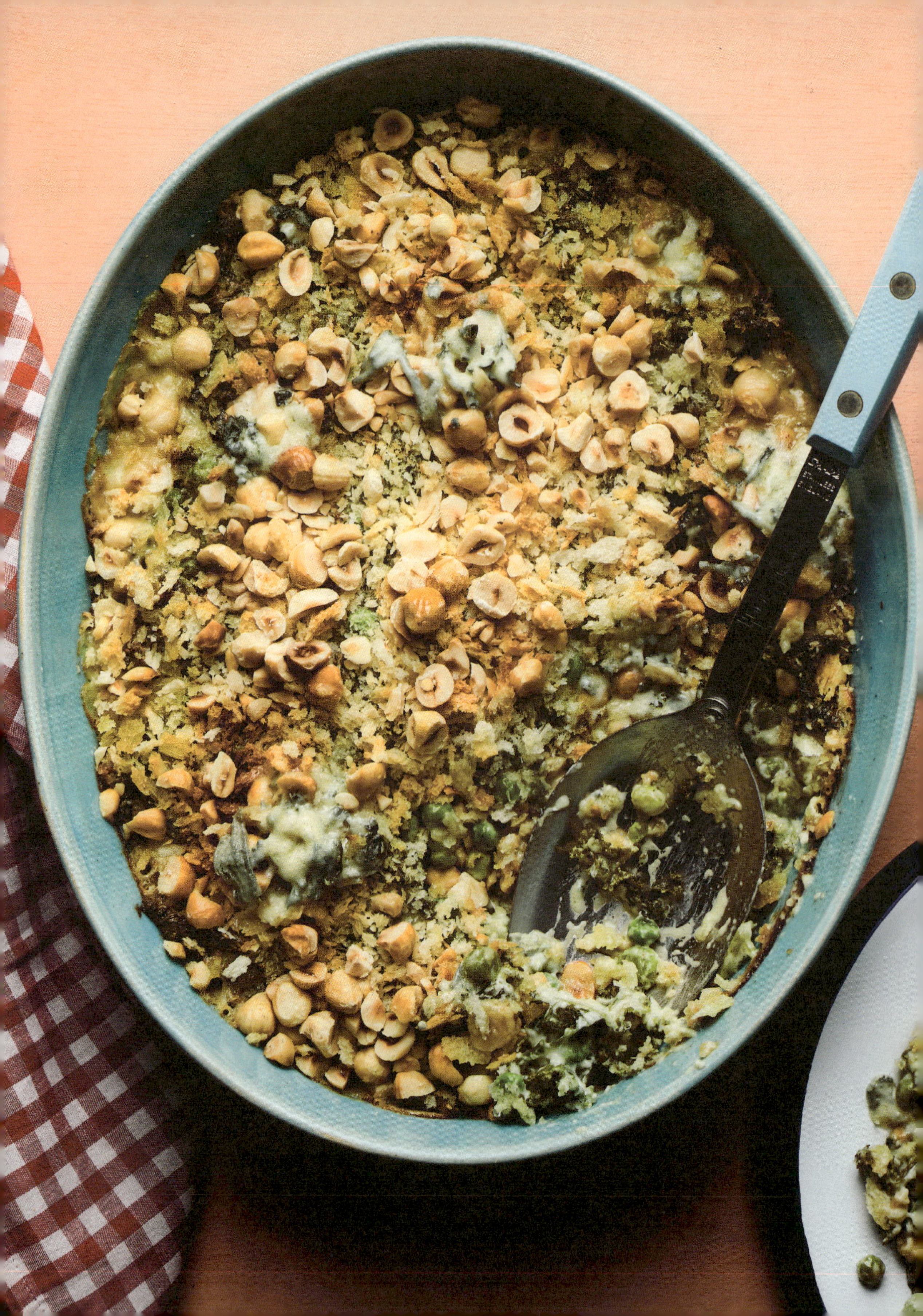

Kale, Pea and Blue Cheese Gratin

Although I originally conceived this as a side, it's also a lovely comforting main dish when served either with some sautéed potatoes to complement the cheesy sauce or a green, leafy salad.

SERVES 4 AS A MAIN OR 6 AS A SIDE

2 tablespoons olive oil
2 shallots, finely diced
200g (7oz) kale or cavolo nero, sliced
250g (9oz) frozen peas
2 tablespoons plain (all-purpose) flour
250ml (9fl oz) double (heavy) cream
150ml (5fl oz) whole (full-fat) milk
50g (1¾oz) Parmesan or vegetarian Italian hard cheese, finely grated (shredded)
150g (5½oz) blue cheese (such as Stilton), crumbled
Nutmeg, for grating
75g (2½oz) panko breadcrumbs (optional)
75g (2½oz) hazelnuts, roughly chopped

Preheat the oven to 200°C/180°C fan/390°F/gas 6.

Heat the oil in a large pan or frying pan (skillet) over a medium-low heat. Add the shallots and fry for 6–8 minutes or until softened. Stir in the kale – you may need to do this gradually – until wilted, then stir in the frozen peas and cook for 2 minutes. Scatter in the flour and season well before mixing everything together.

Pour in the cream and milk and bring to a simmer while stirring. Remove the pan from the heat and stir in the Parmesan and blue cheese until melted.

Tip the gratin mixture into an ovenproof dish and grate over a little nutmeg. Scatter over the breadcrumbs, if using.

Bake in the preheated oven for 20 minutes, then scatter over the hazelnuts. Bake for a further 5–10 minutes or until the sauce has firmed up a little and is bubbling.

Variation: Spinach, mushroom and blue cheese gratin Anyone who has watched *Ratatouille* will know that mushrooms and blue cheese is a winning combination (albeit with added lightning). If you'd fancy a twist on the above, swap out the kale for 200g (7oz) spinach and 250g (9oz) sliced chestnut mushrooms. Fry the mushrooms until golden and the spinach until wilted, then continue following the above recipe.

Potato Salad

Because I don't like a sloppy potato salad, this one is lightly dressed, but you can add more mayo, if you like. The lemon juice dulls the peas, so if you want a pop of vibrancy, defrost the peas separately and fold through before serving.

% V GF

SERVES 4 AS A SIDE

600g (1lb 5oz) new potatoes or Jersey royals, larger ones halved
150g (5½oz) frozen peas
2 tablespoons mayonnaise
1 tablespoon extra virgin olive oil
Juice of ½ lemon (about 1 tablespoon)
½ small red onion, very finely chopped
4–6 cornichons (dill pickles), finely chopped (optional)
Handful of chives, finely sliced
Paprika, to garnish (optional)
Salt and freshly ground black pepper

Put the potatoes in a saucepan of salted water and bring to the boil. Cook for 10–15 minutes or until the potatoes are tender (insert a sharp knife to test). Turn off the heat. Tip the frozen peas into the pan with the potatoes and leave them for a few minutes to defrost. Drain the potatoes and peas, then leave them to dry for a few minutes.

Combine the mayonnaise, oil and lemon juice in a large mixing bowl, then stir in the red onion and cornichons, if using, along with the chives.

Tip the potatoes and peas into the mixing bowl and fold into the dressing, then season well. Leave the potato salad to chill, if you like. Transfer the salad to a serving dish and dust with some paprika, if using.

Fennel, Orange and Pea Salad

When the sun surprises us all with a last-minute visit, it's great to have a quick salad up your sleeve. This one takes mere minutes to put together. If you don't feel confident cutting segments out of the oranges, slice them into rounds – it still looks pretty, you might just have a little less juice in the dressing.

% V GF DF

SERVES 4 AS A SIDE

2 large oranges or 2 blood oranges (when in season)
150g (5½oz) frozen peas
1 fennel bulb, very thinly sliced
50g (1¾oz) spinach or lamb's lettuce (cornsalad/mache)
1 tablespoon extra virgin olive oil
½ tablespoon white wine or cider vinegar
½ teaspoon Dijon mustard

Slice around the oranges to remove the skin. Squeeze any juice from the skins into a small bowl or jug (pitcher). Cut the oranges into segments (or thinly slice them, if you find that tricky). Set the segments or slices aside, then squeeze any juice from the core of the orange into the bowl or jug.

Defrost the frozen peas by covering them with freshly boiled water. Leave them for a few minutes, then drain. Leave to dry.

Toss the fennel, spinach or lamb's lettuce and peas together and arrange over a serving platter, then tuck in the orange segments or slices.

Combine the oil, vinegar and mustard with the orange juice in the bowl or jug, then drizzle over the salad before serving.

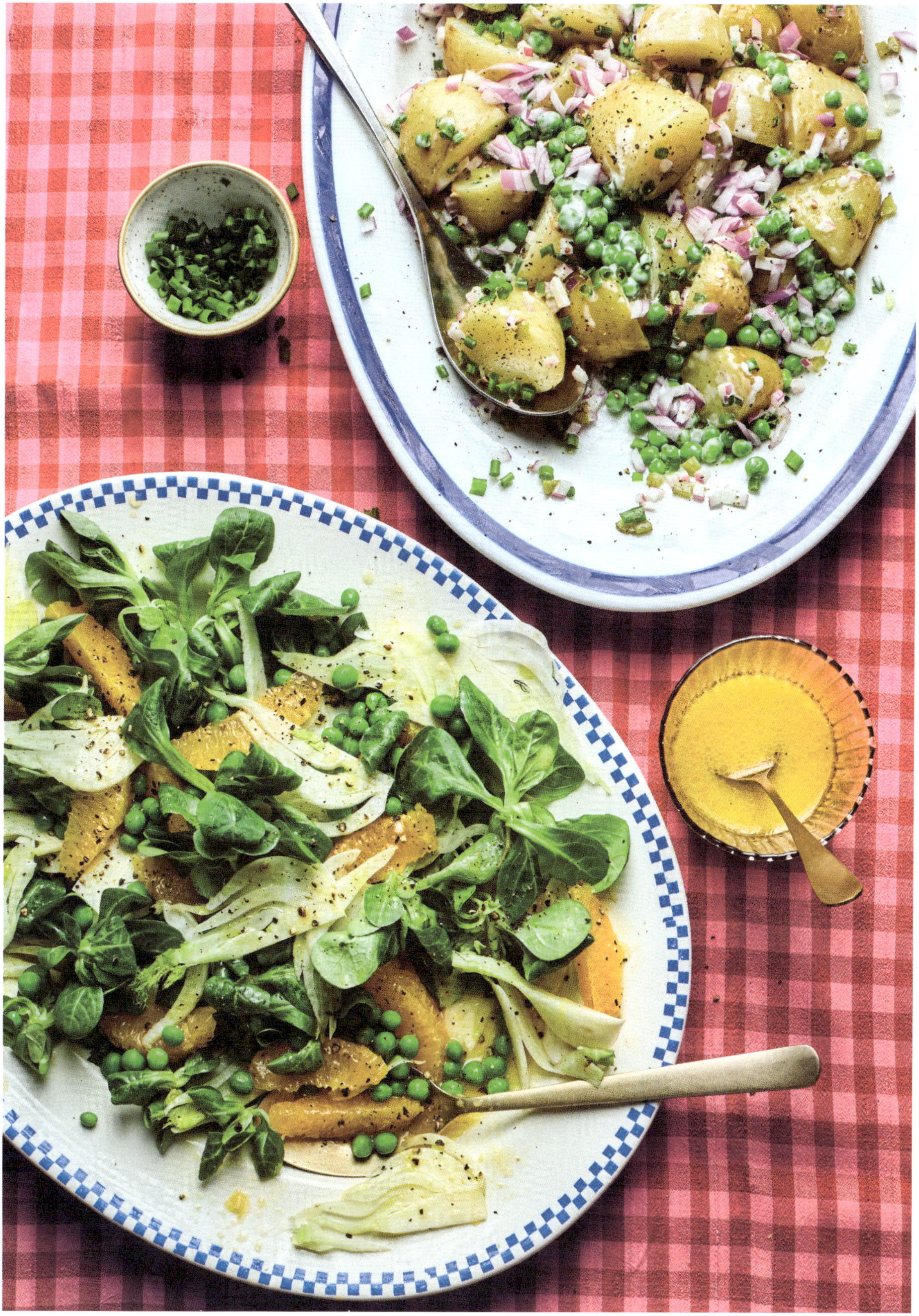

Pea Pesto

This is my basic pea pesto recipe from which you can create your own favourite. Of course, it's wonderful stirred through freshly cooked pasta as well as dolloped onto pizza or whisked into a salad dressing.

SERVES 6–8

300g (10½oz) frozen peas
Zest and juice of ½ lemon (around 1 tablespoon juice)
Handful of parsley (around 15g/½oz)
75g (2½oz) pine nuts
50g (1¾oz) Parmesan or vegetarian Italian hard cheese, grated (shredded)
3 garlic cloves
6–8 tablespoons olive oil
Salt and freshly ground black pepper

Place the frozen peas in a heatproof bowl and cover with freshly boiled water to defrost. Leave for a few minutes, then drain well. (Alternatively, microwave the peas for 2 minutes.)

Put the peas and all the remaining ingredients (except the oil) into a food processor, season with salt and pepper, and pulse until everything is finely chopped.

Drizzle in the oil while blending to make a thick paste.

Spoon into a sterilised jar or reusable container and chill until needed. The pesto should keep for 3–5 days when stored in the fridge. The oil will rise a little, so give the pesto a good mix before using.

Rocket and Pea Pesto

The pepperiness of rocket (arugula) and the sweetness of peas perform a lovely dance in this spin on the classic version.

SERVES 6–8

100g (3½oz) frozen peas
50g (1¾oz) rocket (arugula), roughly chopped
75g (2½oz) pine nuts
50g (1¾oz) Parmesan or vegetarian Italian hard cheese, grated (shredded)
2 garlic cloves
6–8 tablespoons olive oil
Salt and freshly ground black pepper

Place the frozen peas in a heatproof bowl and cover with freshly boiled water to defrost. Leave for a few minutes, then drain well. (Alternatively, microwave the peas for 2 minutes.)

Put the peas and all the remaining ingredients (except the oil) into a food processor, season with salt and pepper, and pulse until everything is finely chopped.

Drizzle in the oil while blending to make a thick paste.

Spoon into a sterilised jar or reusable container and chill until needed. The pesto should keep for 3–5 days when stored in the fridge. The oil will rise a little, so give the pesto a good mix before using.

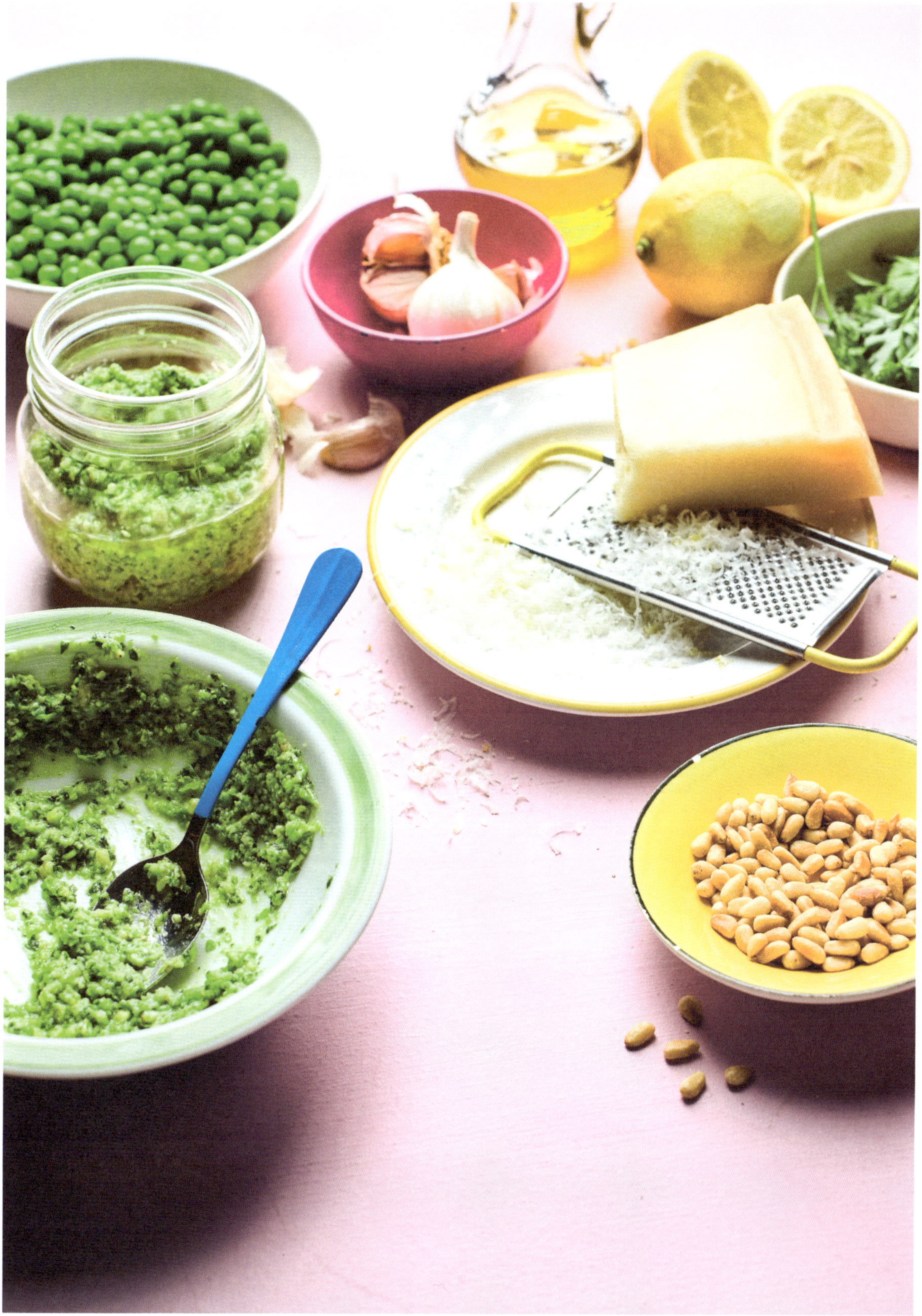

SIDES, SAUCES AND SNACKS

Walnut and Pea Pesto

Using walnuts makes pesto feel grown up. It also reminds me of holidaying with friends in northern Italy where walnut sauce is a delicacy. The peas ensure a vibrant green pesto so the brown of the walnuts doesn't dull things.

SERVES 8 (AROUND 375G/13OZ)

- 150g (5½oz) frozen peas
- 50g (1¾oz) walnuts
- Handful of mint leaves (10g/⅓oz)
- 50g (1¾oz) Parmesan or vegetarian Italian hard cheese, grated (shredded)
- 2 small garlic cloves
- Zest and juice of ½ lemon (around 1 tablespoon juice)
- 6–8 tablespoons olive oil
- Salt and freshly ground black pepper

Place the frozen peas in a heatproof bowl and cover with freshly boiled water to defrost. Leave for a few minutes, then drain well. (Alternatively, microwave the peas for 2 minutes.)

Put the peas and all the remaining ingredients (except the oil) into a food processor, season with salt and pepper, and pulse until everything is finely chopped.

Drizzle in the oil while blending to make a thick paste.

Spoon into a sterilised jar or reusable container and chill until needed. The pesto should keep for 3–5 days when stored in the fridge. The oil will rise a little, so give the pesto a good mix before using.

Pea-sta Sauce

This sauce is great for batching and freezing, ready for when you've run out of other ingredients. It's a good base for sneaking in extra veg. If you want to bulk it out, bacon or ham are classic companions; you can add spinach and broccoli without having to blend it in, or do blitz it in if you want to – the choice is yours.

SERVES 4 (MAKES AROUND 1 LITRE)

- 2 tablespoons olive oil
- 1 onion, finely chopped
- 8 spring onions (scallions), roughly chopped
- 2 garlic cloves, crushed or finely grated (shredded)
- 750g (1lb 10oz) frozen peas
- 250ml (9fl oz) vegetable stock
- Salt and freshly ground black pepper

Heat the oil in a frying pan (skillet) with a lid over a gentle heat. Add the onions and fry, covered, for 10–12 minutes or until soft but not golden.

Stir in the spring onions, turn up the heat to medium and fry for a couple of minutes before adding the garlic and cooking for a minute longer.

Tip in the frozen peas, season with salt and pepper, and cook for a few minutes, then pour in the stock and simmer for 2–3 minutes or until the peas are cooked through.

Tip everything into a blender, or use a handheld stick (immersion) blender, and blitz until smooth.

Four Dips

Peas are the perfect dip maker – they're a bit chunky when blended, have a lovely colour and go well with a variety of flavours. Serve up any single one (or all four) of these dips for a gathering of family or friends. If you're making a dip in advance, be sure to give it a good stir before serving.

Pea and Mint Dip

% ❄ V VG GF DF

SERVES 4 (MAKES ABOUT 500G/1LB 2OZ)

250g (9oz) frozen peas
1 tablespoon extra virgin olive oil (or the best quality you have)
3–4 mint sprigs, leaves picked and chopped (around 20 leaves)
2 tablespoons tahini
125ml (4½fl oz) thick Greek yogurt or plant-based yogurt alternative
Zest and juice of ½–1 lemon
Crackers, crudités or bread, to serve

Place the frozen peas in a heatproof bowl and cover with freshly boiled water to defrost. Leave for a few minutes, then drain well. Repeat if not fully defrosted. Once drained, leave the peas to dry for 5 minutes.

Tip the peas into a food processor or blender along with all the remaining ingredients, using the juice of half a lemon to begin with. Pulse to make a chunky dip – the peas should be roughly chopped. If you prefer, blitz until smooth (or as smooth as you can get it). Drizzle in the remaining lemon juice to taste.

Pea and Miso Dip

% ❄ V VG GF DF

SERVES 4 (MAKES ABOUT 400G/14OZ)

250g (9oz) frozen peas
3 tablespoons extra virgin olive oil
1 red chilli, chopped (optional)
2 level tablespoons white miso
4 spring onions (scallions), trimmed and roughly chopped
Zest and juice of 1 lime
½ teaspoon wasabi paste (optional)
Salt and freshly ground black pepper
Crackers, crudités or bread, to serve

Place the frozen peas in a heatproof bowl and cover with freshly boiled water to defrost. Leave for a few minutes, then drain well. Repeat if not fully defrosted. Once drained, leave the peas to dry for 5 minutes.

Tip the peas into a food processor or blender along with all the remaining ingredients. Pulse to make a chunky dip (you may need to add a little water to get a good dip consistency). Season with salt and pepper to taste.

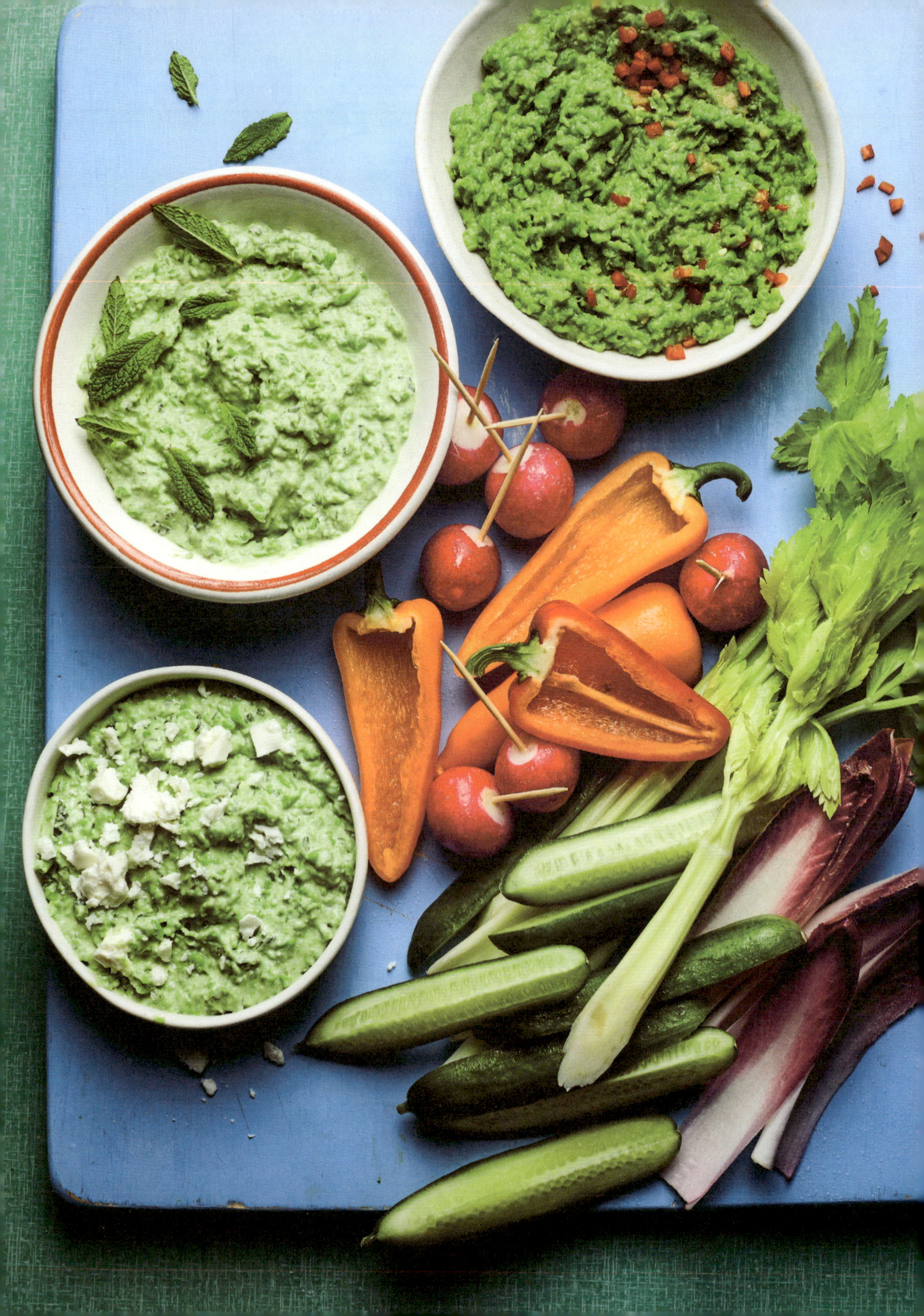

SIDES, SAUCES AND SNACKS

Pea and Feta Dip

% ❄ V GF

SERVES 4

250g (9oz) frozen peas
150g (5½oz) feta
50g (1¾oz) natural or Greek yogurt
2 tablespoons extra virgin olive oil
Zest and juice of ½ lemon
Handful of mint leaves (around 15g/½oz)

Place the frozen peas in a heatproof bowl and cover with freshly boiled water to defrost. Leave for a few minutes, then drain well. Repeat if not fully defrosted. Once drained, leave the peas to dry for 5 minutes.

Put the feta in a blender with the yogurt and blitz until smooth. Whip the mixture a little, then add the peas and all the remaining ingredients. Pulse to make a chunky dip (you may need to add a little water to get a good dip consistency).

> **Cook's tip** Due to the lemon juice, this dip will dull in colour if made too far in advance. It's best to make it just before serving.

Zesty Pea and Herb Dip

% ❄ V VG GF DF

SERVES 4

350g (12½oz) frozen peas
3 tablespoons cold pressed rapeseed oil or extra virgin olive oil
Small handful of mint leaves (about 5g/⅙oz), roughly chopped
Small handful of dill (about 5g/⅙oz), roughly chopped
Large handful of chives (about 10g/⅓oz), roughly chopped
2 tablespoons za'atar
Juice of ½–1 lime
Salt and freshly ground black pepper

Place the frozen peas in a large heatproof bowl or jug (pitcher) and cover with freshly boiled water to defrost. Leave for a few minutes to warm through a little, then drain. Repeat if not fully defrosted. Once drained, leave the peas to dry for 5 minutes.

Put all the ingredients (except the lime juice) into a food processor and blend until you have a thick dip. (It may not be completely smooth.)

Season the dip with salt and freshly ground black pepper to taste. Squeeze in the lime juice, again to taste. Mix or blitz again before serving.

Avocado and Pea Guacamole

This classic dip, often used for nachos and chilli, gets more vibrant with the addition of peas. They add a sweeter flavour that cuts through the avocado. You can make this guac without the avocado – you'll just need to up the peas. If you're making the dip ahead of time, give it a good mix before serving.

% V VG GF DF

SERVES 4–6 AS A DIP (MAKES 500G/1LB 2OZ)

250g (9oz) frozen peas or petits pois
1 avocado, peeled and stoned
2 garlic cloves, crushed or finely grated (shredded)
1 small red onion or shallot, finely diced
1 ripe tomato, finely diced (optional)
Zest and juice of 1 lime
10g (⅓oz) coriander (cilantro), chopped
Salt and freshly ground black pepper

Place the frozen peas in a heatproof bowl and cover with freshly boiled water to defrost. Leave for a few minutes, then drain well. Repeat if not fully defrosted. Once drained, leave the peas to dry for 5 minutes.

Tip the peas into a food processor or blender and blitz until almost smooth. (There will still be a few chunky pea skins remaining.) Add the avocado and garlic to the food processor and pulse until combined and a little chunky.

Transfer the avocado and pea purée to a bowl, then mix through the onion, tomato, if using, lime zest and juice, coriander and a good pinch each of salt and freshly ground black pepper. If you're not a huge lime fan, add the juice to taste.

Pea 'Hummus'

Strictly speaking, hummus means chickpea in Arabic. As this dip has no chickpeas in it, it's not really a hummus at all, however, as it's so similar that's how I describe it when I'm offering it to guests at home. The peas make for a sweeter dip, but you get a nuttiness from the tahini – together they go great with all the usual hummus accompaniments.

% ❄ V VG GF DF

SERVES 4

250g (9oz) frozen peas
1 garlic clove, roughly chopped
3 tablespoons tahini
Juice of ½–1 lemon
4 tablespoons extra virgin olive oil (or the best quality you have)
Crudités, bread stick or crackers, to serve

Place the frozen peas in a heatproof bowl and cover with freshly boiled water to defrost. Leave for a few minutes, then drain well. Repeat if not fully defrosted. Once drained, leave the peas to dry for 5 minutes.

Tip the peas into a food processor or blender with all the remaining ingredients and blitz to a chunky dip.

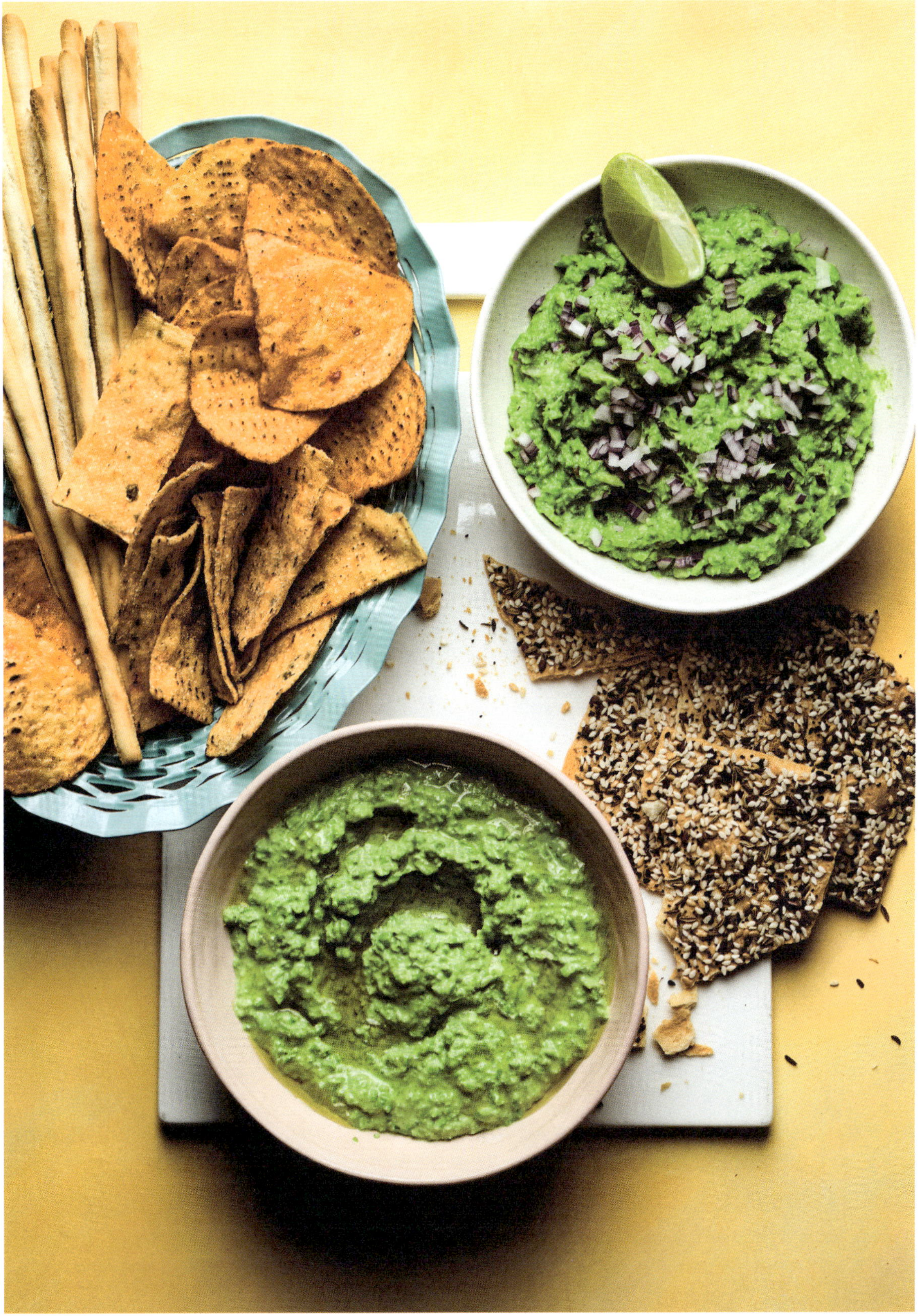

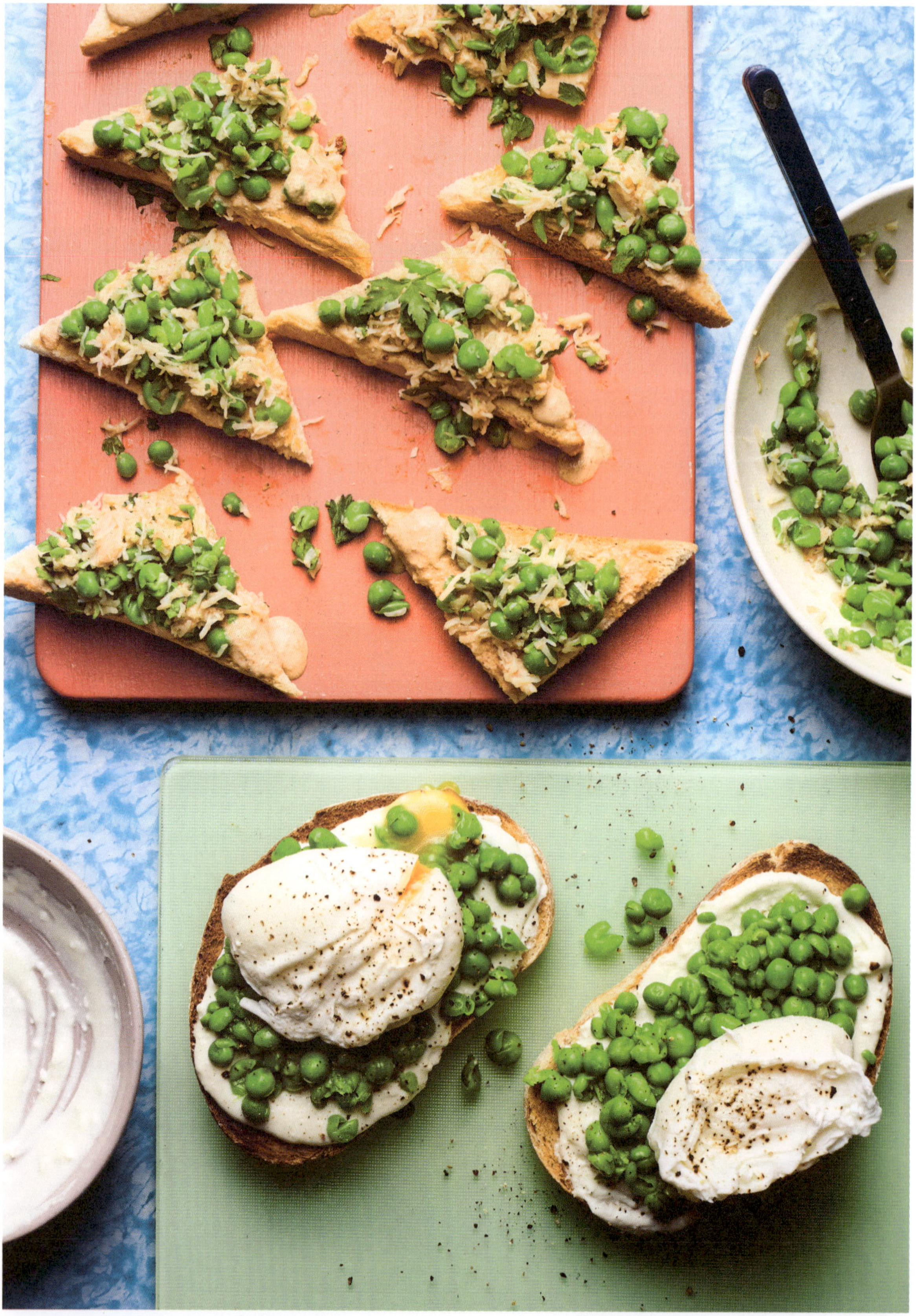

SIDES, SAUCES AND SNACKS

Peas on Toast

Some people put the resurgence in popularity of frozen peas down to the 'on toast' craze (although I like to think it's mainly down to Nigella). There are a few different ways I like to use peas on toasted bread: firstly, as a simple brunch-style dish with feta; secondly, with crab, where the delicate flavour of the meat matches the peas so well (this one is more for dinner parties or an alfresco lunch); finally, with burrata and prosciutto, which I like to say is pintxos-style for no other reason than it brings back memories of visiting San Sebastian.

Smashed Peas, Whipped Feta and Poached Eggs on Toast

% V

SERVES 2

100g (3½oz) feta
2–3 tablespoons Greek or natural yogurt
Handful of mint leaves, sliced
175g (6oz) frozen peas
Zest of 1 small lemon, plus a squeeze of lemon juice
2 eggs, one for each slice of bread (optional)
2 large or 4 small slices of sourdough or white bread
½ tablespoon extra virgin olive oil
Salt and freshly ground black pepper

Place the feta and 2 tablespoons of the yogurt in a food processor and blitz to create a smooth whip, adding an extra tablespoon of yogurt, if necessary. Scrape into a bowl, season to taste with salt and pepper and mix through half of the mint. Set aside.

Place the frozen peas in a heatproof bowl, cover with freshly boiled water and leave for a few minutes to defrost. Drain and shake well in a sieve (strainer) or colander to dry. Roughly mash or chop the peas until broken down a little but not smooth. Stir in the remaining mint, lemon zest and a squeeze of lemon juice to taste. Season then set aside.

If topping with eggs, poach the eggs to your preference in a pan of simmering salted water; usually 2–3 minutes for a runny yolk and a firm white and up to 5–6 minutes for a firm yolk. Using a slotted spoon, lift the poached eggs from the pan and set on a plate – you can lay the eggs on kitchen paper or a clean dish towel to remove any moisture.

When ready to serve, toast the bread until lightly golden. Spread the whipped feta over each slice of toast, then spoon on the smashed peas, drizzle over a little olive oil and top with the poached eggs.

Crab and Pea Toasts

MAKES 16

200g (7oz) frozen peas
100g (3½oz) mixed white and brown crab meat or 50g (1¾oz) of each
2 tablespoons crème fraîche
Zest and juice of 1 lime
Handful of parsley, finely chopped, plus extra to garnish, if you like
4 slices of white bread

Place the frozen peas in a heatproof bowl and cover with freshly boiled water to defrost. Leave for a few minutes, then drain. Shake well to dry. Roughly smash or chop and set aside.

If you're using mixed crab meat, separate the white meat from the brown meat as far as possible (it doesn't matter if there's a little brown meat mixed in with the white).

Combine the brown crab meat with the crème fraîche and set aside.

Fold the white crab meat into the smashed peas along with the lime zest and parsley. Season with salt, pepper and lime juice to taste, then set aside.

When ready to serve, toast the bread until lightly golden. Divide the brown crab meat mixture between the slices of toast, then spread out to the edges. Top with the white crab meat and pea mixture.

Cut each slice of toast into 4 small triangles, then top with a scattering of parsley, if you like.

Prosciutto, Burrata and Pea Pintxos

MAKES 14–16

150g (5½oz) frozen peas
2 tablespoons extra virgin olive oil
1 long baguette
8 slices of prosciutto
Around 250g (9oz) burrata (drained weight)
Freshly ground black pepper

Cook's tip Choose a burrata with a firm centre and store it in the fridge until just before serving – it'll warm up as you tear it. Alternatively, use mini balls of mozzarella – put one on each slice, but this requires a toothpick.

Place the frozen peas in a heatproof bowl and cover with freshly boiled water to defrost. Leave for a few minutes, then drain. Tip the peas into a food processor with ½ tablespoon of the olive oil and a good pinch of salt and freshly ground black pepper, blitz until almost smooth then set aside.

Cut the baguette into 14–16 thin slices, depending on the length of the baguette. For pintxos, the bread isn't actually toasted but you're more than welcome to toast it, if you like.

Drizzle the bread with a little olive oil then spread over the pea purée. Tear or cut each piece of prosciutto in half and lay on top of the peas. Tear the burrata into chunks and place on top of the prosciutto.

If you're worried about the ingredients sliding off, spear them with a small wooden skewer or toothpick (but be sure to warn your guests so they don't bite into it). Crack a little black pepper over the top before serving.

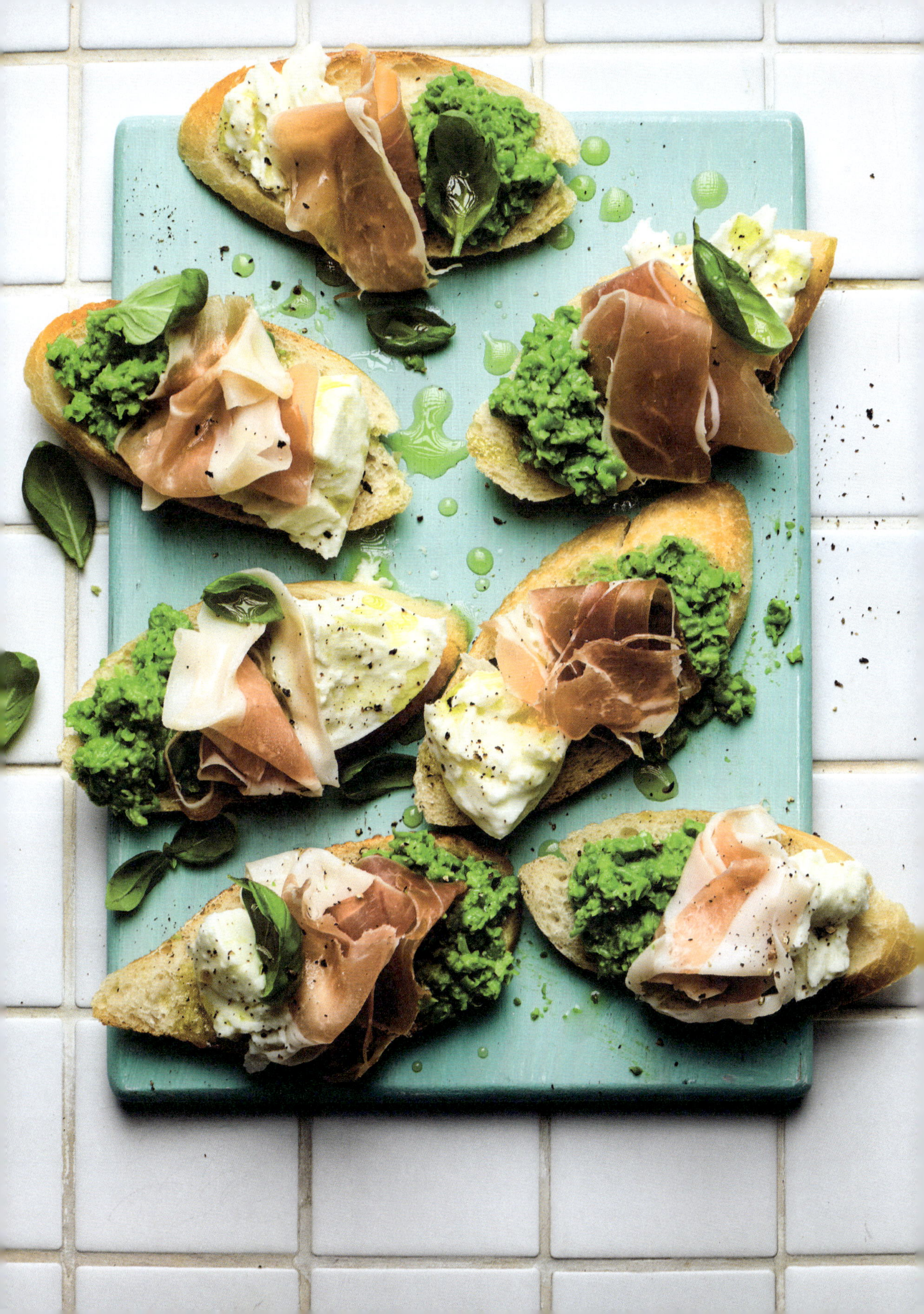

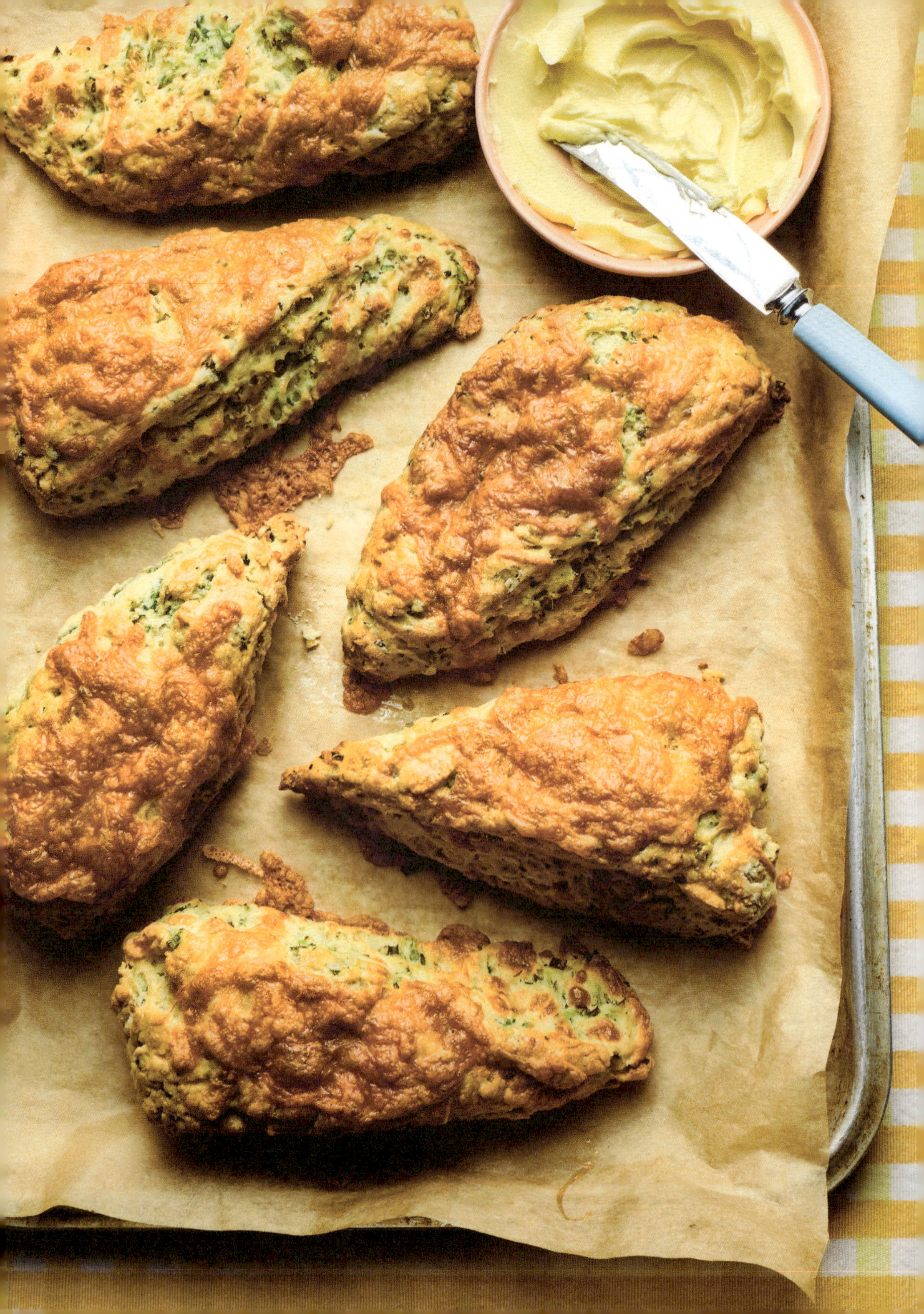

SIDES, SAUCES AND SNACKS

Cheese and Pea Scones

I made these scones just before I took a 16-hour train journey from London to Copenhagen – they made terrific train snacks and were still tasting great five days into our holiday. I love how vibrant the peas make the scones and their flavour really pops with the cheese and chives.

MAKES 6–8

115g (4oz) frozen peas
150ml (5fl oz) cultured buttermilk
2 tablespoons chopped chives
300g (10½oz) self-raising flour, plus extra for the surface
50g (1¾oz) butter, cut into cubes
½ teaspoon baking powder
100g (3½oz) mature Cheddar cheese, grated (shredded)
1 egg, beaten or milk, to glaze

Place the frozen peas in a heatproof bowl and cover with freshly boiled water to defrost. Leave for a few minutes, then drain.

Tip the peas into a food processor, add 2 tablespoons of the buttermilk and a pinch each of salt and pepper, then blend to create a smooth-ish paste.

Transfer the pea paste to a bowl or jug (pitcher) and combine with the remaining buttermilk and chopped chives.

Preheat the oven to 200°C/180°C fan/390°F/gas 6.

Sift the flour into a large mixing bowl and rub in the butter until you have a fine breadcrumb-like texture. Stir in the baking powder and then 75g (2½oz) of the Cheddar.

Mix the pea and buttermilk mixture into the flour to form a soft dough. I find it easier to use my hands to mix everything so I can tell exactly how the dough feels. If it feels too dry, add an extra splash of buttermilk, milk or water until soft.

Tip the dough onto a lightly floured work surface and flatten to 4–5cm (1½ inches) thick. Use a 6–8cm (2½–3 inches) circular cutter to punch out rounds or a sharp knife to cut into triangles. If you need to, reform the scraps of dough to make more scones. Arrange the scones on a baking tray, brush with beaten egg or milk and scatter the remaining cheese on top.

Bake the scones in the hot oven for 20–25 minutes until golden and risen. (If you know you have a hot oven, keep an eye after 15 minutes.) Once cooked, the scones should sound hollow when tapped on their bottoms.

Cook's tip Scones always taste best when served fresh, however, they can be frozen. If you do freeze them, be sure to warm them in an oven or microwave before serving. This helps to soften them.

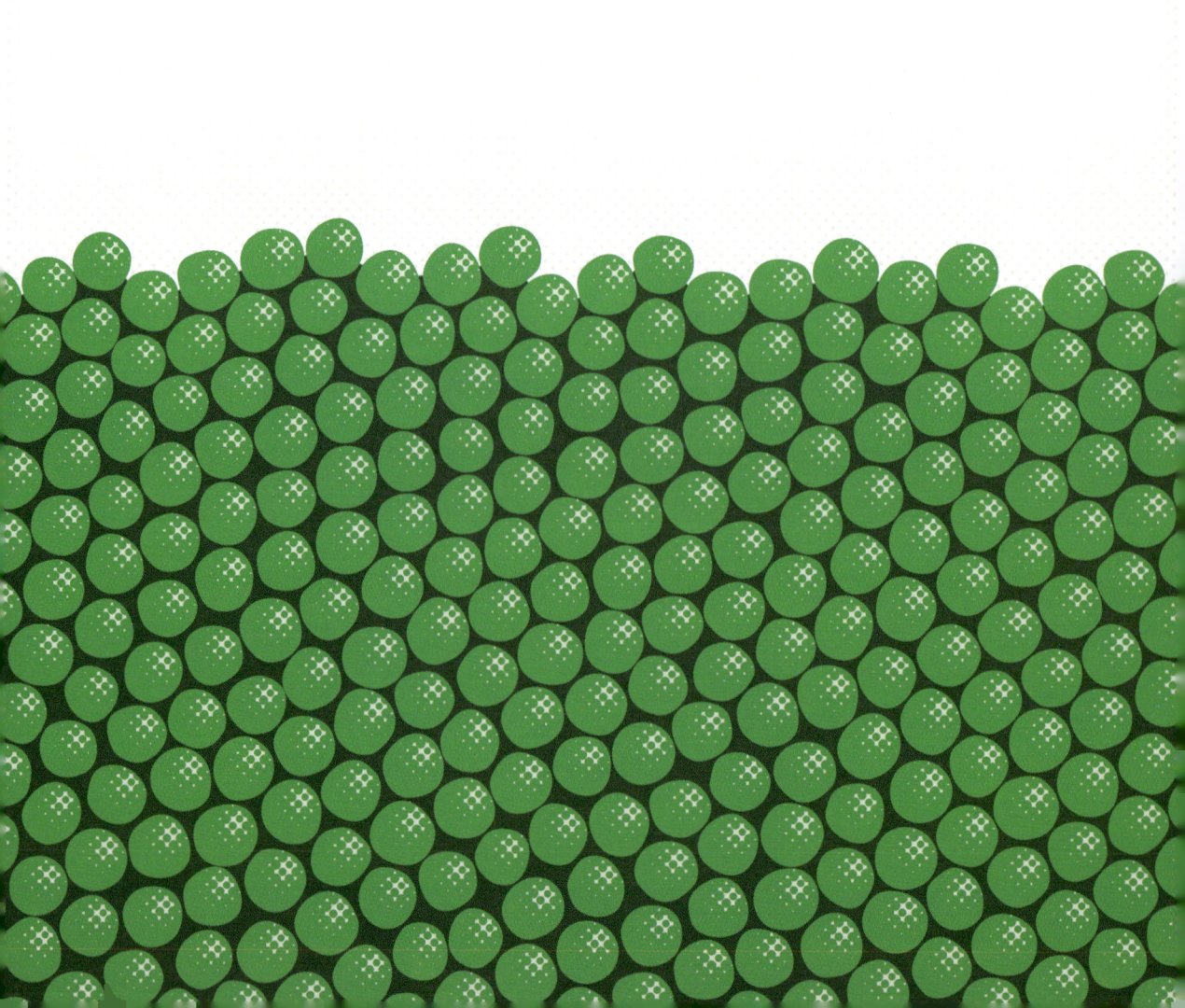

Sweet Peas

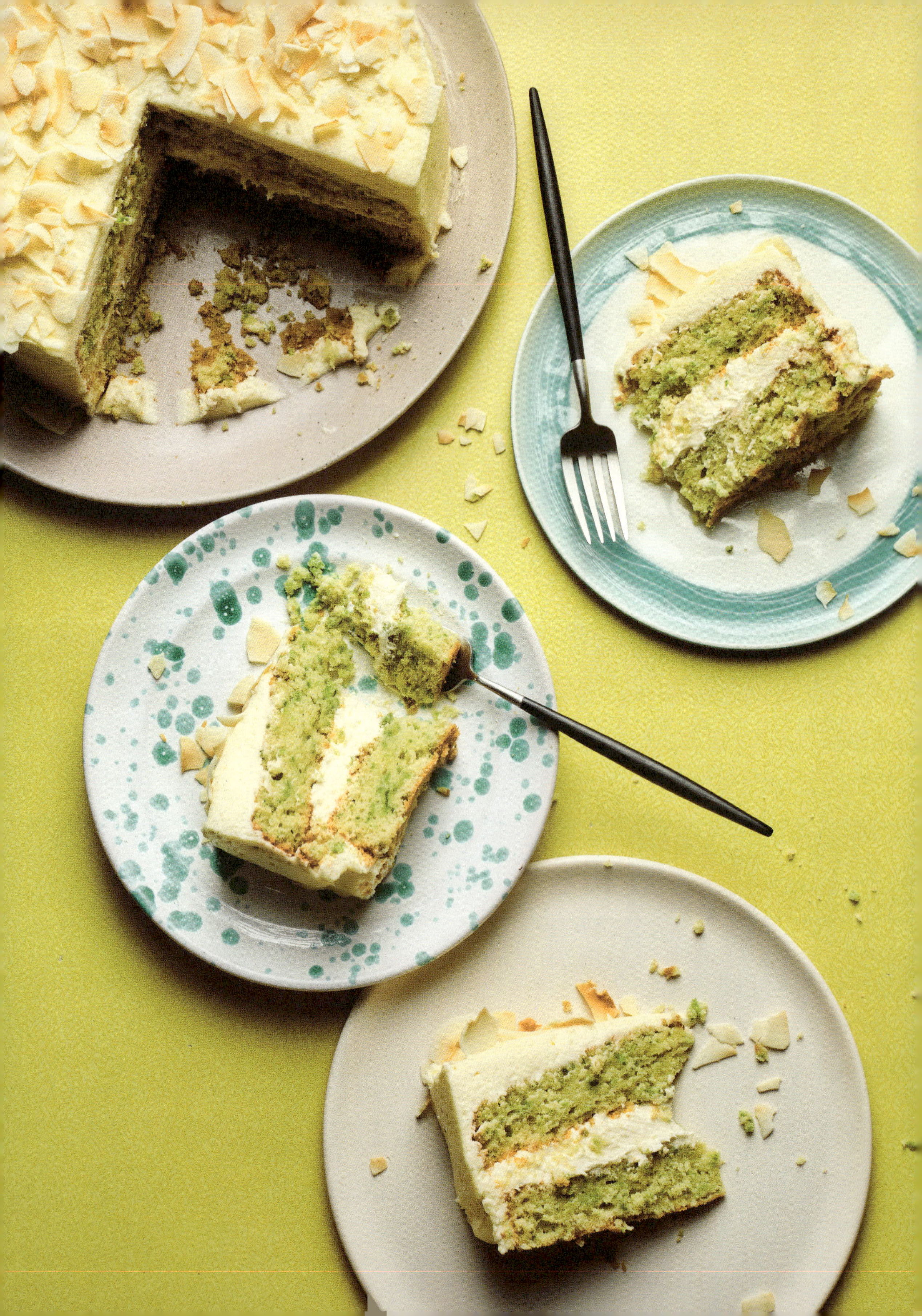

Pea Cake with Coconut Frosting

When you cut into this cake, you'll immediately notice the striking contrast between the green sponge and white frosting. The peas don't overwhelm the flavour, instead they add a little sweetness to the sponge and a vibrancy of colour. When it comes to sweet things, coconut is one of my all-time favourite flavours; even though you don't use much of the extract, it's worth investing in otherwise the flavour won't be quite so intense. A small bottle goes a long way.

(SUITABLE FOR FREEZING WITHOUT FROSTING)

SERVES 10–12

225g (8oz) butter, softened, plus extra for greasing the tin
175g (6oz) frozen peas
200g (7oz) caster (superfine) sugar
4 eggs
250g (9oz) self-raising flour
2 teaspoons vanilla extract
Zest of 1 lemon
Toasted coconut flakes or fresh grated (shredded) coconut, to garnish (optional)

FOR THE COCONUT FROSTING

300g (10½oz) butter, softened
600g (1lb 5oz) icing (confectioner's) sugar
120ml (4fl oz) coconut cream
¾ teaspoon coconut extract or natural flavouring

Preheat the oven to 180°C/160°C fan/350°F/gas 4. Grease two 20-cm (8-inch) cake tins (pans) with butter and then line with parchment paper.

Place the frozen peas in a heatproof bowl and cover with freshly boiled water to defrost. Leave for a few minutes, then drain. Tip the peas into a food processor and pulse until as finally chopped as possible but not puréed. Set aside.

Cream the butter and sugar together until light, fluffy and doubled in volume. Beat in the eggs one at a time, adding a spoonful of flour after each egg to stop the mixture from splitting. Gradually fold in the remaining flour then mix in the vanilla extract and lemon zest. Fold in the chopped peas.

Divide the cake batter between the two tins and bake in the hot oven for 20–25 minutes until the sponges are golden, risen and a skewer inserted into the centre comes out clean. Remove from the oven and leave the sponges to cool in the tins for 15 minutes before removing them from the tin and leaving to cool on a wire rack until completely cool.

While the sponges cool, make the frosting. Cream the butter and sugar together until light and fluffy, then fold in the coconut cream and coconut extract until combined. Chill until needed.

To assemble, put one of the sponges onto a serving plate or cake stand then spread one-third of the frosting on top. Place the second sponge on top then use the remaining frosting to coat the top and sides of the cake. Decorate with toasted or fresh coconut, if you like.

Pea Muffins with Cream Cheese Frosting

Carrots, courgettes (zucchini) and beetroot (beets) are all well-tested in sweet bakes, but I've not seen much around when it comes to using peas. I'm surprised because their flavour works well and the bright green colour doesn't dull during baking, which is especially true in these muffins.

(SUITABLE FOR FREEZING WITHOUT FROSTING)

MAKES 12

175g (6oz) frozen peas
150ml (5fl oz) sunflower or vegetable oil
1 teaspoon vanilla extract
2 eggs
2 tablespoons milk
250g (9oz) self-raising flour
175g (6oz) caster (superfine) sugar

FOR THE FROSTING

75g (2½oz) butter, softened
125g (4½oz) icing (confectioner's) sugar
200g (7oz) full-fat cream cheese

Cook's tip If you want to decorate these muffins further, add some chopped nuts, hundreds and thousands or find some bright green sweets to adorn them with. Even better if they look like peas!

Preheat the oven to 180°C/160°C fan/350°F/gas 4.

Place the frozen peas in a heatproof bowl and cover with freshly boiled water to defrost. Leave for a few minutes, then drain. Tip the peas into a food processor and blitz until finely chopped. Pour the oil into the food processor with the peas and blitz further until well combined.

Tip the pea purée into a bowl and beat in the vanilla extract, eggs and milk. Set aside.

Sift the flour into a bowl and mix in the sugar. Make a well in the centre and stir in the pea purée until everything is just combined – it doesn't matter if there are a few specks of flour.

Put 12 paper cases into a muffin tin and divide the muffin mixture between the cases.

Bake the muffins in the hot oven for 20–25 minutes or until the muffins have risen and a skewer inserted into the centre comes out clean. Remove to a wire rack and leave to cool.

While the muffins cool, make the frosting. Put the butter into a large bowl and sift in the icing (confectioner's) sugar, then cream together until smooth and light, around 5–6 minutes with an electric beater.

Using a silicone spatula or wooden spoon, gently fold or mix the cream cheese into the beaten butter and sugar until just combined. It's important not to beat too vigorously here as the cheese can loosen and make a wet frosting. Chill until needed.

Once the muffins are completely cool, spoon or pipe the frosting on top of the muffins.

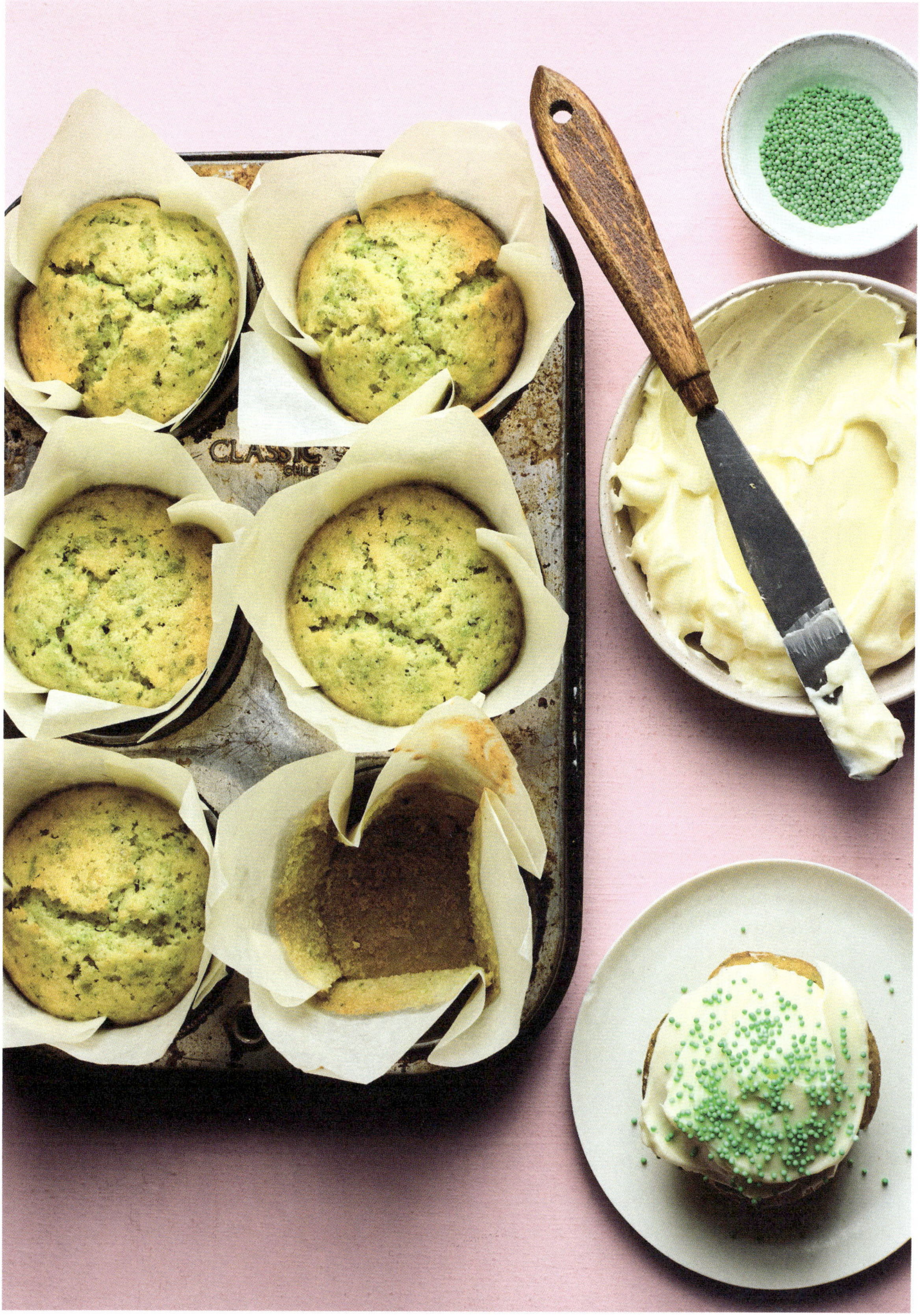
CLASSIC

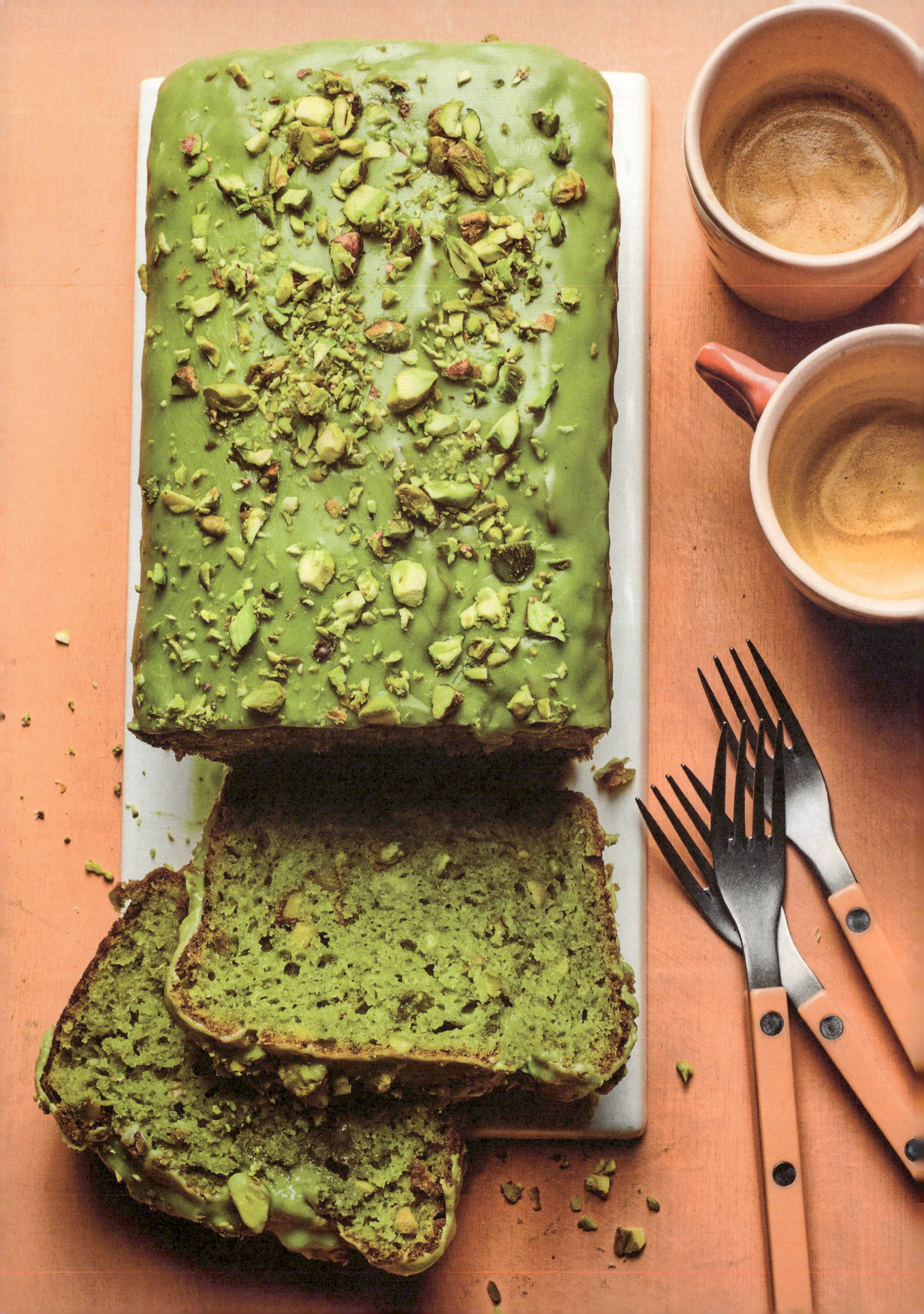

Pea, Pistachio and Matcha Cake

This cake is a real green extravaganza. I love matcha; this is mostly down to my fabulous colleague, Helz, who would regularly make us matcha lattes to kick off our day. I think the flavour goes well here – with the peas and pistachios, it's a green triple threat. I use lime juice in the glaze to add a bit of zing, but you can use milk if you're not a lime fiend.

(SUITABLE FOR FREEZING WITHOUT GLAZE)

SERVES 10–12

- 115ml (4fl oz) sunflower or vegetable oil, plus extra for greasing the tin
- 125g (4½oz) frozen peas
- 200g (7oz) natural yogurt
- 75g (2½oz) pistachios, plus extra for decorating, if you like
- 1 teaspoon vanilla extract
- 3 eggs
- 175g (6oz) caster (superfine) sugar
- 200g (7oz) self-raising flour
- ½ teaspoon baking powder
- 1 tablespoon matcha powder
- Zest of 1 lime

FOR THE GLAZE
- 125g (4½oz) icing (confectioner's) sugar
- ½ teaspoon matcha powder
- 1½ tablespoons lime juice (or you can use milk)

Preheat the oven to 180°C/160°C fan/350°F/gas 4. Oil a 1.5-litre (2-lb) loaf tin and line with parchment paper.

Place the frozen peas in a heatproof bowl and cover with freshly boiled water to defrost. Leave for a few minutes, then drain. Tip the peas into a food processor, add half of the yogurt and blitz until smooth. Throw in the pistachios and blitz until coarsely chopped. Set aside.

In a mixing bowl, combine the oil, vanilla extract and eggs, then stir in the remaining yogurt, sugar and pea and pistachio mixture. Fold in the flour, baking powder and matcha powder along with the zest of 1 lime.

Pour the cake batter into the prepared loaf tin and bake in the hot oven for 45 minutes–1 hour or until risen, golden and a skewer inserted into the cake comes out clean. Remove the cake from the oven and leave to cool in the tin for 15 minutes before lifting out onto a wire rack and cooling completely.

While the cake cools, make the glaze. Mix together the icing sugar with the matcha powder and enough milk or lime juice to make a thick, smooth paste.

Once the cake is cool, pour the glaze over the cake. It's fine if the glaze dribbles down the sides of the cake as this only adds to its beauty. Scatter over a few extra chopped pistachios, if you like.

Cook's tip Matcha is a very specific flavour. If you haven't tried it before, I recommend grabbing an iced matcha or similar drink at a coffee shop before trying this recipe, especially as it's a more expensive ingredient. If you don't like matcha or don't want to use it, just leave it out and glaze the cake with a simple icing (frosting) and scatter over some pistachios.

SWEET PEAS

Green Smoothie

During my last health kick, I used to have one of these smoothies after doing my couch-to-5k run. If you want a good start to the day, I highly recommend one. I prefer a more savoury smoothie because I find I'm not starving by around 11am. Because it's heavy on the green veg, the smoothie is not overly sweet so if your banana is not very ripe, I recommend including the honey or maple syrup. If you're used to a fruit smoothie, this is very different.

% ❄ V VG GF DF

SERVES 2

75g (2¾oz) frozen peas, defrosted according to the packet instructions
200ml (7fl oz) coconut water (or use apple juice which will also sweeten)
½ cucumber, roughly chopped
1 apple, cored and roughly chopped
1 banana, roughly chopped
½ avocado, peeled and roughly chopped
50g (1¾oz) spinach
1 teaspoon spirulina (optional)
1–2 teaspoons honey (or use maple syrup to make it vegan)

Put the peas in a blender, pour in the coconut water and blitz until finely chopped.

Add in the cucumber, apple and banana and blitz again for a few seconds before adding in the remaining ingredients except the honey or maple syrup. Blend again until smooth.

Taste and add the honey or maple syrup, if you like. Add a few ice cubes to the blender and blitz again to chill the smoothie before pouring into two glasses.

Index

A

anchovies
  chicken peasar salad 104
  green beans and peas with anchovies 138
apple
  green goddess salad 110
  green smoothie 166
arroz de primavera 51
asparagus
  arroz de primavera 51
  asparagus and pea linguine 33
  asparagus, pea and mozzarella salad 107
avocado
  avocado and pea guacamole 150
  baked breakfast eggs 132
  green goddess salad 110
  green smoothie 166

B

bacon
  cheesy peas pasta 34
  egg fried rice 28
  macaroni cheese with bacon breadcrumbs 21
  one-pot orzo with peas, mushrooms and bacon 42
  orecchiette with peas and pancetta 38
  pan-fried gnocchi with peas in a creamy tarragon sauce 118
  petits pois à la française 135
  rosie's carbonara 41
baked beans: rhinestone cowboy pie 121
baked breakfast eggs 132
bakes
  baked breakfast eggs 132
  chicken, pea and pesto lasagne 91
  kale, pea and blue cheese gratin 141
  macaroni cheese 21
  rhinestone cowboy pie 121
  salmon and pea pasta bake 37
  tuna cheesy pasta bake 22
barbecue sauce: rhinestone cowboy pie 121
basil: tomato and pea galette 98
beans: quick rustic chicken and bean stew 15
beef
  beef and frozen veg pasties 27
  keema curry 85
  one-pan steak with mushrooms, peas and greens 79
  spiced beef and peanut butter noodles 125
bread
  chicken peasar salad 104
  crab and pea toasts 154
  prosciutto, burrata and pea pintxos 154
  smashed peas, whipped feta and poached eggs on toast 153
broad (fava) beans: hake with braised peas, broad beans and pancetta 97
broccoli: zesty pan-fried purple sprouting broccoli 138
bulgur wheat: lamb kofta with pea tabbouleh 82
burrata: prosciutto, burrata and pea pintxos 154
buttermilk: cheese and pea scones 157

C

cabbage: roast chicken with cabbage and peas 88
cake
  pea cake with coconut frosting 161
  pea muffins with cream cheese frosting 162
  pea, pistachio and matcha cake 165
carrots
  chicken and ham pie 92
  chicken and mushroom pot pie 76
  norwegian-esque fish soup 58
  quick rustic chicken and bean stew 15
cavolo nero
  green shakshuka 67
  harissa chicken and green veg pasta 70
  kale, pea and blue cheese gratin 141
  one-pan steak with mushrooms, peas and greens 79
cheat's mushy peas 136
cheese, blue
  blue cheese and pea tart 95
  blue cheese leeks and peas 137
  kale, pea and blue cheese gratin 141
  spinach, mushroom and blue cheese gratin 141
cheese, cheddar
  cheese and pea omelette 23
  cheese and pea scones 157
  cheesy leeks and peas 137
  chicken, pea and pesto lasagne 91
  chorizo, potato and pea frittata 113
  keema curry pie 85
  loaded jackets 111
  macaroni cheese 21
  macaroni cheese with bacon breadcrumbs 21
  orecchiette with peas and pancetta 38
  rhinestone cowboy pie 121
  salmon and pea pasta bake 37
  tuna cheesy pasta bake 22
cheese, feta
  leek and feta frittata 113
  pea and feta dip 149
  pea, feta and harissa fritters 116
  smashed peas, whipped feta and poached eggs on toast 153
cheese, goats': harissa couscous salad with goats' cheese 108
cheese, mozzarella: asparagus, pea and mozzarella salad 107
cheese, parmesan
  cheesy leeks and peas 137
  cheesy peas pasta 34

INDEX

chicken, pea and pesto
  lasagne 91
chicken peasar salad 104
creamy chicken, tarragon and
  peas with cheesy polenta 94
ham and cheese pasta 34
kale, pea and blue cheese
  gratin 141
orecchiette with peas and
  pancetta 38
pea pesto 144
pea risotto 47
ravioli with sage brown butter 45
risi e bisi 48
rocket and pea pesto 144
rosie's carbonara 41
walnut and pea pesto 146
see also types of cheese
chicken
  chicken and ham pie 92
  chicken and mushroom pot pie 76
  chicken and spring veg
    traybake 74
  chicken and squash curry 117
  chicken, pea and pesto
    lasagne 91
  chicken peasar salad 104
  chicken tikka masala pasties 27
  creamy chicken, tarragon and
    peas with cheesy polenta 94
  frozen veg and pea broth 16
  harissa chicken and green veg
    pasta 70
  jerk-spiced chicken with coconut
    rice with peas 122
  quick rustic chicken and bean
    stew 15
  roast chicken with cabbage and
    peas 88
chickpeas (garbanzo beans): pea
  falafel pittas 101
chillies
  frozen pea dal 71
  keema curry 85
  mattar paneer 73
  pea and courgette pakora 87
  pea and miso dip 147
  pea and onion bhaji 86
  pea, sweetcorn and halloumi
    fritters 116
  spiced beef and peanut butter
    noodles 125
chives
  blue cheese and pea tart 95
  cheese and pea scones 157

green goddess salad 110
loaded jackets 111
norwegian-esque fish soup 58
pea, sweetcorn and halloumi
  fritters 116
potato salad 142
chorizo
  chorizo and pea pasta 46
  chorizo, pea and pearl barley
    stew 64
  chorizo, potato and pea
    frittata 113
coconut cream: pea cake with
  coconut frosting 161
coconut flakes: pea cake with
  coconut frosting 161
coconut milk
  chicken and squash curry 117
  frozen pea dal 71
  jerk-spiced chicken with coconut
    rice with peas 122
  thai-spiced pea and coconut
    soup 61
coriander (cilantro)
  avocado and pea guacamole 150
  baked breakfast eggs 132
  jewelled couscous 52
  keema curry 85
  lamb kofta with pea tabbouleh 82
  mattar paneer 73
  pea and courgette pakora 87
  pea falafel pittas 101
  spiced beef and peanut butter
    noodles 125
  thai-spiced pea and coconut
    soup 61
cornichons (dill pickles): potato
  salad 142
courgette (zucchini)
  pea and courgette pakora 87
  pea risotto 47
  sausage, courgette, pea and
    harissa pasta 18
couscous
  harissa couscous salad with
    goats' cheese 108
  jewelled couscous 52
crab and pea toasts 154
cream
  asparagus and pea linguine 33
  blue cheese and pea tart 95
  cheat's mushy peas 136
  cheesy peas pasta 34
  chicken and spring veg
    traybake 74

creamy chicken, tarragon and
  peas with cheesy polenta 94
kale, pea and blue cheese
  gratin 141
loaded jackets 111
mussels in a creamy white wine
  sauce 68
pan-fried gnocchi with peas in a
  creamy tarragon sauce 118
cucumber
  green goddess salad 110
  green smoothie 166
  lamb kofta with pea tabbouleh 82
  minty peas with warm cucumber
    ribbons 135
curry
  chicken and squash curry 117
  frozen pea dal 71
  keema curry 85
  mattar paneer 73

D

dill: simple salmon and pea
  fishcakes 126
dips
  avocado and pea guacamole 150
  pea and feta dip 149
  pea and mint dip 147
  pea and miso dip 147
  pea 'hummus' 150
  zesty pea and herb dip 149

E

eggs
  asparagus, pea and mozzarella
    salad 107
  baked breakfast eggs 132
  blue cheese and pea tart 95
  cheese and pea omelette 23
  chorizo, potato and pea
    frittata 113
  egg fried rice 28
  green goddess salad 110
  green shakshuka 67
  kedgeree 55
  pea fritters 114
  rosie's carbonara 41
  smashed peas, whipped feta and
    poached eggs on toast 153
  toad in the hole 77

F

falafel
  pea falafel pittas 101
family feasts 80–101

INDEX

fennel, orange and pea salad 142
fish
   hake with braised peas, broad beans and pancetta 97
   kedgeree 55
   mash 'n' pea fish pie 129
   norwegian-esque fish soup 58
   salmon and pea pasta bake 37
   simple salmon and pea fiscakes 126
   tuna and pea pasta 46
   tuna cheesy pasta bake 22
frittatas
   chorizo, potato and pea frittata 113
   leek and feta frittata 113
   red bell pepper and pea frittata 113
fritters
   pea, feta and harissa fritters 116
   pea fritters 114
   pea, sweetcorn and halloumi fritters 116
frozen pea dal 71
frozen veg and pea broth 16

G

gnocchi: pan-fried gnocchi with peas in a creamy tarragon sauce 118
gratin
   kale, pea and blue cheese gratin 141
   spinach, mushroom and blue cheese gratin 141
green beans: green beans and peas with anchovies 138
green goddess salad 110
green shakshuka 67
green smoothie 166
greens: one-pan steak with mushrooms, peas and greens 79
gruyère: tomato and pea galette 98

H

hake with braised peas, broad beans and pancetta 97
halloumi: pea, sweetcorn and halloumi fritters 116
ham
   cheesy peas pasta 34
   chicken and ham pie 92
   frozen veg and pea broth 16
   ham and cheese pasta 34
   pea and ham soup 63
harissa
   harissa chicken and green veg pasta 70
   harissa couscous salad with goats' cheese 108
   pea, feta and harissa fritters 116
   sausage, courgette, pea and harissa pasta 18
herbs
spring pea soup 12
see also types of herbs
hummus
   pea falafel pittas 101
   pea 'hummus' 150

J

jerk-spiced chicken with coconut rice with peas 122
jewelled couscous 52

K

kale
   green shakshuka 67
   harissa chicken and green veg pasta 70
   kale, pea and blue cheese gratin 141
   ramen noodles with pea and miso broth 17
kedgeree 55
kofta, lamb with pea tabbouleh 82

L

lamb
   keema curry 85
   lamb kofta with pea tabbouleh 82
leeks
   blue cheese leeks and peas 137
   cheesy leeks and peas 137
   chicken and spring veg traybake 74
   toad in the hole 77
lemon
   smashed peas, whipped feta and poached eggs on toast 153
   zesty mashed peas 136
   zesty pan-fried purple sprouting broccoli 138
lemongrass
   spiced beef and peanut butter noodles 125
   thai-spiced pea and coconut soup 61
lentils: frozen pea dal 71
lettuce
   chicken peasar salad 104
   green goddess salad 110
   petits pois à la française 135
loaded jackets 111

M

macaroni cheese 21
mascarpone
   blue cheese and pea tart 95
   chicken, pea and pesto lasagne 91
   salmon and pea pasta bake 37
matcha: pea, pistachio and matcha cake 165
mattar paneer 73
midweek meals 102–129
mint
   minty peas with warm cucumber ribbons 135
   pea and feta dip 149
   pea and mint dip 147
   pea and mint soup 62
   petits pois à la française 135
   smashed peas, whipped feta and poached eggs on toast 153
   walnut and pea pesto 146
miso
   pea and miso dip 147
   ramen noodles with pea and miso broth 17
muffins: pea muffins with cream cheese frosting 162
mushrooms
   chicken and mushroom pot pie 76
   one-pan steak with mushrooms, peas and greens 79
   one-pot orzo with peas, mushrooms and bacon 42
   spinach, mushroom and blue cheese gratin 141
mussels in a creamy white wine sauce 68
mustard
   cheesy leeks and peas 137
   chicken and spring veg traybake 74
   one-pan steak with mushrooms, peas and greens 79

N

noodles
   ramen noodles with pea and miso broth 17

INDEX

spiced beef and peanut butter noodles 125
norwegian-esque fish soup 58
nuts
  asparagus, pea and mozzarella salad 107
  jewelled couscous 52
  kale, pea and blue cheese gratin 141
  pea pesto 144
  pea, pistachio and matcha cake 165
  rocket and pea pesto 144
  spiced beef and peanut butter noodles 125
  thai-spiced pea and coconut soup 61
  walnut and pea pesto 146

O

one-pan steak with mushrooms, peas and greens 79
one-pot orzo with peas, mushrooms and bacon 42
one-pot wonders 56–79
onion: pea and onion bhaji 86
orange: fennel, orange and pea salad 142
orecchiette with peas and pancetta 38
orzo, one-pot with peas, mushrooms and bacon 42

P

pancetta
  hake with braised peas, broad beans and pancetta 97
  orecchiette with peas and pancetta 38
  risi e bisi 48
  rosie's carbonara 41
paneer: mattar paneer 73
pan-fried gnocchi with peas in a creamy tarragon sauce 118
panko breadcrumbs
  cheesy leeks and peas 137
  kale, pea and blue cheese gratin 141
  macaroni cheese with bacon breadcrumbs 21
  salmon and pea pasta bake 37
  tuna cheesy pasta bake 22
pasta
  asparagus and pea linguine 33
  cheesy peas pasta 34

  chicken, pea and pesto lasagne 91
  chorizo and pea pasta 46
  harissa chicken and green veg pasta 70
  macaroni cheese 21
  one-pot orzo with peas, mushrooms and bacon 42
  orecchiette with peas and pancetta 38
  ravioli with sage brown butter 45
  rosie's carbonara 41
  salmon and pea pasta bake 37
  sausage, courgette, pea and harissa pasta 18
  tuna and pea pasta 46
  tuna cheesy pasta bake 22
pasta sauces: pea-sta sauce 146
pastry
  beef and frozen veg pasties 27
  blue cheese and pea tart 95
  chicken and ham pie 92
  chicken and mushroom pot pie 76
  chicken tikka masala pasties 27
  ricotta, pea and pesto tart 24
  tomato and pea galette 98
peanut butter: spiced beef and peanut butter noodles 125
pearl barley: chorizo, pea and pearl barley stew 64
pea-sta sauce 146
peppers (bell)
  jewelled couscous 52
  rhinestone cowboy pie 121
  sausage, courgette, pea and harissa pasta 18
  spiced beef and peanut butter noodles 125
pesto
  chicken, pea and pesto lasagne 91
  pea pesto 144
  ricotta, pea and pesto tart 24
  rocket and pea pesto 144
  tomato and pea galette 98
petits pois à la française 135
pies
  chicken and ham pie 92
  chicken and mushroom pot pie 76
  keema curry pie 85
  mash 'n' pea fish pie 129
  rhinestone cowboy pie 121
pittas
  pea falafel pittas 101
polenta, creamy chicken, tarragon and peas with cheesy 94
pomegranate: jewelled couscous 52

potatoes
  chicken and spring veg traybake 74
  chorizo, potato and pea frittata 113
  keema curry pie 85
  loaded jackets 111
  mash 'n' pea fish pie 129
  norwegian-esque fish soup 58
  pea and ham soup 63
  pea and mint soup 62
  pea and watercress soup 62
  potato salad 142
  quick rustic chicken and bean stew 15
  rhinestone cowboy pie 121
  simple salmon and pea fiscakes 126
prawns (shrimp)
  norwegian-esque fish soup 58
prosciutto, burrata and pea pintxos 154
pumpkin seeds (pepitas): green goddess salad 110

Q

quick rustic chicken and bean stew 15

R

ramen noodles with pea and miso broth 17
ravioli with sage brown butter 45
rice
  arroz de primavera 51
  egg fried rice 28
  jerk-spiced chicken with coconut rice with peas 122
  kedgeree 55
  pea risotto 47
  risi e bisi 48
ricotta: ricotta, pea and pesto tart 24
risotto, pea 47
rocket (arugula)
  harissa couscous salad with goats' cheese 108
  rocket and pea pesto 144
rosemary
  chicken and spring veg traybake 74
  frozen veg and pea broth 16
  quick rustic chicken and bean stew 15
rosie's carbonara 41

INDEX

S

sage: ravioli with sage brown butter 45
salads
   asparagus, pea and mozzarella salad 107
   fennel, orange and pea salad 142
   green goddess salad 110
   harissa couscous salad with goats' cheese 108
salmon
   salmon and pea pasta bake 37
   simple salmon and pea fiscakes 126
sauces
   pea-sta sauce 146
sausages
   rhinestone cowboy pie 121
   sausage, courgette, pea and harissa pasta 18
   toad in the hole 77
scones: cheese and pea scones 157
shakshuka, green 67
sides, sauces and snacks 130–157
smashed peas, whipped feta and poached eggs on toast 153
smoothie, green 166
soups
   frozen veg and pea broth 16
   norwegian-esque fish soup 58
   pea and ham soup 63
   pea and mint soup 62
   pea and watercress soup 62
   spring pea soup 12
spiced beef and peanut butter noodles 125
spinach
   arroz de primavera 51
   chicken and squash curry 117
   chicken, pea and pesto lasagne 91
   fennel, orange and pea salad 142
   frozen pea dal 71
   frozen veg and pea broth 16
   green smoothie 166
   harissa chicken and green veg pasta 70
   spinach, mushroom and blue cheese gratin 141
split peas: frozen pea dal 71
spring onions (scallions)
   egg fried rice 28
   jerk-spiced chicken with coconut rice with peas 122
   loaded jackets 111

pea and miso dip 147
pea and watercress soup 62
pea falafel pittas 101
pea, feta and harissa fritters 116
pea fritters 114
pea-sta sauce 146
petits pois à la française 135
ramen noodles with pea and miso broth 17
spring pea soup 12
squash: chicken and squash curry 117
storecupboard saviours 10–29
sweetcorn: pea, sweetcorn and halloumi fritters 116
sweet peas 158–166

T

tabbouleh, lamb kofta with pea 82
tahini
   pea and mint dip 147
   pea falafel pittas 101
   pea 'hummus' 150
tarragon
   creamy chicken, tarragon and peas with cheesy polenta 94
   pan-fried gnocchi with peas in a creamy tarragon sauce 118
tart
   blue cheese and pea tart 95
   ricotta, pea and pesto tart 24
   tomato and pea galette 98
thai-spiced pea and coconut soup 61
thyme
   chicken and ham pie 92
   chicken and mushroom pot pie 76
   chicken and spring veg traybake 74
   frozen veg and pea broth 16
   pea risotto 47
   quick rustic chicken and bean stew 15
   roast chicken with cabbage and peas 88
toasts
   smashed peas, whipped feta and poached eggs on toast 153
tomato and pea galette 98
tomatoes, cherry
   avocado and pea guacamole 150
   baked breakfast eggs 132
   jewelled couscous 52
tomatoes, tinned chopped
   chicken and squash curry 117

chorizo and pea pasta 46
keema curry 85
mattar paneer 73
orecchiette with peas and pancetta 38
quick rustic chicken and bean stew 15
traybake, chicken and spring veg 74
tuna
   tuna and pea pasta 46
   tuna cheesy pasta bake 22

V

vegetables
   beef and frozen veg pasties 27
   frozen veg and pea broth 16
see also types of vegetables

W

walnut and pea pesto 146
wasabi: pea and miso dip 147
watercress
   asparagus, pea and mozzarella salad 107
   pea and watercress soup 62

Y

yogurt
   green shakshuka 67
   keema curry 85
   pea and feta dip 149
   pea and mint dip 147
   pea and onion bhaji 86
   pea, pistachio and matcha cake 165
   smashed peas, whipped feta and poached eggs on toast 153
   spring pea soup 12

Z

zesty mashed peas 136
zesty pan-fried purple sprouting broccoli 138
zesty pea and herb dip 149

Cook's Index

Cooks in 30 Minutes or Less
arroz de primavera 51
asparagus and pea linguine 33
asparagus, pea and mozzarella salad 107
avocado and pea guacamole 150
baked breakfast eggs 132
cheat's mushy peas 136
cheese and pea omelette 23
cheese and pea scones 157
cheesy peas pasta 34
chorizo and pea pasta 46
crab and pea toasts 154
creamy chicken, tarragon and peas with cheesy polenta 94
egg fried rice 28
fennel, orange and pea salad 142
frozen veg and pea broth 16
green beans and peas with anchovies 138
green goddess salad 110
green shakshuka 67
green smoothie 166
hake with braised peas, broad beans and pancetta 97
harissa chicken and green veg pasta 70
harissa couscous salad with goats' cheese 108
jewelled couscous 52
kedgeree 55
lamb kofta with pea tabbouleh 82
mattar paneer 73
minty peas with warm cucumber ribbons 135
mussels in a creamy white wine sauce 68
norwegian-esque fish soup 58
one-pan steak with mushrooms, peas and greens 79
one-pot orzo with peas, mushrooms and bacon 42
orecchiette with peas and pancetta 38
pan-fried gnocchi with peas in a creamy tarragon sauce 118
pea and courgette pakora 87
pea and feta dip 149

pea and ham soup 63
pea and mint dip 147
pea and mint soup 62
pea and miso dip 147
pea and onion bhaji 86
pea and watercress soup 62
pea cake with coconut frosting 161
pea falafel pittas 101
pea, feta and harissa fritters 116
pea fritters 114
pea 'hummus' 150
pea muffins with cream cheese frosting 162
pea pesto 144
pea-sta sauce 146
pea, sweetcorn and halloumi fritters 116
petits pois à la française 135
potato salad 142
prosciutto, burrata and pea pintxos 154
quick rustic chicken and bean stew 15
ramen noodles with pea and miso broth 17
ravioli with sage brown butter 45
ricotta, pea and pesto tart 24
risi e bisi 48
rocket and pea pesto 144
rosie's carbonara 41
sausage, courgette, pea and harissa pasta 18
smashed peas, whipped feta and poached eggs on toast 153
spiced beef and peanut butter noodles 125
spring pea soup 12
thai-spiced pea and coconut soup 61
tuna and pea pasta 46
walnut and pea pesto 146
zesty mashed peas 136
zesty pan-fried purple sprouting broccoli 138

Batch Cooking
Can be easily doubled, stored and reheated until piping hot
arroz de primavera 51
asparagus and pea linguine 33
baked breakfast eggs 132
beef and frozen veg pasties 27
cheat's mushy peas 136
cheesy leeks and peas 137
chicken and spring veg traybake 74
chicken and squash curry 117
chicken, pea and pesto lasagne 91
chorizo and pea pasta 46
chorizo, pea and pearl barley stew 64
chorizo, potato and pea frittata 113
creamy chicken, tarragon and peas with cheesy polenta 94
egg fried rice 28
frozen pea dal 71
frozen veg and pea broth 16
green beans and peas with anchovies 138
green shakshuka 67
hake with braised peas, broad beans and pancetta 97
harissa chicken and green veg pasta 70
jerk-spiced chicken with coconut rice with peas 122
kale, pea and blue cheese gratin 141
kedgeree 55
keema curry 85
loaded jackets 111
macaroni cheese 21
mash 'n' pea fish pie 129
mattar paneer 73
mussels in a creamy white wine sauce 68
norwegian-esque fish soup 58
one-pan steak with mushrooms, peas and greens 79
one-pot orzo with peas, mushrooms and bacon 42
orecchiette with peas and pancetta 38
pan-fried gnocchi with peas in a creamy tarragon sauce 118

pea and blue cheese tart 95
pea and courgette pakora 87
pea and ham soup 63
pea and mint soup 62
pea and onion bhaji 86
pea and watercress soup 62
pea falafel pittas 101
pea, feta and harissa fritters 116
pea fritters 114
pea risotto 47
pea-sta sauce 146
pea, sweetcorn and halloumi fritters 116
petits pois à la française 135
quick rustic chicken and bean stew 15
ramen noodles with pea and miso broth 17
rhinestone cowboy pie 121
risi e bisi 48
roast chicken with cabbage and peas 88
rosie's carbonara 41
salmon and pea pasta bake 37
sausage, courgette, pea and harissa pasta 18
simple salmon and pea fishcakes 126
spiced beef and peanut butter noodles 125
spring pea soup 12
thai-spiced pea and coconut soup 61
tuna and pea pasta 46
tuna cheesy pasta bake 22
zesty mashed peas 136

Freezer Friendly
Can be safely frozen, stored for up to 3 months, defrosted and reheated until piping hot
arroz de primavera 51
beef and frozen veg pasties 27
cheat's mushy peas 136
cheese and pea scones 157
cheesy leeks and peas 137
cheesy peas pasta 34
chicken and ham pie 92
chicken and mushroom pot pie 76
chicken and spring veg traybake 74
chicken and squash curry 117
chicken, pea and pesto lasagne 91
chorizo and pea pasta 46
chorizo, pea and pearl barley stew 64
chorizo, potato and pea frittata 113
creamy chicken, tarragon and peas with cheesy polenta 94

frozen pea dal 71
frozen veg and pea broth 16
green smoothie 166
hake with braised peas, broad beans and pancetta 97
harissa chicken and green veg pasta 70
jewelled couscous 52
jerk-spiced chicken with coconut rice with peas 122
kale, pea and blue cheese gratin 141
keema curry 85
lamb kofta with pea tabbouleh 82
loaded jackets 111
macaroni cheese 21
mash 'n' pea fish pie 129
mattar paneer 73
one-pan steak with mushrooms, peas and greens 79
one-pot orzo with peas, mushrooms and bacon 42
orecchiette with peas and pancetta 38
pea and blue cheese tart 95
pea and courgette pakora 87
pea and feta dip 149
pea and ham soup 63
pea and mint dip 147
pea and mint soup 62
pea and miso dip 147
pea and onion bhaji 86
pea and watercress soup 62
pea cake with coconut frosting 161
pea falafel pittas 101
pea, feta and harissa fritters 116
pea fritters 114
pea 'hummus' 150
pea muffins with cream cheese frosting 162
pea pesto 144
pea, pistachio and matcha cake 165
pea risotto 47
pea-sta sauce 146
pea, sweetcorn and halloumi fritters 116
quick rustic chicken and bean stew 15
ramen noodles with pea and miso broth 17
rhinestone cowboy pie 121
ricotta, pea and pesto tart 24
roast chicken with cabbage and peas 88
rocket and pea pesto 144
salmon and pea pasta bake 37

sausage, courgette, pea and harissa pasta 18
simple salmon and pea fishcakes 126
spiced beef and peanut butter noodles 125
spring pea soup 12
thai-spiced pea and coconut soup 61
toad in the hole 77
tuna and pea pasta 46
tuna cheesy pasta bake 22
walnut and pea pesto 146
zesty mashed peas 136

Vegetarian
Always check the information on the packet to ensure all ingredients are vegetarian
arroz de primavera 51
asparagus and pea linguine 33
asparagus, pea and mozzarella salad 107
avocado and pea guacamole 150
baked breakfast eggs 132
cheat's mushy peas 136
cheese and pea omelette 23
cheese and pea scones 157
cheesy leeks and peas 137
fennel, orange and pea salad 142
frozen pea dal 71
green goddess salad 110
green shakshuka 67
green smoothie 166
harissa couscous salad with goats' cheese 108
jewelled couscous 52
kale, pea and blue cheese gratin 141
loaded jackets 111
macaroni cheese 21
mattar paneer 73
minty peas with warm cucumber ribbons 135
pea and blue cheese tart 95
pea and courgette pakora 87
pea and feta dip 149
pea and mint dip 147
pea and mint soup 62
pea and miso dip 147
pea and onion bhaji 86
pea and watercress soup 62
pea cake with coconut frosting 161
pea falafel pittas 101
pea, feta and harissa fritters 116
pea fritters 114
pea 'hummus' 150

pea muffins with cream cheese
    frosting 162
pea pesto 144
pea, pistachio and matcha cake 165
pea risotto 47
pea-sta sauce 146
pea, sweetcorn and halloumi
    fritters 116
potato salad 142
ramen noodles with pea and miso
    broth 17
ravioli with sage brown butter 45
rhinestone cowboy pie 121
rocket and pea pesto 144
smashed peas, whipped feta and
    poached eggs on toast 153
spring pea soup 12
thai-spiced pea and coconut
    soup 61
tomato and pea galette 98
walnut and pea pesto 146
zesty mashed peas 136
zesty pan-fried purple sprouting
    broccoli 138

Vegan
Always check the information on
the packet to ensure all ingredients
are vegan
arroz de primavera 51
avocado and pea guacamole 150
frozen pea dal 71
green smoothie 166
jewelled couscous 52
pea and courgette pakora 87
pea and mint dip 147
pea and mint soup 62
pea and miso dip 147
pea and watercress soup 62
pea falafel pittas 101
pea 'hummus' 150
pea-sta sauce 146
ramen noodles with pea and miso
    broth 17
spring pea soup 12
thai-spiced pea and coconut
    soup 61
zesty mashed peas 136
zesty pan-fried purple sprouting
    broccoli 138

Gluten-free
Always check the information on
the packet to ensure all ingredients
are gluten-free
arroz de primavera 51

asparagus, pea and mozzarella
    salad 107
avocado and pea guacamole 150
baked breakfast eggs 132
cheat's mushy peas 136
cheese and pea omelette 23
chicken and spring veg traybake 74
chicken and squash curry 117
chorizo, potato and pea frittata 113
creamy chicken, tarragon and peas
    with cheesy polenta 94
egg fried rice 28
fennel, orange and pea salad 142
frozen pea dal 71
frozen veg and pea broth 16
green beans and peas with
    anchovies 138
green goddess salad 110
green shakshuka 67
green smoothie 166
hake with braised peas, broad beans
    and pancetta 97
jerk-spiced chicken with coconut
    rice with peas 122
jewelled couscous 52
kedgeree 55
keema curry 85
loaded jackets 111
mattar paneer 73
minty peas with warm cucumber
    ribbons 135
mussels in a creamy white wine
    sauce 68
norwegian-esque fish soup 58
pea and courgette pakora 87
pea and feta dip 149
pea and ham soup 63
pea and mint dip 147
pea and mint soup 62
pea and miso dip 147
pea and onion bhaji 86
pea and watercress soup 62
pea falafel pittas 101
pea 'hummus' 150
pea pesto 144
pea risotto 47
pea-sta sauce 146
petits pois à la française 135
potato salad 142
quick rustic chicken and bean
    stew 15
risi e bisi 48
roast chicken with cabbage and
    peas 88
rocket and pea pesto 144

spring pea soup 12
thai-spiced pea and coconut
    soup 61
walnut and pea pesto 146
zesty mashed peas 136
zesty pan-fried purple sprouting
    broccoli 138

Dairy-free
Always check the information on
the packet to ensure all ingredients
are dairy-free
arroz de primavera 51
avocado and pea guacamole 150
baked breakfast eggs 132
chorizo and pea pasta 46
chorizo, pea and pearl barley
    stew 64
egg fried rice 28
fennel, orange and pea salad 142
frozen pea dal 71
frozen veg and pea broth 16
green beans and peas with
    anchovies 138
green shakshuka 67
green smoothie 166
harissa chicken and green veg
    pasta 70
jerk-spiced chicken with coconut
    rice with peas 122
jewelled couscous 52
pea and courgette pakora 87
pea and mint dip 147
pea and mint soup 62
pea and miso dip 147
pea and watercress soup 62
pea falafel pittas 101
pea 'hummus' 150
pea-sta sauce 146
quick rustic chicken and bean
    stew 15
ramen noodles with pea and miso
    broth 17
sausage, courgette, pea and harissa
    pasta 18
simple salmon and pea
    fishcakes 126
spiced beef and peanut butter
    noodles 125
spring pea soup 12
thai-spiced pea and coconut
    soup 61
zesty mashed peas 136
zesty pan-fried purple sprouting
    broccoli 138

Acknowledgements

I always feel guilty when writing thank yous, like I've forgotten someone, so I end up thanking everyone in my life. To avoid repeating myself, here's a blanket acknowledgement to those I mentioned in *The Tinned Tomatoes Cookbook*, because you have all pitched in and supported me throughout to get me to this point. The following thanks are targeted to those who have helped out during this project.

I couldn't believe my luck when the gang got back together to make this follow-up. It felt like a Spice Girls reunion. Thanks to Céline for putting your faith in me again – especially after my drunken insistence that we get a McDonald's after one too many – and for your general greatness. Lisa, the book wouldn't be what it is without your skill and vision (and nagging). To the team that bring the recipes to life: Mowie, you're a genius and make it all look so effortless – thanks also for photoshopping the peas out of my teeth in my headshot; Troy, from hairdresser to the best food stylist in the world – my food never looks as good as you make it look; Jess, they say behind every great man is an even greater woman (don't tell Troy I said that) – thank you for ranting about politics and recommending Gill. To designers Clare and Megan, I'm thrilled that this book looks just as good as the last one and that's due to your vision and creativity. Thanks, too, to Lorna Wing who helped with recipe testing.

A huge thank you to Elly for your guidance, faith and just being a really great agent – and for accepting my calls when I really should email (it's just easier when I'm walking, you know).

I'm lucky to have a day job working with THE best in the business. There are too many people to name them all, but thanks to everyone on the 5th floor, in the shows team and on the podcast team, you all know who you are. I will just mention the food team: Lulu, Cassie, Barney, Anna, Ailsa, Helz and Rach because they're all especially amazing. Also, to Jessica, Lily, Simon and Katherine for supporting me in this endeavour.

To all my friends who have championed the previous book and this one, thank you so much. It means a huge amount to have your friendship. You all know who you are, but a special shout out to Rosie for her recipe testing, Lisa and Sam for the constant support from NL, Felicity for not only being an inspiration but for encouraging me to watch MAFSA, Xanthe for her friendship and being the best dinner companion, The Library for the support and friendship, Chetna for the constant nagging and infectious happiness. To Lindsay and Louise for their support and advice, Lesley for your unwavering friendship and faith in me, the Soz Huns crew for the laughs when I most definitely need them, the Leonardis for all the pasta we've shared that inevitably inspired half of this book and to my GNIM family: Katie, Kristen, Pauline, Orlando, Rosie and Susan for the regular writing support.

A big thanks to everyone at The Guild of Food Writers who has provided support and stepped in when I've needed you. Thanks especially to everyone on the committee and to Julie, my fabulous Vice Chair, for everything she does.

A massive thanks to my family for their continual support. To Mum, Dad and Sarah (especially for all the recipe testing), Nan and Grandad, Ali (even though you said you won't buy this book) and Dave, Jean (especially for buying everyone you have ever known a copy of my first book) and Mike, Will and Dan, Mel and Paul, Nats, Anja and my wonderful nieces Charley and Jojo. Thanks to you all, for everything.

Finally, to Gareth. First it was tinned tomatoes and now it's frozen peas. I don't know what will be next but I'm glad you'll be by my side. Thank you for your constant belief in me and being my biggest champion. There is a certificate in the post.

About the author

Samuel Goldsmith is Senior Food Editor and Podcast Editor at Immediate Media, where he works on the UK's No.1 food media brand, Good Food. He has over 15 years' experience working in the food and drink industry as an editor, writer, educator and cook. He has written features and recipes, developed recipes, and styled shoots for national and international publications such as *Waitrose Kitchen* and Australian *delicious*; consulted on a number of best-selling food and drink books; and was a nutritional consultant for BBC's *Eat Well for Less*. He is a founding director of award-winning CIC, 91 Ways, and is Chair of the Guild of Food Writers. *The Tinned Tomatoes Cookbook* was his debut book.

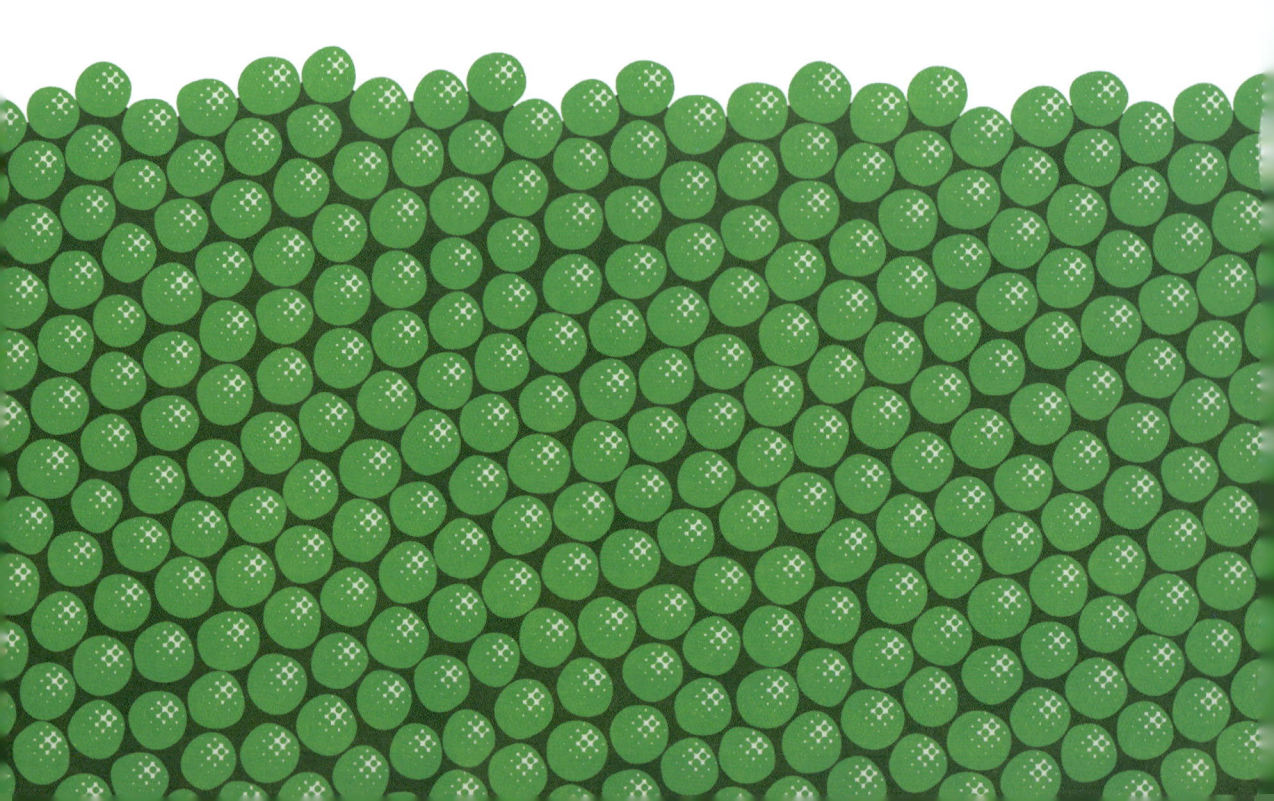